THE EVANGELISM HANDBOOK

The
Evangelism
Handbook

Gaining the World
Without Losing Your Soul

Graham Warner

eagle

Guildford

Copyright © 2000 Graham Warner

The right of Graham Warner to be identified as author of this work has been asserted by him in accordance with the Copyright, Design and Patents Act 1988.

British Library Cataloguing in Publication Data. A catalogue record for this book is available from the British Library.

Published by Eagle, an imprint of Inter Publishing Service (IPS) Ltd, PO Box 530, Guildford, Surrey GU2 5FH.

Scripture quotations unless otherwise noted are taken from the HOLY BIBLE, NEW INTERNATIONAL VERSION. Copyright © 1973, 1978, 1984 by International Bible Society. Used by permission of Hodder & Stoughton, a Division of Hodder Headline.

Typeset by Eagle
Printed by Cox & Wyman, Reading
ISBN No: 0 86347 368 7

Contents

Acknowledgements   11
Foreword   13
Introduction   19

PART ONE – 131 EVANGELISTIC PRINCIPLES
1. **The Morale of the Members**   25
    Move non-Christians to jealousy, Rom 11:14   25
    Christianity is caught not just taught, Ps 42:7   27
    The kingdom is about joy, Mt 13:44; Rom 14:17   29
    Joy even in rejection, Mt 5:11-12; Lk 6:23   30
    You shall go out with joy, Is 55:12   31
    You shall return with joy, Lk 10:17   33
    The joy of fulfilling the task, 1 Thess 3:9,
        3 Jn 1:4, Ac 20:24   34
    The joy of meeting needs, Ac 8:8, Jn 17:13   35
    The joy of rewards, Mt 25:21   36

2. **The Mandate of the Mission**   37
    We are appointed . . . to bear much fruit,
        Jn 15:1-8, 16   37
    Each seed reproduces, Mt 13:8   38
    Abiding – the key to fruitfulness, Jn 15:1   39
    The harvest is plentiful, Mt 9:36-38, Jn 4:35-38   39
    The right seeds for our soil, 2 Cor 9:10   41
    Break up your fallow ground, Jer 4:3   42
    Pray for light to shine out of our hearts
        2 Cor 4:6   43
    Pray for authorities, 1 Tim 2:1-4   45
    Pray that Jesus 'sends us' into evangelism, Mt 9:38   46
    Pray for open doors of opportunity, Jn 17:9,
        Col 4:3   46
    Pray for boldness to speak as we ought,
        Eph 6:19   48
    We are comissioned to go to the world,
        Mt 28:18   50
    Evangelism is primary function of the church,
        Mt 28:1820   51

Pastors, teachers and prophets in
    evangelism, Eph 4:11   52
Blessing every family of the earth, Gen 12:3;
    22:18   54
Witness for Jesus on earth and he will witness
    for us in heaven, Mt 10:32-33; Lk 9:26   55

3. **The Magnitude of the Magnetism**   56
Everyone knows of his existence, his power and
    his character, Rom 1:19-23   56
God is not willing that any should perish,
    2 Pet 3:9, 1 Tim 2:4   58
Jesus draws *all men*, Jn 12:32   59
Christ died for the sins of the whole world,
    1 Jn 2:2   60
The Holy Spirit convinces the world of sin,
    righteousness and judgment, Jn 16:8–11   62
The Holy Spirit is poured out on *all* flesh, Ac 2:17   64
Spiritual power = power to witness, Ac 1:8   66
Unity is the key – the world will know, Jn 17:21-23   67
Love is the key – *all will know,* Jn 13:35   68
A little bit of yeast leavens the whole lump,
    Lk 13:21   69
The true light lightens *every man,* Jn 1:9   70
The end comes when the gospel is preached
    in *all the earth,* Mt 24:14   71
Preach where Christ is not already named,
    Rom 15:20-21   73

4. **The Model of the Master**   75
Jesus invested time   75
Jesus worked spontaneously, Jn 5:19   76
Jesus did what he saw the father doing   77
Jesus had no set techniques   78
Jesus presented the toughest of terms, Lk 14:33   82
Jesus uses the art of conversation, Jn 4:1-7   83
Jesus uses dialogue not monologue   83
Jesus gives individual attention   84
Jesus uses questions   85

Jesus uses words of knowledge 88
Jesus uses picture language 90
Jesus uses parables, Mt 13:10-13 93
Jesus uses 'miracle language', Mt 12:28 95
Jesus uses social action 97
Jesus is motivated by compassion 99
Jesus uses hospitality 100
Jesus uses the context of a shared meal 102
Jesus encourages the use of money in
    evangelism, Lk 16:9-11 103
Jesus is described as the friend of sinners 105
Jesus only followed up those who followed 105

5. **The Morals of the Messenger** 107
God uses the weak, Mt 5:3 108
We are salt, light and a city, Mt 5:13 109
God uses our actions and reactions, Mt 5:38ff 112
Turn the other cheek, Mt 5:38 112
Give to those who steal from you, Lk 6:28-30 114
Go the second mile, Mt 5:41 117
Give to everyone who asks . . . lend expecting
    nothing back, Lk 6:30-35 118
Love your enemies, Mt 5:43 121
Be perfect, Mt 5:48 123

6. **The Ministry of the Merciful** 124
Repentance and social action 125
Salvation and social action 125
Faith and social action 127
Love and social action 130
Prayer and social action 131
Spiritual warfare and social action 132
Bible reading and social action 135
Worship and social action 137
Giving and social action 138
Work and social action 140
Church and social action 141
Jesus and the cup of cold water 144

7. **The Manifestation of the Miraculous**   146
    Don't look for signs in themselves, Mt 12:39   149
    Beware of false Christs, Mt 24:24   149
    Use signs and wonders, Mt 10:1, 7-8   150
    It is easier to see non-Christians healed than
        Christians, Ac 17-23   151
    Sometimes miracles are a negative use
        power, Ac 13:11   152
    Miracles meet the need   153
    Miracles protect us in the task, Lk 10:19   154
    Tongues can be used in evangelism,
        1 Cor 14:21-23   155
    Spiritual gifts in evangelism, 1 Cor 12:8-11   156
    Words of knowledge in evangelism,
        Acts 9:10-15, 10:4-8   157
    Preach the gospel to *all creation*, Mk 16:15   160

8. **The Maximising of the Message**   163
    Jesus gives us the message   163
    The message is positive – heaven not hellfire
        Mt 10:7   164
    The message is prophetic, Mt 10:19-20   166
    We preach Christ crucified   168
    We offer God's forgiveness   169
    We proclaim a living Saviour   169
    We share our personal testimony   169
    We make much of Jesus   171
    We prove Jesus is the Christ   172
    We preach the gospel fully   174
    We relate to where people are   175
    We explain how our life has changed   175
    We make the introduction between man
        and God   177
    We challenge people to change their lifestyle   177
    We proclaim freedom from all things   178
    We feel so secure that we want everybody to
        be like us   178
    We lead people to the Father   179
    We lead people to Christ   180

We lead people to the Holy Spirit 181
We baptise people in the name of the Father,
Son and Holy Spirit 182
We make disciples, not just converts 183

9. **The Measure of the Man** 184
Receiving a child = receiving Christ, Lk 9:48,
18:16-17 185
Babes receive revelation, Lk 10:21 186
Serving the poor = serving Christ, Mt 25:40f 187
Forgive everybody to be forgiven, Mt 10:40-41 187
Accepting a Christian = accepting Christ,
Mt 10:40-41 189
Rejecting Christians = rejecting Christ,
Mt 10:14-16 190
Men of peace receive peace, Lk 10:6 190
To him who has shall more be given, Mt 13:12 191

10. **The Maintenance of the Multiplication** 193
Church planting provides variety 193
Church planting provides choice 195
Church planting increases the intensity of
light, Rev 1:12 196
Church planting makes church accessible 197
Church planting has the lost as its priority,
Rom 15:20 197
Church planting provides relevant
evangelism, 1 Cor 9:20 198
Church planting provides involvement in the
community, Ac 6:1 200
Church planting provides freedom for
initiatives/vision/gifting 201
Church planting provides task/team orientated
churches, Mt 28:18 202
Church planting provides localised spiritual
warfare, Eph 2:2 204
Church planting because of building size 206
Church planting because of divisions and splits 208

PART TWO – 101 EVANGELISTIC IDEAS

11. The Methods of the Market Place   213

Saturation evangelism   213
Using initiative   213
Being creative   214
The 418 Prayer Projects   218
Letter evangelism   227
Open-air evangelism   230
Banners   236
Posters   239
Leaflets   242
Literature tables   244
Giving to bless   246
Marches and processions   248
Services in public places   251
Door to door   253
Newspapers   256
Free advertising   257
Telephone   258
Institutions   259
Local shopfront   262
Pubs   263
Youth work   266

Acknowledgements

This book has only been made possible by all those who have joined in the teamwork of evangelism alongside me, particularly the members of Ichthus Christian Fellowship and my present church, 'The 418 Project', in Hemel Hempstead. Thank you to all who have been willing to put time and energy into experimenting with such a wide range of new ideas in outreach activities.

Above all, I would like to acknowledge a debt of gratitude to my remarkable wife Sallie and my two wonderful daughters Claire and Sarah, for putting up with our life on the wilder shores of evangelism. I am grateful for their unfailing support and encouragement.

Many thanks also go to Samuel Fogelqvist for his excellent cartoon drawings.

Lastly, but especially, I would like to thank Barbara Newton for the many hours she has spent rearranging my sentences, tidying my punctuation and teaching me to identify a misrelated participle. Without her help, this book would never have reached its final form.

Foreword

Graham Warner's *Evangelism Handbook* is a challenging call for the church of Jesus Christ to go back to its roots and begin afresh with the priorities of its calling; namely winning souls not losing them and gaining the world not abandoning it. So, it is worth noting since Graham, as usual, is being radical and examining church roots, that the great adventure of Christian world mission did not begin with the honoured notables of the nineteenth century such as Carey, Hudson Taylor, C.T. Studd and William Booth to name but a few. Truly these and many others shaped the 1800s, now known in many circles as the 'great missionary century'. However, even though these past spiritual giants are inspiring, this was not the beginning of world mission.

Neither did world mission begin in the eighteenth-cen tury experience of Herrnhut with the 'baptism of the Spirit' upon the disparate and quarrelling Moravians and their multi-denominational adherents. Certainly this experience welded them into a unity forming a mission church community, which began to fill the earth with missionaries and continued in world mission significantly by leading John Wesley to Christ and so fuelling the fires of the Great Awakening.

The Counter-Reformation which was the Roman Catholic response to the sixteenth-century Protestant Reformation, produced Francis Xavier amongst many others and Catholicism spread the name of Jesus through the Americas, Asia and parts of Africa; places where the music of his name had previously been unknown. This period saw the greatest expansion of the Roman Church, but it could hardly be said that it was radical evangelism producing radical Christianity in the sense of original Christianity. Sadly, Protestantism was confined to Northern Europe throughout this period while Xavier preached Christ in fifty-two countries in the ten years between his conversion at the age of thirty-five and his death at forty-five. But neither the Reformation nor its Roman counterpart could be said to be the roots of world mission. The former centuries had seen intrepid pioneers who had been inspired to carry the good news to what was regarded as the ends of the earth. Brendan and his fellow Irish monks negotiated the North Atlantic and probably 'found' America in the sixth century AD simply motivated by the desire to obey Matthew 28 verses 19–20. This was 900 years before Columbus and 500 years before the Vikings arrived there.

Francis of Assisi is in the same spiritual ilk as Brendan's Celtic Christianity which, incidentally, had spread to northern Italy not far from Assisi. Francis founded two missions to Muslims in Syria and Morocco. While sharing with the Celts their evangelistic zeal, he joined them also in his love for nature and simplicity of life. However, it is not for us to look at the evangelistic preaching of Francis as foundational, even though he was restoring the call of God for all mankind, European and Muslim alike. This is not where we are to look for the source of evangelistic zeal.

Not even the resurrection of our Lord in the first century AD, nor his Great Commission in Matthew 28 verses 19–20 strictly begin God's earthly evangelistic purpose. This purpose of God in human history might be called the universal meta-narrative in today's post-modern jargon; that is the great all-embracing overview story which gives meaning to all our smaller stories.

Surprisingly, we return to the first book of the Bible and 4,000 years ago. Abraham was called by God for a particular purpose. Of course, in one sense, world mission begins in the heart of God. It was his idea. He so loved the world he gave his Son to it, who sent his Spirit, for it is the Spirit's presence in the church which is first and foremost that we might be witnesses to the ends of the earth (Acts 1:8). But, in another sense, that is as a movement in humanity's on-going story; God with Abraham begins a new thing in humanity with a view that every family in every ethnic linguistic group might be blessed.

The LORD had said to Abram [Abraham], 'Leave your country, your people and your father's household and go to the land I will show you.

'I will make you into a great nation
and I will bless you;
I will make your name great,
and you will be a blessing.
I will bless those who bless you,
and whoever curses you I will curse;
and all peoples on earth
will be blessed through you.'

So Abram left, as the LORD had told him; and Lot went with him. Abram was seventy-five years old when he set out from Haran.

(Gen 12:1–4; cf Gen 17:1–8; 18:17–18;
22:17–18; 26:18; 28:14)

Now the interesting fact at the beginning of world mission is the use God makes of the word 'bless'. The root of the word 'bless' occurs five times in this covenant statement. Genesis uses the word 88 times and the rest of the Old Testament only a further 310. God's desire to bless both surrounds and saturates the covenant call of Abraham and is the end objective of his mission. The reason for a covenant people, that is, a special people with whom God works for his purpose to be fulfilled, is that the world of nations and families might be blessed.

Now Graham's book is a challenge to recover the roots of the church and so consequently to rediscover the fundamental reasons for which the church exists. That reason is mission or evangelism which consists in using all means to bring blessing to every earthly family. However, what is blessing? Blessing sounds a warm and loving word but rather vague. By following Graham's example of radicalism and examining the roots, an investigation of the beginning of

God's mission in Abraham 4,000 years ago, the blessing God has ordained, might well be defined. This blessing, which is for all mankind and which Abraham and the covenant people Israel and then the church must transport, might then be defined, restated and reaffirmed. Psalm 105 verses 8–15 remind us that Abraham, Sarah, Isaac and Rebekah were all anointed and also were regarded as prophets. 'Do not touch my anointed ones; do my prophets no harm' (v 15). The wives were particularly in view because the stories alluded to refer immediately to the women being touched, then secondarily to the men (Gen 20:6; 26:10–11). It was also made clear in the story that Abraham was a prophet (Gen 20:7). and this calling in Psalm 105 verse 15 is extended to all four; therefore this mission is a ministry for both men and women. The roots of the covenant people who are called into being to bless the families of the earth were anointed prophets, both men and women. They had something of God to carry into the world – the anointing, and they had something from God to say to the world – they were prophets.

So in the epistle to the Galatians chapter 3 verses 8–9, Paul also goes back to those beginnings which precede him by 2,000 years and argues that believers of his day, and so those of today, are 'blessed with Abraham the believer'. The blessing we receive is the anointing, as with Abraham and, incidentally, Sarah, Rebekah and Isaac. This is the Holy Spirit of God. Galatians 3 verse 14 says: 'In order that the blessing given to Abraham might come to the Gentiles through Christ Jesus, so that by faith we might receive the promise of the Spirit.' In order to receive this presence of God by his Spirit we need Abraham's prophetic message, '[Abraham] believed God and it was credited to him as righteousness' (Gal 3:6), or again as in 3 verse 11: 'The righteous will live by faith'. The prophetic ministry gives the message of faith in order to clear the decks to receive the anointing, but the anointing is so that we may carry and convey God's life-giving Spirit to a dying world. This calling and ministry is not just for the exceptional worthies of the past but every branch and twig of the covenant tree so that they may fulfil their purpose. What could be a more thrilling or meaningful existence than to be a part of the covenanted people bringing the anointing which is God's presence to each human being we meet? This calling is perfectly exemplified by Jesus who demonstrates what world mission is. Of Jesus it is said, 'God anointed Jesus of Nazareth with the Holy Spirit and power, and how he went around doing good and healing all who were under the power of the devil, because God was with him' (Acts 10:38).

Graham's contribution to the church in this book is an antidote to the twenty-first-century self-occupied church, full of evangelistic panic, consumerism addiction, affluence pursuit, exhaustion shopping and the frenetic demand for instantaneous satisfaction culminating in entertainment stupefaction, all of which war against the believer laying hold of the magnificent vision of being the people of God. This antidote is first and foremost thoroughly biblical. In these pages we find strategies, tactics, disciplines and training all sharpening the mind, motives and emotions. It is a sort of compendium of neglected truths of God's mind for service and battle. He is reminding us that the first lesson before any other that Jesus taught his disciples is Matthew 4 verse 19: 'I will make you fishers of men.' How far down the line of Christian maturity can we be if we have never learnt the first lesson. This lesson was given in the context of presence, power, proclamation and persuasion evangelism, being done by Jesus (see Matt 4:12–5:2). In other words, by all means win some just as Jesus did. Winning men and women to discipleship is multi-faceted in its comprehensive embrace of all sorts and conditions of the human race, but in a word it is blessing them.

The mind of God for blessing all sinners and all nations was revealed at the time of the first sin. God prophesied that through the seed of woman would come the defeat of the devil and the death of the death he had brought. That Jesus through his blood and resurrection fulfilled this prophecy and accomplished salvation for humankind most Christians would agree. However, the final application of this victory is to be demonstrated and accomplished through the church, the covenant body of Jesus. This Paul declares in Romans 16 verse 20: 'The God of peace will soon crush Satan under your feet.' God's plan requires the church's feet, that is the church that at last sees its purpose here on earth in fighting Satan and bringing God's blessing of the Spirit to all those who will believe. Graham's book will help us to 'hasten that day' for which a groaning world has waited too long as it waits for the church to be the adventurous covenant church of God's intention and purpose and not the church of our own convenience. God wants to bless every family of the earth; so should and must we, Christ's Body. The blessing of God is the source, inspiration, activity and content of world evangelisation.

Roger T. Forster
January 2000

Introduction

The current expectation that revival is coming has a tendency to lead us into evangelistic passivity; after all, when it comes, thousands will suddenly flock through our doors. But, while we wait, society is becoming more and more secular and church membership continues to decline. We might hope for some easy 'cure all', some instant 'world-winning' solution. The harsh reality is, however, that we will never win the world without evangelising it. It seems that God has so designed it that it takes energy on our part to create change in society or in individuals' lives. 'Good works' are often going to be 'hard works'. Scientists prove that it is easier to bring about disorder than it is to produce order. Life without input seems to dissipate and run down. Just as the garden becomes overrun, or the house becomes dusty and messy, so society, without active intervention, becomes disorderly. This book is a challenge for the church to get involved in the task of changing the world. We *can* make an impact on society, but this will require some effort on our part.

I don't particularly see myself as an expert in these things. During much of my twenty-eight years of experience in evangelism, social action and church planting, I have acted rather like a manager of a football team. My role has been largely in encouraging the various team members, who have often been far more able and better equipped than I, to play their game. Instrumentalists in an orchestra often play with skills beyond the conductor's personal ability. He, nevertheless, wants to get the best out of each musician, emphasising their strengths and expertise. The material in these chapters has formed a basis for lectures and training seminars for many years. I personally find these principles incredibly exciting and stimulating and trust that they will bring out the evangelistic potential in others.

I am not sure that we ever lose our 'L' plates in evangelism. The world's scene shifts so rapidly. Our evangelism of tomorrow will be a far cry from our experiences of today. I hope therefore that this material will provoke some fresh, creative ways of communicating the gospel for the next phase of church outreach. I am sure that some of the keys to evangelising in the future are to be found by investigating the past. That is why I seek to identify 131 biblical principles taken from the earthly ministry of Jesus and from the experiences of the first generation of Christians. The second part of the book looks at more contemporary, personal examples and makes 101 practical suggestions. Hopefully these will spark 1,001 fresh ideas, using the reader's own creativity, leisure interests, personality and gifting.

I grew up with the statistic that it took 1,000 Christians a whole year to win just one convert to Christ. This seemed to highlight a real lack of motivation for a movement which has the 'Great Commission' as its 'job description'. My experience of church seemed to bear out the truth of that statistic. Yet I began to find 'evangelistic faith' through looking at the amazing promises, descriptions and definitions of the kingdom in the New Testament. In the chapter entitled 'The Magnitude of the Magnetism' I seek to show how spiritual dynamics are at work in society even before we lift a finger. Similarly, in 'The Manifestation of the Miraculous' we see that, when we do turn our focus to evangelise, there are remarkable supernatural aids available to us, making the task of evangelism really easy. I hope you will find as you read through these principles that your evangelistic faith will grow too.

I joined Ichthus Christian Fellowship in its early days in London, back in 1975, and was privileged to be part of it as it became one of the fastest-growing churches in the country. This experience inspired me to believe that people get saved when we proclaim the good news, because they did. It is exciting when the Lord gives words of knowledge, e.g. 'Five people will be saved on the High Street tomorrow', and sure enough, before the end of a two-hour open-air meeting, five people have given their lives to the Lord. Of course, in some parts of the world hundreds may be converted through street evangelism. However, we were finding new faith because we were seeing signs of breakthrough which previously had not been happening on the streets of London.

There is nothing more wonderful than observing dramatic conversions and we have witnessed a few. Of course, we have also seen many other conversions that are perhaps a little less dramatic, but these are nevertheless just as wonderful. I will share some of these stories in the following pages. Interestingly, even when we don't see a breakthrough with people becoming Christians we can still be effective in evangelism. You could compare unsuccessful evangelists to the returning fisherman, who, when asked what he had caught, replied, 'I caught nothing, but I influenced loads!' There is an ironic truth here. There are amazing dynamics influencing society even if we don't find converts. I do fully believe, however, that we are in this business to catch people and if we fish much we shall also catch much (to mix a Galatian metaphor!). But we will also look at how our evangelism can make the whole pond a better environment for even the 'uncaught' fish to live in.

We were asked recently by our local authority to help, quite literally, clean up a local pond. Putting on our 'wellies' to do this is just part of our strategy of serving people, and that really did provide a better environment for some fish, as well as for the local community. From time to time we get involved in such projects. For example, we built a log maze in a local school playground, and we helped redevelop the gardens of our local Old People's Home. We get so excited about serving society in these practical ways that we have started a training programme, called WorldShapers,* specifically aimed at social action. It is a Bible School on the job, where the trainees learn in the process of serving the needs of society.

I remember sharing some of this training material at a school of evangelism in Holland, after which a young man approached me, saying, 'I wish I could do all these things, only I have a problem, I don't have a calling for it.' My reply seemed to take him by surprise, 'I don't have a calling for these things either. I just know that God loves people and wants them saved. I want to go and do whatever I can to make disciples. You don't have to have a calling to be a witness or to serve; it is already commanded for us all.' My hope is that in reading this material you will find some avenue of witnessing which inspires you enough to make fresh evangelistic inroads into the world!

The Evangelism Handbook, is a challenge to go further than some of our conventional forms of evangelism have done. We need to put some colour and character, i.e. 'soul', into our strategies for winning the world. At first sight, it may look as if I am contradicting what Jesus said. He asked, 'What good will it be for a man if he gains the whole world, yet forfeits his soul?' (Mt 16:26). Our title uses the terms of Jesus' statement as the basis for the idea that finding our souls spiritually, opens the door for us to gain the world evangelistically.

* Information about WorldShapers is available at
  http://come.to/Worldshapers

Part One

131 Evangelistic Principles

CHAPTER 1

THE MORALE OF THE MEMBERS

PRINCIPLE 1

Move non-Christians to jealousy . . . and save some

Romans 11:14

We were in the middle of a mission on a university campus in Greater Manchester. I had been warned that the President of the Atheist Society would strenuously oppose anything we did. That afternoon, going round the halls of residence, I happened to knock on her door. She harangued me for about an hour. I didn't get the chance to say very much, but before I left, I asked if I could pray with her. 'Oh no, you don't get me on that one,' she replied. Nevertheless, I told her that I would pray for her as would the other Christian students. At the feedback session later that day the whole Christian Union started interceding for her.

The following afternoon, I knocked on her door again to see how the Lord was getting on. Amazingly, she greeted me with the words, 'I am no longer an atheist,' adding after a little pause, 'I am now an agnostic.' This seemed a major move in the right direction, and she invited us in. This time she allowed us to talk to her, even letting us pray for her.

The next day, she sent for me declaring that she wanted to become a Christian. Four of us sat in a car together in the university car park and, sitting on the back seat, she gave her life to the Lord. After praying, she looked out of the car window. 'The world is completely different,' she said. I was so elated that I didn't sleep that night. The following day, out of sheer excitement I led seven other people to Christ. I think they could sense just how thrilling Christianity can be.

The Apostle Paul expressed the hope that somehow he 'might move to jealousy [his] fellow countrymen and save some of them' (Rom 11:14, NASB). This is an interesting concept – the church needs to project an image which makes outsiders feel that they are missing out. It's great when non-Christians come to the conclusion that we enjoy the Lord far more than they enjoy their leisure pursuits. We need to provoke the world to become jealous of what we have in Christ.

A couple of years ago, I was preaching and teaching in India. I was staying for a few days at an apartment in New Delhi which overlooked the Indian army barracks. We would sit out on the balcony in the evenings listening to the soldiers gathered around the camp fire. They would spend their evenings enthusiastically singing songs and clapping in time to the music. I found their camaraderie so attractive that I said to the friends with whom I was staying, 'If I lived here, I would definitely join the army.' The soldiers' singing was almost Christian in its intensity of expression, although I am sure it was in fact anything but spiritually edifying. Nevertheless, it provoked in me a feeling of jealousy.

A sense of camaraderie and good team dynamics characterise growing churches. Where Christians relate together in friendship with enthusiasm, energy and life, converts seem eager to join them. I can understand why revivals have caused such rapid growth in the church. Everybody starts talking about Jesus and there is a general sense of excitement. Outsiders become inquisitive to find out more. When Jesus' disciples went through the towns and villages gathering up the sick and the demon possessed, there was a certain exhilaration as they passed the word around. Something supernatural was happening and the world at large could sense it. As a result, people gathered together in their thousands. It was the same in the early church when people were being healed. The grapevine was buzzing with the news.

PRINCIPLE 2

Christianity is caught not just taught

Psalm 42:7

Those listening to the Samaritan woman at the well could sense the thrill behind her words, 'Come, see a man who told me everything I ever did' (Jn 4:29). It is not surprising that so many came out of the city to find Jesus. This woman was genuinely excited that she had found someone who was possibly the Messiah. I am challenged by this. How much excitement do people read behind my words when I knock on their door and invite them along to our next service? We of course have to be honest, but how can we describe, with superlatives, the brilliance of the Christian life? How can we get non-Christians excited about our church? What real-life stories can we share which communicate something of our passion and enthusiasm?

There is a spectacular follow-up to John's story about the woman at the well, if this is indeed the same city which Philip comes to in Acts 8 verses 5–8. Multitudes responded to Philip's preaching. It could be that the message had been buzzing round this town ever since Jesus sat on their well, offering eternally living water.

It is well known that communication is, amazingly, far more body language and tone of voice than the actual words we speak. Words on their own amount to only about 7 per cent of actual communication, tone of voice 35 per cent and body language a staggering 58 per cent. Most people are pretty observant and they know when we are genuinely excited by our faith. For some months we had an elderly gentleman living with us who had been redeemed from a rather colourful life of crime. He had spent much of his adult life in and out of prison, so he probably wasn't much good as a con man, even though that had been his life's occupation. After his conversion he came with us to church each Sunday. He wasn't used to sitting listening to sermons and didn't understand a lot of what was being said, but each

Sunday he would make the same comment on the way home. 'I didn't understand any of that – but he *really sounded as if he meant it!*' He had caught the enthusiasm and the spirit of what was being shared and it stirred a flame in his own heart. For this reason, one of the most crucial strategies in church evangelism must be first of all to raise the morale of our troops, to increase their level of excitement about Jesus and the message.

Some years ago, we took a group away for a holiday to the West Country. On the second day, a non-Christian member of the group came up to me and started to name church members who he thought were genuine Christians and others who he perceived were not. He went through six names before I got the chance to stop him. As I walked away, I was asking myself some questions about what he was saying. How was he making his assessments? Was there any truth behind his words? The problem was that some of his negative observations were actually referring to leaders in our church! Outwardly, we were all saying the same things, living by the same principles, yet this non-Christian was reading something deeper.

The psalmist said, 'Deep calls to deep' (Ps 42:7). As God works deeply in us, something deep happens in those with whom we share. Too often, though, our experience is so shallow that we have a very superficial effect on those around us. People can't receive from us any more than we have. Christianity is caught not just taught. We need to create a paradigm shift in the way the world views the church, because, on the whole, they have picked up the impression that Christianity is boring and not particularly relevant to life. Unfortunately, what they have seen in the church they have not wanted to catch.

PRINCIPLE 3

The kingdom is about joy

Matthew 13:44; Romans 14:17

Christian joy has to be one of the most powerful means of attracting people to the Christian faith. The ability to rejoice in the ups and downs of life even when we are experiencing extreme pressures, seems to have no parallel in the world. There is nothing so compelling as a group of Christians radiating the joy of the kingdom. Perhaps sometimes 'miserable sinners' find this difficult to take. I shall never forget one lady taking a swing at us with her handbag, as we were singing on the street, accusing us of being too happy. She described herself as being religious, and she was obviously not allowed to enjoy it.

Jesus was described as being anointed 'above [his] companions . . . with the oil of joy' (Heb 1:9). Then three times he tells us that this joy is now ours and that his joy can be made full in us (Jn 15:11; 16:24; 17:13). So, we too should have more joy than any of our non-Christian companions. Once, as I was travelling from Marseilles to London by train, I got deep into conversation with a fellow passenger. The moment he discovered I was a Christian, he tried to attack my faith on every level he could think of and, being a psychiatrist, he tried to explain away every reason I had for it. The conversation lasted more than ten hours. As the train eventually approached London, he said, 'Well, you haven't converted me, but I have to admit you are a much happier person than I am, and even if your faith isn't true, you are much better off believing what you do, than I am in not believing.' We then shared a taxi cab into the centre of London from the station and during this short trip he offered me a job. I think he wanted me to cheer up some of his patients!

This joy was always intended to be the answer to the world's deepest longings. As the psalmist observes, 'In his presence there is fullness of joy' (Ps 16:11, NASB).

Evangelism is, therefore, about bringing genuine satisfaction and fulfilment, which was intended by the Creator, to every desperate, aching heart. The kingdom of God is about righteousness, peace and joy in the Holy Spirit (Rom 14:17). When people look for this fulfilment in other things which often lead to addictions, I encourage them to repeat this phrase, 'This hunger is not for .... (e.g. alcohol, sex) it is for you, Lord'. The more intense a person's addiction, the greater their potential hunger for the Lord, and the greater their fulfilment in his joy.

PRINCIPLE 4

Joy even in rejection

Matthew 5:11–12; Luke 6:23

Strangely, one of the highest expressions of joy in the New Testament is at the very point when naturally we would lose all joy, that is when people persecute us or say all kinds of evil about us falsely. Jesus says we can then rejoice and be exceedingly glad, or literally leap for joy.

Joy, like the rest of the fruit of the Spirit, seems to flourish under pressure. For example, if you ask the Lord for more patience, he will cause it to grow through testing circumstances. If we ask the Lord for more love, he will usually send someone along to stretch our capacity for care and compassion. The fruit of peace is not cultivated by sitting on a mountain top in a serene environment but is created by the Lord in the panic and pressure of everyday life. The peace of God grows on the inside as the adverse stress increases on the outside. Jesus is making the observation that joy, too, increases under pressure (Lk 6:23). Maximise the opposition and you maximise the potential of your personal joy. This is God's way of 'beating the living daylights' out of a Christian. The batterings of life break the outer shell and release the glory of the Lord within us.

James tells us to, 'Consider it pure joy, my brothers,

whenever you face trials of many kinds, because you know that the testing of your faith develops perseverance' (Jas 1:2–4). This encourages us to enjoy the process, whatever the pressures life can throw at us. Just like hot water is necessary to make a good cup of tea, so the heat of life brings out our flavour. If the water isn't hot the tea is insipid and tasteless. The longer the teabag is in the hot water the stronger the tea becomes.

If it is actually possible to be glad when we are being rejected, or when our evangelism fails, or when we are denigrated or persecuted, we have surely a key to overcoming the most debilitating of our fears regarding evangelism. To be able to walk away from rejection, or should I say leap away, being exceedingly glad, surely gives us an incentive to chance the risks of rejection, which are perhaps inevitable if we are to see anyone converted. So, in the worst-case scenario, when our evangelism goes pear-shaped, we can still leave with a smile on our face.

PRINCIPLE 5

You shall go out with joy

Isaiah 55:12

It is a shame that so often evangelism carries threatening connotations when there are many scriptures emphasising the potential joy which is involved in sharing our faith. 'You will go out in joy and be led forth in peace' (Is 55:12). Even though the psalmist says that we will sometimes sow in tears, we will still reap in joy. Psychologists talk about the pleasure/pain principle as the motivation for all human behaviour. Often it is the pain that has been the motivating factor in evangelism. We witness because we need to escape the pain of guilt. We have to do it because we know we should. Then we find it painful even when we do do it, because of the hurts of rejection and failure.

To link pleasure and evangelism seems like a complete

contradiction in terms. 'Surely,' we think, 'witnessing is a necessity to be endured not a service to be enjoyed.' We do as little as possible in order to balance carefully the pain of actually having to do it, against the pain of the guilt of not doing it. Because we have not experienced joy in evangelism, most of us conclude that evangelism is, therefore, not our gift and we seek to serve in some other field in the church.

It would be so good if we could change our general mental focus and find ways to link pleasurable associations and motivations with our evangelism. We need to enjoy it and, consequently, our joy will rub off on the environment around us. Isaiah tells us that even the hills and trees will shout for joy and clap their hands. We need to start asking ourselves more empowering questions, not just, 'What should we do?' but, 'How can we enjoy the process of doing evangelism?'

For sure, teamwork provides an answer to these questions. With a team, it becomes amazingly easy to do things which you would never dare to do on your own. I remember watching an elderly gentleman standing in the middle of St Paul's Square, before I was ever involved in evangelistic work. He sang 'Amazing grace' and then preached, on his own, to the hundreds of people gathered around the bars in the square. I couldn't help admiring his courage and wishing that somehow I could witness with similar boldness. But I knew that for me this was an impossibility. I was terrified of speaking in public under any circumstances. At that time, I felt that standing on the street and sharing the gospel was utterly beyond my capability. Little did I know that I would soon be doing this regularly and in fact be thoroughly enjoying the experience. Teamwork made it easy. I have to say, however, after years of experience, that I would still find it impossible to stand in St Paul's Square on my own and sing 'Amazing grace'!

PRINCIPLE 6

You shall return with joy

Luke 10:17

The early disciples returned from their evangelistic campaigns with real delight: 'The seventy-two returned with joy and said, "Lord, even the demons submit to us in your name." '(Lk 10:17). Jesus showed this joy to be a little misplaced and reminded them that they should never be glad at someone else's downfall, even if it is the devil's. But Jesus himself seemed then to express a real sense of joy at the kinds of people who were receiving the kingdom. 'I praise you, Father . . . you have hidden these things from the wise and learned, and revealed them to little children' (Lk 10:21). He seemed to be enjoying the irony of this.

Flicking through the pages of Acts, we read of tremendous joy being released, whether it is the Ethiopian eunuch returning home, *rejoicing* after his baptism in the desert (Acts 8:39), or a whole city like Samaria, where there was *much rejoicing* after the preaching of Philip (Acts 8:8). Maybe this was the natural overflow of the fact that the early disciples were meeting together with *gladness* and sincerity of heart (Acts 2:46). We had a Danish student working with us last year for a few months and he regularly used to say: 'It's true, you can get "high" on evangelism.' Certainly, it has been our experience that people returning from evangelism have a real sense of excitement and elation, which is more than just relief that it is all over!

From time to time, we have delayed the start of our midweek prayer meeting and given everybody a couple of leaflets and said: 'We are all going out to knock on a couple of doors each and invite those we meet along to church. Then we will pray when everybody has returned.' I can honestly say that these prayer meetings have been some of the liveliest that I have ever attended because the members of the group would all return with such joy.

PRINCIPLE 7

The joy of fulfilling the task

1 Thessalonians 3:9; 3 John v 4; Acts 20:24

We hardly ever reach the joy of fulfilling a task without perseverance. Imagine the joy of that woman when she found her lost coin, having swept the whole house from top to bottom (Lk 15:8), or the shepherd as he found the straying sheep having sought high and low for it (Lk 15:4). Even the angels are excited when they see the results of our labours (Lk 15:10). They have a party every time someone repents, so it is not surprising that they are watching our evangelism (1 Pet 1:12). If the father in the story of the prodigal son portrays the feelings of our heavenly Father, we see that it is more than just the angels of heaven who are rejoicing when someone is found. We, like Jesus, need to persevere until the task is finished because of the joy that is set before us (Heb 12:2).

There must have been tremendous satisfaction as the Lord rested on the seventh day and looked at all he had made. It was good, good, good, good, good, and very good, (Gen 1:4, 10, 12, 18, 21, 25 and 31). I enjoy a bit of DIY, but I have to say that I enjoy finishing it even more. It is an immense satisfaction to see a job done. Paul talks of his joy in finishing the course that was set for him and of fighting a good fight. Maybe sometimes we don't think we accomplish quite as much as others do, but the real question to ask is 'Are we finishing the tasks that God has given us to do?' The ultimate task that the Lord has entrusted to us is to evangelise the whole world in our generation. It would be a fantastic joy if we could fulfil this task and finish this phase of world history during our lifetime.

The expressions that were given in the Old Testament regarding the joys of harvest are just as appropriate for the spiritual harvests of the New Testament. Consider, for example, Isaiah 9 verse 3: 'You have enlarged the nation and have increased their joy; they rejoice before you as people rejoice at the harvest, as men rejoice when dividing the plunder.'

PRINCIPLE 8

The joy of meeting needs

Acts 8:8; John 17:13

One of the key ways of proclaiming the gospel is through social action, in meeting the needs of others. This brings us one of the profoundest joys in life, which is often sensed by the people we are serving. Last year, I had the opportunity of praying round the house of a lady who had just been converted from a Buddhist cult. We were doing some spiritual house cleaning. She had become a Christian through reading Paul's remark, quoting Jesus, 'It is more blessed to give than to receive' (Acts 20:35). It gave her a totally new revelation on life. She suddenly became aware that her Buddhist training was all about herself. It was fundamentally selfish, but Jesus was saying that happiness was about serving others. That one sentence changed her whole life.

Some years ago, I was sitting in an airport reading a magazine, which had an article entitled 'Get as much as you can, and can as much as you get'. Currently in the bestseller lists is John Gray's *How to Get What You Want and Want What You Have*. This has become one of the deceits of our times; that happiness is somehow wrapped up in getting more things. The early Christians discovered true joy by giving things away. Sometimes they begged for the opportunity to give, even giving beyond their means and making themselves poor in the process (2 Cor 8–9). This will be developed in a later chapter, but it is appropriate to say now that this joy is not just ours. It is for those whom we seek to serve. Like Jesus, our anointing should be to give a garland instead of ashes and the oil of gladness instead of mourning (Is 61:3).

I have often had people apologise to me for being such a trouble when they have had to call upon me for help in some form or other. They don't really understand the truth behind my response to their thanks, 'It's a pleasure.' They think they have been a burden, but they haven't, quite the opposite in fact, they have been the cause of release of joy in my life. What a delight to be able to help someone, to make a difference in someone's life – no matter how small! They shouldn't have to thank us, we should be thanking them for giving us the opportunity to serve them.

PRINCIPLE 9

The joy of rewards

Matthew 25:21

Fishermen still enjoy the process of fishing even if they don't catch anything – hope drives them on. There is nothing like the hope that today may be the day that we catch the next fish for the kingdom of God. Evangelism is a win-win situation because it wins people in the present and rewards in the future. We can enjoy both the process and the results of our labours in the here and now, and Jesus will also bless us with additional rewards at the end of the day. He couches it in terms like, 'Well done, good and faithful servant . . . Come and share your master's happiness!' (Mt 25:21). I have always had a problem with the concept of working for the payment of rewards. It seems like a wrong incentive. Of course that is not why we serve. We serve because we love the Lord and the people. But nevertheless, God promises to recompense every kindness shown and every sacrifice made with rewards multiplied a hundredfold.

There is no doubt that when we eventually stand before the Lord not only will we say that any efforts invested were totally worthwhile, but I think most of us are going to wish we had given a little bit more. There will be no one on that day who will wish he had spent more time at the office. This book has been written to stir our hearts to live for the Lord's priorities, to encourage one another to make our days count for the kingdom of God. Life is so short and the mandate is so big, but the rewards are really great.

CHAPTER 2

THE MANDATE OF
THE MISSION

PRINCIPLE 10

We are appointed . . . to bear much fruit

John 15:1–8, 16

Taking some time out from a fairly busy teaching schedule on a church houseparty, I took a stroll along some Danish country lanes. Dusk was just beginning to fall and I was enjoying a few moments of privacy, singing and praying out loud in the quietness of the half light. With almost every step that I took, I could hear the scurrying feet of wildlife, probably desperate to escape the dreadful singing, scuttling this way and that in the roadside ditches. Suddenly my mind grasped the words of the old hymn that I was singing 'Something lives in every hue, Christless eyes have never seen'. The truth of this came home to me. How incredibly fruitful life in nature is.

Almost everywhere you look in the world, vegetation, along with animal and insect life, flourishes, most of it quite spontaneously. How wonderfully nature has fulfilled the commands of its Creator to reproduce and fill up the earth. As I walked along, my mind ran back to similar lanes along which I would pray back home. How many times had I watched the seedtimes turn to harvests. I had often marvelled at the combine harvesters, reaping amazingly vast quantities of crops. They seemed to rebuke the smallness of my own fruitfulness for God. Why is it that the God of life and abundant fruitfulness is so successful in every sphere of life, except the very one for which he gave his own life?

PRINCIPLE 11

Each seed reproduces

Matthew 13:8

Fruitfulness is God's intention for every disciple. Painfully, he prunes some of us to make us more fruitful and expresses his ultimate desire that we bear much fruit. By our fruitfulness the Father is glorified and, in this way, we also prove ourselves to be real disciples (Jn 15:8). Certainly, some of this fruit refers to our qualities of character, defined as the fruit of the Spirit's character in Galatians 5 verse 22. We recognise one another by these fruits, which is why, of course, they prove our discipleship. You will know them by their fruits, Jesus said (Mt 7:16, 20). But, nevertheless, the illustration of nature surely challenges us to increase our productivity, to produce fruit not just within ourselves but also in the world around us. Jesus' parable of the sower sets a target to reproduce thirtyfold, sixtyfold or one hundredfold. We should set this as a minimum objective for every church member, to reproduce at least thirtyfold in their lifetime. How about setting the objective to see the seed of your life bring between thirty to one hundred people to new life in Christ before you die? The church would grow phenomenally if this became our yearly target.

Jesus also adds, in John 15, that our fruit should 'remain'. If it wasn't for the Apostle Paul's honesty in admitting that some of his converts had reverted to the world (2 Tim 1:15; 4:10) I would feel very condemned by this statement. I have to admit that some of those whom I have led to the Lord have slipped away. I think of one man who gave up his faith and went on to commit murder, or the lady who forsook the church to enter into an informal marriage covenant with someone of her own sex. I grieve for them even though I am sure that God's grace still follows them. However, it is so good to see many whose fruit has remained, and it is particularly encouraging to see your fruit go on to yield yet more fruit in others through them.

PRINCIPLE 12

Abiding – the key to fruitfulness

John 15:1

The key to this fruitfulness is in recognising that we are unable to produce anything on our own, but if we 'abide in the vine' his fruitfulness becomes ours. What does this mean? In a way it seems a contradiction in terms to say 'abide' and then to say 'go' and bear fruit. On the one hand, this seems to emphasise the importance of 'resting' in the Lord, but it is counterbalanced by the activity of the go-getter for Jesus. We must go and bear this fruit and not just sit back and wait for it to grow on its own. But we also have to remain firmly grounded in the Lord. If you keep digging up potatoes to see how they are growing, they will cease to grow. In the same way, our abiding has to be continuous. We must abide in the vine for the whole season of fruit bearing. We cannot be in Christ one day and out the next and still expect a fruitful season.

PRINCIPLE 13

The harvest is plentiful

Matthew 9:36–38; John 4:35–38

In fact, the fruitfulness of nature is mirrored by the fruitfulness of the kingdom. The harvest is not only ripe but also plentiful. We do not need to pray for a harvest. Harvest, according to Jesus, is no problem. The problem is the lack of workers. The ripeness of harvest is produced by the Creator and that is why he is described as the 'Lord of the harvest'. We will examine a little later some of the ways in which the Lord produces supernatural harvest. Certainly, we see described for us throughout the pages of the book of Acts the reality of this principle of abundant harvest, in that we read of thousands being converted, sometimes in vast multitudes.

If we believe that the harvest is plentiful, we will surely be motivated to go and gather the fruit. Every church, according to Jesus, is surrounded by many who are actively or passively seeking him. Potential converts, like ripe fruit, are waiting to be picked. Often our experience is that no one seems interested in God's kingdom, and it is true that many are not, but Jesus sees society as being made up of many who are still seeking God. Our task is to find these lost sheep. It might require some diligence on our part in seeking them out, but they are certainly there.

It is challenging to read the Old Testament laws regarding harvesting. The poor were allowed to enter the fields and pick the grapes and the olives, but they were not allowed to harvest them. They could pick them and eat them, but they were not allowed to put them in their baskets (Dt 23:24). Does the rather sparse picking of converts in our spiritual harvests today perhaps make a statement about our spiritual poverty? When we are in partnership with the One who owns the fields, we are free to harvest in a big way. At present, it is as if we are gleaning in the fields rather than harvesting.

We have to further explore the question, 'Is there anything we should be doing towards producing the harvest?' Not being an expert on farming or agriculture, my thinking is probably a little simplistic, but success in arable farming seems dependent on three things: 1) The right seed, 2) The right soil, and 3) The right climate. Some areas just don't suit cereal crops and, no matter how much you sow them, they won't grow there. In those areas, it is better to grow timber or to convert everything to grasslands. Perhaps, when we don't see a lot of spiritual fruit for our labours, we need to ask whether we are sowing the right kind of seeds for the ground available to us. What does this mean?

PRINCIPLE 14

The right seeds for our soil

2 Corinthians 9:10

1) The right seed

Although the statement that the Lord 'multiplies your seed for sowing' is more to do with financial giving than evangelism, I am sure the principles are nevertheless the same. We will look at the principle 'Freely you have received so freely give' a little later. But here in 2 Corinthians 9 verse 10 we are told that 'He who supplies seed to the sower and bread for food will also supply and increase your store of seed and will enlarge the harvest of your righteousness'. The Lord is promising to supply the seed for us and this will probably need to vary for use from one place to another. So we can perhaps presume that he furnishes us with different kinds of seeds for our varying sowing situations – alternative methods of evangelism for different social conditions. What works in one place might not work somewhere else. Every farmer has to learn what grows best on his land. As with natural fruit, the seed grows within itself and then gets planted out. What are the seeds which are growing within us as a church fellowship? We need to recognise what grows well in our situation and to seek to plant these seeds into others' lives.

PRINCIPLE 15

Break up your fallow ground

Jeremiah 4:3

2) The right soil

The Bible says that the Lord teaches the farmer everything he needs to know about ploughing, sowing and threshing (Is 28:23–29). We desperately need to learn more about these for our spiritual farming. It has surprised me to see how much time and energy farmers put into preparing their ground before sowing. Alongside my church work, I also run a property business and last year we were involved in converting a barn into a four-bedroomed house. It took over a year to complete the project and so we saw the whole process of sowing and reaping going on in the surrounding fields.

We were amazed at how quickly the ploughing followed the harvesting. The farm workers had toiled so hard at reaping the crops that we had quite expected that they would take a well-earned rest. But, to our surprise, the ploughing for the next crop started the very next day. The field was so large that it took the farmer on his tractor three days to complete, working from early morning till late evening. Having finished, we expected to see the sowing start, but were astounded to discover the next day that the plough was back in the field. We marvelled at that poor farmer's perseverance as he sat on his tractor for a another three days, while he ploughed the same ground again. In fact, he then came and ploughed it a third and fourth time before he eventually sowed his seed.

No farmer would just sow without first breaking up the ground and there must be a spiritual equivalent to this ploughing and loosening of the soil. We often sow seeds without taking much thought for the condition of the earth. I now find myself asking questions as to how we can best cultivate society to become more receptive to the seeds that we plant. It brings into play a concept that has been called 'pre-evangelism'. Pre-evangelism is doing anything that creates more receptive attitudes towards the gospel. Some classic examples would be social action, the use of prophecy and of course the proven course of friendship. Social action, like friendship, often gives us the right to be heard. As people accept our kindnesses, they often take into their hearts what we stand for too.

3) The right climate
The next question to ask is 'Can we affect the climate?' Mark 4 verses 26–29 tells us that Jesus said,

> 'This is what the kingdom of God is like. A man scatters seed on the ground. Night and day, whether he sleeps or gets up, the seed sprouts and grows, though he does not know how. All by itself the soil produces corn – first the stalk, then the ear, then the full grain in the ear. As soon as the grain is ripe, he puts the sickle to it, because the harvest has come.'

Both the growing and the ripeness of the harvest are in God's hands. Nevertheless, we are essential in the processes of sowing and reaping. Maybe one sows and another reaps as in 1 Corinthians 3 verses 6–9, or perhaps we all need to sow and we all need to reap where we have the opportunity. Much of the rest of this chapter looks at the place of prayer in providing the right conditions for growth and particularly how we pray to be effective in providing the right climate for harvest.

PRINCIPLE 16

Pray for light to shine out of our hearts
2 Corinthians 4:6

After many years of open air meetings and praise marches around the estates of South East London, I think it became easier for people to become Christians. The Apostle Paul says, 'The god of this age has blinded the minds of unbelievers, so that they cannot see the light of the gospel of the glory of Christ, who is the image of God' (2 Cor 4:4). The real way to overcome darkness is to cause the light of Jesus to shine. Just as God commanded light to shine in the beginning (Gen 1) we now pray that he will cause his light to radiate out of our hearts. If we hide the gospel by failing to proclaim it, the devil, it seems, can blind the eyes of the unbelieving. We need to evangelise as aggressively as we can. The more evangelisation goes on, the lighter the atmosphere becomes. This undermines the devil's kingdom and provides the light necessary for the growth of the seed.

This world is filled with the darkness of evil and unbelief. We need to be able to punch a hole through to heaven to bring light to people who are sitting in darkness. The message of the gospel is spiritually discerned. It is not primarily grasped intellectually or apprehended emotionally. Some-times you can explain the gospel as simply as possible, use every illustration, every anecdote, and a person will still fail to understand, yet then you can go back to the same person and say the same thing and suddenly it clicks. They've seen the light.

We had a mission in the West Country some years ago with dramatic results. Every non-Christian who came to the meetings was either healed or saved. People just walked in off the street remarking on the changed atmosphere in the town, as if an umbrella of love was over it. They had come to the meeting to find out what was going on. The reason for the breakthrough was a group praying over the town from a local hillside with almost non-stop intercession. The growth of the seed and the ripening of the crops are totally dependent on the effect of the sunshine. Prayer creates the 'Sonshine' (i.e. the radiance of Jesus' glory), not just from heaven but out of our hearts and our churches.

PRINCIPLE 17

Pray for authorities

1 Timothy 2:1-4

Paul's instructions to Timothy are that entreaties and prayers, petitions and thankgivings should be made on behalf of all men. It is one of the passages which show us that we can affect the whole of society. In fact, when we pray for kings and those in authority, it leads to peace and quietness of life for all, allowing people to live with godliness and dignity. But the climax of these verses, as far as I am concerned, is verse 4 which talks about 'God our Saviour, who wants all men to be saved and to come to a knowledge of the truth'. It is our responsibility, by our prayers, to provide a spiritual environment in our country which makes it easy for people to find the Lord.

The church has for too long, I think, ignored the world of politics. We are, of course, part of a kingdom that is not of this world, but we are here to influence this world and its systems. I have enjoyed the process of getting to know some of the people in authority in our town, so that I can pray for them a little more intelligently. We have tried to discuss our plans and visions as a church with those in authority, like our MP, our county and local councillors, and the mayor of the town. I sat yesterday in the public gallery of the Social Services County Councillors Forum thinking that we should certainly have Christians involved in all such gatherings, just to pray and to listen. When I was in London, I had a friend who would spend much of his time praying around the Houses of Parliament and, sitting in the public gallery, he was able to pray specifically for those in authority and to pray over their decisions as they were being made.

PRINCIPLE 18

Pray that Jesus 'sends us' into evangelism

Matthew 9:38

The key to getting into the harvest is also prayer. Jesus doesn't just say 'Go', he says we must ask the Father to 'send us' out. Being sent out means that we go carrying the Father's authority. So we read, 'He called his twelve disciples to him and gave them authority over . . .' (Mt 10:1). This mission is God's and we go out in his name, to do his bidding.

The words 'send out' are strong words. In the Greek, the word '*ekballo*' is used, from which we get our English word 'ballistic', as in ballistic missile. This gives the sense of thrust, of a supernatural push into evangelism. In fact, it is the same word that is used in Matthew 10 verse 1 for 'cast out' demons. So, quite literally, we pray that the Lord would cast out Christians. Perhaps this is the only way to get us out of our Christian ghettos into the harvest fields. The Lord knows how difficult we find this task and, without this push from heaven, I'm not sure that the job of winning the world is ever going to get done. However, surely one of the keys to seeing our nation evangelised is to pray this particular prayer. With the Lord of the harvest helping us, witnessing suddenly becomes easier.

PRINCIPLE 19

Pray for open doors of opportunity

John 17:9, Colossians 4:3

Paul asked people to pray for him that he would have an open door of opportunity. Notice that he doesn't tell the

Colossians to pray for the non-Christians to whom he is witnessing (Col 4:3), instead he says, 'Pray for us, too, that God may open a door for our message.' We need open doors of opportunity for the gospel. Paul said of his stay in Corinth, that God opened a 'wide and effective door'. If the Lord opens a door for you, then you will be amazed at how easy evangelism can be.

At one stage of my work in London, I worked nights at an alcoholics' rehabilitation centre. Before going on duty for my first night, I sat with a friend in my home and we prayed that the Lord would give me an open door of opportunity to present the gospel. Off I went, arriving at 10 pm just as the day staff were locking the office. 'You have to stay with the residents in the lounge during the night duty,' they said. That was fine by me as contact with the residents was what I wanted. But when I got to their lounge I was in for a shock. As I walked in I found a large room full of blaspheming alcoholics. The foul atmosphere of blue jokes and abusive language hit me like a wall. I felt I had stepped into an alien environment. However, mustering my courage, I went over to the first group of men and tried to introduce myself. But they totally ignored me. They seemed to have decided on a strategy to shut me out as if I didn't exist. I went round the whole room like this, to every group, and they all refused even to acknowledge my presence. I was so completely at a loss that I sat in a corner by myself and picked up a newspaper, pretending to read but really thinking about that prayer we had prayed such a short time before. I thought to myself that there was no way I could share my faith in that environment.

But suddenly, after about half an hour, somebody shouted a question at me from the other side of the room. It was a question about Christianity. I cannot now remember what it was, but everyone in the room fell silent and turned to look at me. I had got my Bible in my bag so I quickly took it out and read a verse, using it to answer the question. No sooner had I concluded my answer than another resident fired a question at me, and then another, and another. Four hours later we were still debating Christian issues until at last I decided it was time to send everybody to bed.

The following night, when I came on duty, immediately a man stood up in the lounge and, banging on the table, said, 'Quiet everybody, it's Christian time.' This went on for a week until one night one of the residents waited behind after everyone else had gone to bed. He came and sat down beside me and said, 'Graham, can you get this Jesus into my life?' With an open Bible, we knelt on the floor in the middle of that room which just a few days earlier had been such a foul place and he gave his life to Christ. Over the next few nights four more alcoholics did the same, and it was wonderful because as they did so, Jesus broke the power of alcohol on them. Just in giving their lives to Christ they were set free from the alcohol.

Now, they weren't very diplomatic because they went to the people running the centre and said, 'Do you know, you're wasting your time here. It's Jesus that sets people free from alcohol.' When they had been questioned a little bit further, I got the sack from my job. But it didn't really matter because I left five evangelists behind in that place. The last I heard, four of them were still off the drink and one of those, having started his own business and family, named his first son Graham after me. What a privilege to have played a part in seeing their lives transformed. But that all happened, if I am honest, in a place where I would not have dared to share my faith. The Lord opened a door of opportunity, and if the Lord does that, then suddenly you find it's incredibly easy.

PRINCIPLE 20

Pray for boldness to speak as we ought
Ephesians 6:19

In Ephesians 6:19, Paul asks others to pray for him to 'have boldness to speak as I ought to speak' (NASB). It is one thing to have an open door but quite another to have the boldness to walk through it. Many of us feel inadequate for the task of presenting the gospel. I have always been so encouraged by the thought that if we feel we can't do something, this feeling of inadequacy actually qualifies us for the action of the Holy Spirit. The weaker we are, the more the Lord can use us, because we are forced to act in the power of the Holy Spirit. It is only if we face up to our fears and inadequacies and pray to the Lord for help, that the Holy Spirit will speak through us.

I remember a salutary example of this one Sunday afternoon when I led a team from Scandinavia in an 'open air' at Speakers' Corner, the part of Hyde Park which every Sunday transforms itself into what I call a 'nutters' paradise'. Anyone can stand on a soapbox and say anything they like. When you go there, you find that anyone with an axe to grind is standing on a milk crate sounding off about their favourite issue. The moment you release the Holy Spirit by preaching there, the professional hecklers and the demon possessed all make a beeline for you. I always considered that it provided a useful training to get us inured to persecution. On this particular Sunday, I preached my heart out for about half an hour. It is an amazing experience just to stand there and preach with people yelling their heads off at you. It is also very exhausting and, after half an hour, I ran out of things to say, so I stepped down off our little makeshift platform. On the spur of the moment, I just grabbed the nearest girl team member and said, 'Come on, you have a go.' As I said it, her face went white. As she stepped up onto the crate, she was completely drained of colour and obviously scared witless. She was almost speechless with terror. Eventually, shaking and stammering, she stumbled out one or two barely coherent sentences and as she did so all the hecklers fell silent. A hush fell on the crowd and a man pushed his way to the front, in tears, and said, 'I want to give my life to Jesus.' God had been able to use the girl's weakness to break through.

I am so grateful that we have a God who works like that. He does not work through slick presentations and pat programmes but he comes through where there is a weak but willing channel. Paul, writing to the Corinthians, reminded them of how he came to them in 'weakness and fear, and with much trembling' (1 Cor 2:3). If that is how Paul felt, it is not surprising that we also feel like that. The good news is that the Holy Spirit can take us in our weakness and use us, even if we perhaps don't look too good to our team mates. The Lord can give us the boldness to do what we wouldn't normally do.

PRINCIPLE 21

We are commissioned to go to the world

We have looked at our responsibility to bear fruit, and at the way that prayer provides not only the right environment to open people's hearts but also opens doors of opportunity and gives boldness to walk through them. These are essential if we are to fulfil our commission. Nowhere do we get a clearer mandate than in the last words of Jesus before he returned to heaven. He commissions us to go and make disciples of all nations. It is as though he is summarising the whole emphasis of his heart and teaching in one last parting shot. Too often we as a church have sat back and expected the world to come to us. Jesus definitely gives the responsibility to the Christians to invade the world's territory rather than the other way round.

Again there is a link between authority and evangelism. Most people, if asked to quote the Great Commission, will respond by quoting, 'Therefore go and make disciples of all nations.' The word 'therefore' actually links our mandate to the previous statement of Jesus that 'All authority belongs to me in heaven and on earth'. It is for this reason that we go and seek to make disciples and to bring them under his authority. The Great Commission finishes by saying, 'Teach them to observe everything that I have commanded.' This commission certainly underlines what is expected by the Lord in the life of each disciple, not just lifestyle or character but also effectiveness in evangelism.

PRINCIPLE 22

Evangelism is the primary function of the church

Matthew 28:18–20

It is no surprise to me that out of the 183 different situations in which we find Jesus throughout the Gospel records, half are in what can only be described as evangelistic situations, i.e. where he is relating to people who are either neutral or negative towards him. If you then look at the occasions where he is teaching or training his followers, much of his emphasis is still on evangelism. In other words, when Jesus isn't out there doing evangelism, he is talking about getting out there to do evangelism.

A quick scan through the five sermons of Jesus in Matthew's Gospel shows an evangelistic theme or emphasis in all of them.

Five Sermons of Jesus in Matthew

1.	Light of the World	chs 5–7
2.	The Twelve sent out to win the world	ch 10
3.	Parables of kingdom growing	ch 13
4.	Seek and save the lost	ch 18
5.	Take gospel into all the earth – end times come	chs 24–25

I have been glad to be involved with Ichthus Christian Fellowship through the years and have so appreciated Roger Forster's heart and teaching that evangelism is the 'raison d'être' of the church. He often says that the church is 'the only society that exists totally for non-members'. A church will often get into a cycle where all its energies are taken up with running itself and then it has nothing left with which to bless the world around it. A church without evangelism is like an oil refinery without a shipping or dispatching department. If all the oil produced by a refinery was used in order to run the refinery, it would be a total waste of space. In the same way, the church becomes pointless if it ceases to affect, bless and win the world. When we understand the mandate of the church, everything else slots into its place to serve the overall focus of evangelising the world.

Often, individual churches have only carried this 'reason for being' if they are led by evangelists. Churches led by pastors, teachers or prophets have more often than not carried a different agenda. I have always been disappointed that those with certain gifts presume that their sphere of operation is solely Christian or church based. We need prophets in the church who will prophesy for non-Christians. Prophets can so easily create a 'God framework' for the unconverted. Where unbelievers have dismissed the Lord as being irrelevant, distant or even dead, a prophetic word can shatter these 'unbelief systems'. We need prophets in evangelism, who can prophesy on the High Street and on the doors, prophesying directly to the authorities or simply providing the evangelists with their message for the town. We need prophets who think evangelism, so that, even when they are speaking into the church, their strategy is to equip the saints to fulfil the mandate of reaching the world.

PRINCIPLE 23

Pastors, teachers and prophets in evangelism

Ephesians 4:11

Why do teachers presume that their gifting is to just teach Christians? Surely, their gift is to be able to put over the principles of the kingdom of God whether the hearer is Christian or non-Christian. We used to say in London that the teachers in the church should train on the High Street. The real test of a teaching gift is whether you can grab the attention of those who are not particularly interested and get them to understand the Word of God. It is easy to teach in church as most churchgoers are polite enough to at least look as if they are listening to you, even if they are bored stiff. But put a church teacher in front of the local comprehensive school sixth formers and they would quickly be made aware of whether or not the pupils think they have a teaching gift.

Some years ago, I was invited to give a lecture on the main tenets of the Christian faith to the combined sixth forms of a public school in South East London. On my arrival at the school, I was whisked off to the headmaster's office, where he quizzed me on all I had intended to say. On every topic I raised, he immediately closed the subject by saying 'No I don't want you to mention anything about that.' Having dismantled my entire lecture, he suggested that I just say something about myself and my role as a church worker and then open it to the floor for questions. If I was nervous before, now I was terrified. I was introduced by the headmaster to a full auditorium, for a double period, unable to say anything that I had planned.

I started with a few introductory remarks and, as he had suggested, opened it up for questions. Inevitably, the first question was on a topic that I had been asked to say nothing on, and in fact, so were the majority of the other questions asked that afternoon. On hearing that first question, my mind raced as to how I could get out of this hole. I wished the earth could have opened up and swallowed me. Not daring to look in the direction of the headmaster, I decided to throw caution to the wind and give a straight answer. That seemed to provoke a stream of questions on forbidden topics, and I responded with equally forbidden answers.

An hour and half later, at the end of the session, the headmaster came to the front of the lecture theatre and, instead of publicly rebuking me as I had expected, reached out his hand and shook mine vigorously. To my total surprise he said, 'That was the best sixth form lecture I have ever attended.' Again he whisked me off to his office. This time it was for a congratulatory glass of sherry, over which he asked if I would become chaplain to the school. Although

I never took him up on his offer, he did invite me back every year to take this sixth form lecture. In fact, I was highly amused the next year when he took me into his office before we started and told me to say this and that, and tell this story and recount that miracle, all of which had been initially strictly off limits the previous year.

I could only presume that he had never really heard before what Christianity was all about, and his own preconceived ideas had held him back from wanting to discover more. He seemed genuinely amazed at things that to us are simple, basic, Christian truths. It is therefore essential that the teachers, like the prophets, have as part of their agenda how to teach the world the objective truths of God's kingdom. God's moral values, for example, need to be taught to society along with the gospel. Not only should our teachers seek to find direct avenues to teach non-Christians, but they should also see that the end result of their teaching in the church is to motivate the members also to reach the lost.

Likewise, pastors should care as much for the lost sheep as for those already in the fold. Our pastors need to carry the Anglican sense of pastorate who see that their responsibility for care is for all living in the community around their churches. Society desperately needs caring shepherds who can bring help and direction to the multitudes who, as Jesus said, are 'harassed and helpless, like sheep without a shepherd' (Mt 9:36).

PRINCIPLE 24

Blessing every family of the earth

Genesis 12:3; 22:18

The first verse in the New Testament introduces Jesus to us as both the 'Son of David' and the 'Son of Abraham'. There could be no more fitting introductions: Jesus fulfils the promises made to David of a King who ushers in an eternal kingdom, and the promises made to Abraham that through his seed (i.e. Jesus) all the families of the earth would be blessed. It becomes the privilege of the church to complete this promise, that in his name, we should bless all peoples throughout the whole world. It is not surprising that Matthew finishes his Gospel with this great commission to go and make disciples in every 'ethnic group'.

PRINCIPLE 25

Witness for Jesus on earth and he will witness for us in heaven

Matthew 10:32–33; Luke 9:26; Luke 12:8–9

This is such a key part of our mandate that Matthew's Gospel states that Jesus will confess us before the Father in heaven if we confess Jesus before men, whereas Luke's Gospel says that he will confess us before the angels of God. Either way, we see Jesus watching as to whether we are prepared to confess him openly or whether, like Peter, we deny him before men. I don't really know what it means for Jesus to deny us before the angels and the Father, but we get the picture that he is witnessing on our behalf in heaven as we witness for him on earth. This furnishes us with an extra motivation in evangelism, knowing that it triggers a reaction on our behalf in heaven. It is as though Jesus is saying, 'If you will be proud of me, then I will be proud of you.' Perhaps that is why the previous verse talks about us being of more value than many sparrows and that the hairs on our heads are all numbered.

Most of us are happy to sing of our pride in Jesus. We proclaim in the midst of the congregation the greatness of our God. This all seems so easy in the context of worship in the Sunday service, but often feels completely different in the world's environment. But surely, the highest form of worship is to state before the watching world that we are totally proud of our Saviour and his kingdom. I have always felt that evangelism has to be the highest form of worship.

CHAPTER 3

THE MAGNITUDE OF THE MAGNETISM

The earth's gravitational field affects the whole population of the world whether they understand it or not. Even if certain individuals did not believe in it, the influence is, nevertheless, universal. Interestingly, the New Testament describes a similar dynamic regarding the kingdom of God. There are many principles which prove that everybody, regardless of their faith or understanding, is influenced by the spiritual realm of God's activity. God is at work, tugging at the hearts of all men like a great magnet. This chapter will examine some of the scriptures which state God's universal desire for all people, as well as the evident worldwide influence already powerfully at work in the hearts of all mankind. It is also clear in many of these biblical passages that we are to be involved in the process of magnifying this magnetism.

PRINCIPLE 26

Everyone knows of his existence, his power and his character

Romans 1:19–23

Paradoxically, one of the proofs of God's existence is that we don't have to prove that God exists. The whole world appears to be already aware of the presence of a divine being. Mankind has always been, and still is, incurably religious. It is striking that the Bible does not seek to prove God's existence. It pre-assumes this and speaks to us in a way that takes his actuality for granted.

Romans 1 verse 20 defines very clearly for us this presumption: 'For since the creation of the world God's invisible qualities – his eternal power and divine nature – have been clearly seen, being understood from what has been made, so that men are without excuse.' It goes on to say that 'even though they knew God, they did not honour him as God', and resorted to worshipping other idols. The emphasis in these verses is on the fact that we are *all* without excuse. No one will be able to excuse himself on the day of judgment on the basis that he was unaware that God existed. God has gifted each person with an instinct, which is a similar starting point for all in our search for him. Whether we follow this instinct, or not, is up to us. Man can and does sometimes reject this inner sense.

Some of our door-to-door surveys have shown that over 90 per cent of people admit to a belief in a vaguely defined superbeing. Only 10 per cent would profess to be atheists. I often ask why these atheists don't believe in God, and usually get the reply that 'a God of love would not permit suffering in the world'. Since there is so much suffering, they therefore conclude that there is no God. But interestingly, this very argument, which is intended to disprove the existence of God, actually unwittingly admits to the invisible attributes of God. I would often respond to them by asking, 'Who told you that God is a God of love?' This upholds the truth of Romans 1 verse 20. Deep in everyone's heart, everybody knows of the existence of a loving, good and powerful divine being.

It is to this instinct that we appeal in the course of our evangelism. 'We commend ourselves to every man's conscience.' We appeal to the common factor between them and us, that is, a God-given instinct which, either active or dormant, is nevertheless capable of spiritually receiving from the Lord.

PRINCIPLE 27

God is not willing that any should perish

2 Peter 3:9; 1 Timothy 2:4

I love the three *'come to'* invitations which are described in the above verses from Peter's letter and the first letter to Timothy which announce God's threefold desire that everyone should:

1. *Come* to experience salvation (1 Tim 2:4);
2. *Come* to a knowledge of the truth (1 Tim 2:4);
3. *Come* into repentance (2 Pet 3:9).

It is expressing, as clearly as it can be said, that he is *not willing for anyone to perish* and desires *all* men to be saved. Some would argue that God is exclusively selective and that only certain individuals are predestined for heaven. Sadly, it is true that not every person will come into salvation, but nevertheless it is God's earnest desire that everyone should respond to his offer of eternal life. Christ came '. . . to save *the world* through him' (Jn 3:16–17, my emphasis). '[He] gave himself as a ransom for *all men* – the testimony given in its proper time' (1 Tim 2:6, my emphasis).

Any limitation on the numbers of those being saved is dependent, not upon God, but upon man's acceptance of God's offer. The potential is there for all. Just as a wedding is incomplete until both parties have stated their will to participate in the marriage. God has already made his vows; he has already declared, 'I will.' This declaration has been made in respect of every human being, everywhere, throughout time. He has committed himself to the relationship and now waits for each individual to respond.

PRINCIPLE 28

Jesus draws *all men*

John 12:32

Jesus said, 'I, when I am lifted up from the earth, *will draw all men* to myself' (Jn 12:32, my emphasis). Since he was lifted up on the cross, we must presume that this promise is now operative, and that Jesus, like an enormous spiritual magnet, is now divinely drawing the souls of all men. There is no indication that this is a narrow selection process. Quite the opposite: it is a universal, all-embracing assertion. There are many other similar statements which underline God's initiative in bringing us to himself. The following are eight such examples:

1. 'Every plant that my heavenly Father has not planted will be pulled up by the roots' Mt 15:13.
2. 'No-one can come to me unless the Father who sent me draws him' Jn 6:44.
3. 'No-one can come to me unless the Father has enabled him' Jn 6:65.
4. 'Everyone who listens to the Father and learns from him comes to me' Jn 6:45.
5. 'A man can receive only what is given him from heaven' Jn 3:27.
6. 'To those whom you gave me out of the world . . . you gave them to me' Jn 17:6.
7. 'The knowledge of the secrets of the kingdom of heaven has been given to you, but not to them' Mt 13:11.
8. 'Not everyone can accept this word, but only those to whom it has been given' Mt 19:11.

These statements leave us in no doubt that God takes the first initiative in our search for him. But I also believe that man has total freedom of choice as to whether or not he wants to respond to the Lord's drawing. Because this drawing is universal, it means that whoever wishes to come to him can do so. An illustration which I find helpful is the imagery of two fields: one field chosen by God and one which is the choice of the world. In evangelism, we persuade people to move from the world's field into God's chosen one. The Bible sets out the necessary criteria for those desiring to enter God's field such as: humility and understanding, childlike faith and acceptance, poverty in spirit and repentance. The diagram below sets out the two fields and then shows the various ways in which the Lord is working to seek to bring us into his field of selection.

GOD'S FIELD OF SELECTION   THE WORLD

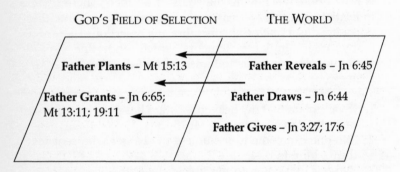

The Divine Perspective

PRINCIPLE 29

Christ died for the sins of the whole world

1 John 2:2

'He is the atoning sacrifice for our sins, and *not only for ours* but also for the sins of the *whole world*.' This surely answers the question as to whether Christ died for all, or whether he died just for those who will be ultimately saved. We all accept that Christ's death atones for our sins but, personally, I believe Jesus died for the sins of *all* mankind, for every generation throughout human history, whether they wanted it or not. The price was paid to the full. It is, however, only when each individual responds and appropriates the gospel that he or she receives salvation. Christ nevertheless died for everyone irrespective of their response or commitment to him. You may remember the chorus we used to sing a few years ago called, 'Bind us together'. One verse of it really hits the nail on the head:

Made for the glory of God
Purchased by his precious blood
Born with a right to be clean
For Jesus the victory has won.
Bob Gillman © Thankyou music, 1977

Since Christ died for all of us, we are all born with the right to be clean from the contamination of sin. The wages of sin have already been paid, providing us all with the right to eternal life. I have always seen evangelism as a campaign for people's rights. Campaigns are made on behalf of people who have been deprived of their just entitlement and everyone has an entitlement to God's eternal kingdom. Through evangelism, we can encourage people to claim their right to life.

I find it amazing that Jesus never actually expressed in words that he would be dying on the cross for our sins. Throughout his ministry reference was made to his impending death and resurrection some forty-seven times in total. But he never actually made the connection that his supreme sacrifice was made to forgive us for our sins. In his characteristic, self-effacing way, Jesus wished us to receive this truth by revelation. There are, however, many instances in the New Testament where others have spoken of his redemptive mission. For example, his ministry on earth was introduced by John the Baptist when he referred to Jesus as 'The Lamb of God who takes away the sin of the *world*' (Jn 1:29, my emphasis). Having begun his Gospel with this statement, John the disciple also refers to Jesus as the Saviour of the *world* in his first epistle (1 Jn 4:14).

Perhaps the most outstanding prophecy about Jesus'

death was made by Caiaphas the high priest in the special council. With the intention of either defending or accusing Jesus, he said, 'It is better for you that one man die for the people than that the whole nation perish' (Jn 11:50). It is difficult to say what his motive was. The Gospel goes on to tell us that Caiaphas did not say this on his own initiative, but that he prophesied that Jesus was going to die for the nation. Caiaphas may have prophesied by the revelation of the Holy Spirit or he may have been referring to a statement from the Old Testament, i.e. Isaiah 53 verses 5–6, 'But he was pierced for our transgressions, he was crushed for our iniquities; the punishment that brought us peace was upon him, and by his wounds we are healed . . . and the LORD has laid on him the iniquity *of us all*' (my emphasis).

PRINCIPLE 30

The Holy Spirit convinces the world of sin, righteousness and judgment

John 16:8–11

Jesus, after his resurrection, returned to heaven so that the Holy Spirit could be sent to us to be our helper. We often think that it is only Christians who have the Holy Spirit, but the help offered is actually to the totality of mankind and is not restricted to the church alone. He helps the church by guiding us into truth, reminding us of Jesus' teachings, disclosing to us the will of the Lord and producing the life of Christ in us. But he is also active in the non-Christian world with a threefold evangelistic operation.

1) Convincing the world of sin

'When [the Holy Spirit] come, he will convict *the world* . . . in regard to sin, because men do not believe in me' (Jn 16:8–9, my emphasis). Surely the worst sin that can be committed by mankind is to reject the Creator, the Sustainer and the

Saviour of the world. The Holy Spirit is active in working on the hearts of men, so that they might become aware of their guilt regarding not believing in Jesus.

Why don't we see more of this conviction from the Spirit of God, convincing sinners of the error of their ways? Perhaps part of the answer is that the church itself has become so worldly, that it has now become necessary for this work to be carried out within it. This may have stopped the flow of the Holy Spirit through the church into the surrounding society. We have all been moved by stories of revivals where unchurched people suddenly sense the weight of their sin. This is often prompted by times of brokenness, repentance and purging in the church.

2) Convincing the world of righteousness

This conviction over sin is followed by an equally dramatic conviction regarding righteousness. So, on the one hand, the Holy Spirit is awakening man's conscience in the area of 'wrong doing' and, on the other hand, he is convincing men of 'right doing'. This is a continuation of Jesus' ministry. Just as he showed righteousness in all that he did, now the Holy Spirit continues to make mankind aware of righteousness. This is an important emphasis, because it shows the area of repentance to be not just overcoming the negative, i.e. sin, but also being convicted about positively doing what is right.

3) Convincing the world of judgment

The Holy Spirit also teaches us of the consequences of points (1) and (2); of sin and of righteousness, and, as a corollary, of the judgments which will be made in respect of both. Every human being senses an awareness, through the conscience, of being accountable for his actions. This is what sets man apart from the animal kingdom. The Holy Spirit also makes us aware of the spiritual personalities behind good and evil. As emphasised in John 16 verses 9–10, Jesus is the power of all goodness. The devil, on the other hand, personifies every evil and has already been judged as the same. '. . . the prince of this world now stands condemned' (v 11). The Holy Spirit therefore makes non-Christians aware of the fact that the devil has already received his judgment. He is on the road to destruction and, by joining him, we too would head for nothing but hopelessness. The Holy Spirit convinces us that life without God is meaningless.

PRINCIPLE 31

The Holy Spirit is poured out on *all* flesh

Acts 2:17

In Joel 2 verses 28–32 predictions had been made that God's Spirit would be poured out on *all* people, thus ushering in a new age. Peter explains the fulfilment of this prophecy in Acts 2 verses 17–18:

> 'In the last days, God says,
>   I will pour out my Spirit on *all people*.
> Your sons and your daughters will prophesy,
>   your young men will see visions,
>   your old men will dream dreams.
> Even on my servants, both men and women,
>   I will pour out my Spirit in those days,
>   and they will prophesy. ' (my emphasis)

The coming of the Holy Spirit has brought God's intimate presence within everyone's reach, and this physical close-ness has opened up new channels of communication: revelations in the form of dreams, visions and prophecies. These are described as being for everyone and not merely for the church. They are for *all flesh,* non-Christians as well as Christians, for the unrighteous as well as the righteous, for every kind of person, particularly those whom we may not consider to be suitable candidates. It is for the children, the old people, the young and even the slaves. This biblical promise is for *all.*

Paul, before his conversion, was adamantly set against the message of Jesus. His conversion needed to have a supernatural element. He would not have been converted by mere discussion. His heart was zealously set in opposition to the faith. God uses these Holy Spirit revelations to break people's belief and unbelief systems. Paul's unbelief was broken by means of a vision, which became the vehicle of his salvation. The good news for us is that, on this basis, anybody can change, even those who are most negative to the gospel. We could see literally overnight a complete turn around in anyone. All we need is for the Lord to give dreams or visions or even a prophecy like that of Caiaphas in John 11 verse 50 which we looked at earlier.

It is great to see Muslims becoming Christians as a result of having personal encounters with the Lord through these visions and dreams. We were once preaching among Muslims in a park in Cyprus and a young man came up to me and said, 'This Jesus you are talking about, I have met him in a dream a few days ago.'

The first time I ever came across people being converted solely through dreams was in Sweden. A lady entered the church for a Sunday service and came straight up to us at the front. She asked if she could join this church. We replied, 'Yes, of course,' and then asked if she was a Christian. When she answered that she was, we enquired further whether she then belonged to another church. 'No,' she replied, 'I have never been to church in my life.' She had become a Christian the previous Wednesday night as a result of a dream. Jesus had appeared to her in the dream and said, 'I died for you, you need my forgiveness. How are you going to respond to this?' In her dream she got on her knees and apologised to the Lord, and woke up a Christian! Now, that's evangelism made easy.

Since then I have met several people who have had similar experiences. I shall never forget speaking in one church where a young lady stood out from the crowd, literally, because of her brightly-coloured, punk-style hair. Unfortunately, everybody else was dressed rather soberly. At the end of the service she ran out before anyone could get to meet her. But as she left she took a leaflet from the back of the church. An hour or so later she phoned the number on the leaflet, and got through to the pastor's home where we happened to be eating our lunch. She recounted how the strangest thing had happened to her in the church that morning. She had felt like she wanted to speak in another language and then explained that ever since she had run out of the church, she had in fact been speaking in another language. She had never heard of speaking in tongues and was phoning to find out what had happened to her. All I could hear of this conversation was the church leader continually asking, 'But have you repented?' Well, she did!

PRINCIPLE 32

Spiritual power = power to witness

Acts 1:8

'You will receive power when the Holy Spirit comes on you; and you will be my witnesses . . . to the ends of the earth' (Acts 1:8). This is the introduction to the Holy Spirit in the book of Acts. It is challenging because it equates our power in the Holy Spirit to our effectiveness as witnesses. Statements like these make us all question our spiritual power. All too often the church has not made this the benchmark of power. Instead we look at other things: freedom of worship, forcefulness of preaching, manner of praying, or boldness in using gifts. Perhaps all these have some kind of bearing on our power but none is more clearly defined in the Bible than this one: SPIRITUAL POWER = WITNESS. We need to keep stating and restating this to re-educate the church and set our expectations in this alternative measure of power.

I was speaking at a YWAM base in Holland a few years ago when I suddenly saw this verse in a totally new light. I was struck by the end of the verse, 'You shall be my witnesses both in Jerusalem and in all Judea and Samaria even to the remotest part of the earth.' I felt the Lord say to me that I would witness him, i.e. experience him, wherever I go in the world. And that is exactly the point. We can't bear witness to something, until we ourselves have witnessed it. Our testimony has to be of our power encounters with the Holy Spirit. As we personally experience, we can, in turn, powerfully release this experience to the world.

The Lord's ultimate objective for the church is to win the whole world but he nevertheless asks the early church to start the process where they are, in Jerusalem. Evangelism always has to start in our Jerusalem. Before we go on to win the world, we have to start witnessing in our home environment: our family, our college friends, our work colleagues, our neighbours, our town. Some people think it is easy to evangelise if you become a missionary or a full-time church worker. When you go on the mission field you discover exactly the same dilemmas as you had back home, because this has now become your home. We need the power of the Holy Spirit to help us break through to evangelise right now, right here!

PRINCIPLE 33

Unity is the key – the world will know

John 17:21–23

Getting the world 'to know' and 'to believe' is therefore the mandate of the church. Interestingly, Jesus uses both of these expressions in his prayer in John 17, and shows us that the key for this to happen is the 'oneness' and 'unity' of the church. 'That all of them may be one, Father, just as you are in me and I am in you. May they also be in us so *that the world may believe* that you have sent me' (v 21, my emphasis). 'May they be brought to complete unity *to let the world know* that you sent me and have loved them . . .' (v 23, my emphasis).

It is extremely challenging to think that it is our relationships with our fellow Christians which become the clearest demonstration to the world of the fact that Jesus was sent by the Father. We should be able to stand on the High

Street and say that we can prove Jesus was the Messiah, the Saviour of the world, by pointing to the church. I am not sure that the world would find this too convincing at the moment. However, I think it has been wonderful to see the coming together of all the different streams and denominations over recent years, much of which is due to inter-church activities such as Spring Harvest or March for Jesus. Even TV's *Songs of Praise* has played a part in opening eyes and hearts to different sections of the church.

Oneness was Jesus' prayer for us and it is not surprising that this is being answered and that in Jesus we do have unity. Certainly, Paul portrays this in Ephesians 2 verse 15 and Colossians 3 verse 11, where he describes the church as being one new man, where there are no racial, religious, cultural or status barriers. None of the barriers which divide people in the world exist in the church (or at least they should not). The harmony between opposing factions becomes a visual aid not only of the unity in the Godhead but also of the reconciliation between God and man.

When 'homogenous units' are propounded as a strategy for church growth I am disappointed. Perhaps churches which contain only people of a restricted socio-economic or cutural group do grow faster, but they do not express the cosmopolitan nature of the kingdom and they lose this strategic visual aid for evangelism. The world believes when they see unity and community between every kindred, tribe and nation. When they see harmony overcoming prejudices and hatred, it suddenly seems possible that Jesus can change the world.

PRINCIPLE 34

Love is the key – *all will know*

John 13:35

'By this all men will know that you are my disciples, if you love one another.' In the previous verses in John 13, Jesus has hinted again at his forthcoming death, which was going to be the ultimate demonstration of his love. He then gives his disciples a new commandment, 'Love one another. As I have loved you, so you must love one another' (v 34). I have a colleague in London who used to say, 'Divine repetition is intentional to emphasise importance.' When Jesus repeats 'Truly, truly' we know we really need to take special notice. When he says, 'Love one another . . . love one another,' we know that we really need to take action. Our action needs to be the same as Jesus' own loving actions.

The specific evangelistic emphasis in this statement is extraordinary, '*All* men will know.' This underlines again the principle regarding 'unity' and proves the evangelistic spin-off from the way that we relate to one another. I have always had a special interest in the word 'all', because often when it is used, it makes an extreme or completely embracing statement. It has become a habit for me to put a circle round each 'all' that I read in the Bible; there are 5,095 of them so it makes quite a word study. These make me stop and meditate for a few moments as to what is being said. Surely, this 'all' in John 13 verse 35, is a major key in evangelising everybody in our community. We just need to love one another as Jesus loved. The world recognises the believer by his love and acknowledges his affiliation with Jesus because he carries the same character traits.

PRINCIPLE 35

A little bit a yeast leavens the whole lump

Luke 13:21

This picture of the kingdom comes as one of the responses to Jesus' own question, 'To what shall I liken the kingdom of God?' He answers it with several different illustrations, many of which show the kingdom as a dynamic growing entity, such as the parables of the sower, the mustard seed, or the wheat and tares. The parable of the leaven carries on the emphasis. A little bit of leaven affects the whole lump; it spreads until the dough is all leavened.

Jesus is showing the spiritual effect of the kingdom on the surrounding society. It is great to know that, just by being in the town, we are affecting the whole place. I am sure that the presence of Spirit-filled Christians means that the devil is unable to do what he would really like to do. I have no doubt that there is a spiritual blessing affecting the lives of the non-Christians living around us. I have always thought that a non-Christian is privileged to live next door to a Christian.

Luke 13 verse 21 tells of a woman who hides leaven in a large amount of flour 'until it was all leavened'. This hints that the process of the kingdom leavening society is not yet complete, but is definitely happening and will be accomplished. When we planted a church in Soho, in central London's red light district, we were really pleased to see many of the sex shops closing down. When we planted a church in a north Peckham estate, which at one time had the highest house-breaking crime statistics in Europe, the crime rate dropped by 20 per cent in the first year of working there. Maybe there are other reasons for these things happening, and there is still a long way to go yet, but I am sure the leaven of the church is affecting the world around us.

PRINCIPLE 36

The true light lightens *every man*

John 1:9

John speaks of the true light which, 'coming into the world, enlightens *every man*'. This is a wonderful statement which shows that every individual, whether they realise it or not, is affected by the light of Jesus. Even though the world has become a pretty dark place, the Scriptures teach us that the light shines in this darkness, and that the darkness cannot overcome it.

The light of Jesus shines for everyone. Not everyone may want to come to this light, either because they love the darkness, or because they are afraid that their hearts and deeds will be exposed by the light, but the universal effect of this light is clearly stated. The analogy of the sun is helpful because everybody is affected by it. You cannot live anywhere in the world without being blessed in some way by the effect of the sun's rays. Its light literally lightens the way for every man. It affects the fruitfulness of the earth, as well as the tides and the seasons. Its gravitational pull holds us and draws us, keeping and moving the earth through its orbit in the universe. Whether people acknowledge it or not, Jesus affects the life of every person. 'He is before all things, and in him all things hold together' (Col 1:17). 'For God was pleased to have all his fulness dwell in him, and through him to reconcile to himself all things, whether things on earth or things in heaven, by making peace through his blood, shed on the cross' (Col 1:19–20).

PRINCIPLE 37

The end comes when the gospel is preached in *all the earth*

Matthew 24:14

Presumably, the Jewish mandate under the old covenant was to be witnesses of God's glory to the whole earth. Unfortunately, they became very parochial and saw the rest of the world as untouchables. Not only was their attitude wrong, but their example did nothing to win the rest of the earth to God's ways. Nevertheless, there are clear glimpses throughout the Old Testament that the message would affect the nations and spread to the uttermost recesses of the globe.

OT affirmation that the gospel reaches out into all the earth

- 'All the ends of the earth will . . . turn to the Lord' Ps 22:27.
- 'All the ends of the earth have seen the salvation of our God' Ps 98:3.
- 'From the west they acclaim the Lord's majesty . . . in the east give glory to the Lord . . . From the ends of the earth . . .' Is 24:14–16.
- 'My salvation [reaches] to the ends of the earth' Is 49:6.
- 'They will proclaim my glory among the nations' Is 66:19–20.
- 'To you the nations will come from the ends of the earth' Jer 16:19.

The Great Commission

Jesus picks up this theme in the various renderings of the Great Commission recorded in Matthew, Mark and Luke. In Matthew and Mark, Jesus is quoted as encouraging us to fulfil this task: 'Go . . . make disciples of *all* nations.' 'Go into *all* the world and preach.' Luke's wording is slightly different. He quotes Jesus as saying, 'It is written . . . repentance for forgiveness of sins should be proclaimed in His name to *all* the nations, beginning from Jerusalem' (my emphases). This is not just an inspiration to go and do it, it's a declaration that the job will be accomplished – just as it was prophesied in the Old Testament. This is why Jesus taught that one of the signs of the end of the age was the fact that the gospel would be preached in the whole world as a witness to all the nations and then the end would come. Peter's words 'Look forward to the day of God and speed its coming' (2 Pet 3:12) encourage us to see that there are things that we can do to hasten the day of the Lord's return. The immediate context talks about holy conduct and godliness, but we also see world evangelism as one of the preconditions for his return.

PRINCIPLE 38

Preach where Christ is not already named

Romans 15:20-21

It has always been my ambition to preach the gospel where Christ was not known, so that I would not be building on someone else's foundation. Rather, as it is written:

'Those who were not told about him will see,
    and those who have not heard will understand.'

Rom 15:20-21

These verses are a fitting end to this chapter, because they describe the drive in the heart of the Apostle Paul to get the gospel out into all the earth. He does not want to preach where others have already been doing the job. He doesn't want to build on another man's foundation. If we are going to win the world, we have to venture into those areas which are as yet unevangelised. The good news is that Isaiah prophesied that these areas would be responsive to the gospel: 'For what they were not told, they will see, and what they have not heard, they will understand' (Is 52:15). This drove Paul to preach the gospel fully all the way from Jerusalem to Macedonia, the former Yugoslavia.

For each succeeding generation, the challenge and the task begin again. There are some places where Christ has been preached before, but that does not necessarily mean that the present population has been evangelised. We need to find those in our communities who have not really heard or understood the gospel. We also need to be looking at the remotest parts of the earth as the culmination of our mission objective. 'Those who were not told about him will see, and those who have not heard will understand.'

CHAPTER 4

THE MODEL OF THE MASTER

Not surprisingly, Jesus is the perfect model for fruitful evangelism. His communication skills were excellent; his lifestyle was outstanding; his attitudes were astounding; his reactions to situations were extraordinary; his healings were compassionate; his miracles were amazing; his teaching was not only perfect but totally challenging and life-changing; his questions searched the soul and his answers left his audiences dumbfounded.

Jesus' impact on people's lives, as indeed on history, has been dramatic, and if we want to be effective in evangelism, we couldn't do better than to follow his example. In fact, the key is really to let Jesus live his life again in us through the Holy Spirit. He is not just a model. His earthly life becomes the focus for our faith. Having understood how he lives and works, we seek to let him live out his own principles again through us. This chapter explores some general observations that have helped me in my learning process in seeking to reach lost souls. Many of these observations are perhaps obvious, while others are seemingly extreme and rather radical.

PRINCIPLE 39

Jesus invested time

Evangelism demands time. You don't change lives without input and we see Jesus spending almost exactly half of his time in direct evangelism. Sometimes this is on an individual level and at other times it is to groups, from small groups to vast crowds. You couldn't get a better balance in ministry than the model he presents to us. He spent half his time on 'in house' Christian activity and the other half of his time seeking to reach those outside the kingdom community. If you were to ask churches to try to put a percentage on how much time is spent on church activity and how much time is spent on evangelism, it would most probably be split around 95 per cent to 5 per cent, with the larger share of time and effort spent on church activity. What a challenge to seek to follow Jesus' model! What a shake-up that would give us in church structures if we allocated 50 per cent of our time and energy to evangelistic activity! It would completely change our ideas on our use of time. It would rewrite our priorities and our churches would definitely start growing.

PRINCIPLE 40

Jesus worked spontaneously

John 5:19

Often, evangelism carried out by churches is carefully planned. We hold an open air service once a month or set aside an evening at regular intervals for door-to-door visiting. I can remember some days of Ministers' Fraternal meetings where for months we would plan an Easter open air event. There would sometimes be even a year of planning but often the result didn't really seem worth it.

For Jesus, spontaneity was the key to evangelism. We need churches filled with people who are constantly looking for ways and opportunities spontaneously to share their faith. It is not that Jesus did not have his overall planned strategy. He wanted to get round all the villages before setting out on his journey to Jerusalem. However, the basic opportunities were spontaneous. In fact, he was often interrupted in the middle of doing what he had planned. On one occasion, he takes the disciples aside for a break and suddenly discovers that 5,000 people have turned up for tea. Another time, he is hurrying to save Jairus' dying daughter when he is interrupted by the woman with the haemorrhage. He stops to deal with her and in the process the little girl dies. No problem, of course, to Jesus. Again and again the needs of those around him provided him with the opportunity to release spontaneously the kingdom of heaven. This shows that evangelism is not so much a planned programme as a lifestyle.

The whole church should be eagerly looking for every possible occasion to touch lives with the kingdom of God. You can't plan to cast out a demon today, neither can you plan to heal someone. These things are need-orientated and require us to be in touch with people and in each instance to seek God's power to meet their needs. I wonder how many people have passed by me in the course of this year who missed some blessing or supernatural miracle just because I wasn't alert to their need or to what Jesus wanted to do in that situation?

The amazing thing about evangelism in the Gospels and in Acts is that it just happened. Peter, in the early church, didn't say, 'We are going to heal the lame man at the gate of the temple today.' They just happened to come across the situation, got involved in it and released the power of God there. As a result, the church grew dramatically. I have always been impressed that they did that miracle on the way into the church. How many of us are in that state of preparedness on Sunday morning before church? I think I would have waited until after the service and have healed the crippled man on the way out, when I was more full of the Spirit.

PRINCIPLE 41

Jesus did what he saw the Father doing

'I tell you the truth, the Son can do nothing by himself; he can do only what he sees his Father doing, because whatever the Father does the Son also does.' 'By myself I can do nothing; I judge . . . I seek not to please myself but him who sent me' (Jn 5:19, 30). I would love to know whether Jesus is seeing the Father working in the very moment of action, or whether this is something shared between him and his Father in advance of each situation. There is perhaps the hint that this is an instant tuning in to the activity of the Father as he says in verse 17, 'My Father is always at his work to this very day, and I, too, am working.' If only our eyes could see more clearly what the Lord is doing around us. We do, of course, have the wonderful privilege of seeing all the kinds of things that Jesus does, because the Gospels provide a record of his earthly life in black and white for us. We can then read these things in advance and by faith say that we too do the things that we see Jesus doing. Surely the four accounts of the life of Christ recorded for us are there to encourage our faith and to direct our paths to bless the world in the same way as he did two thousand years ago.

PRINCIPLE 42

Jesus had no set techniques

I don't know whether you are like me, but I often feel safe with a set technique or a rote-learned presentation. We quote phrases like 'Repetition is the mother of skill' and then try to perfect some repeated pattern. There are 'How to' books written to provide a pattern for every avenue in life, but amazingly Jesus had no set pattern that we can follow when it comes to evangelism. In fact, he never seems to do the same thing twice.

In all the 183 different situations where Jesus confronts individuals or groups in the Gospels, there is a staggering variety in what he does and says each time. There is, of course, a very valid reason for this. Unique individuals deserve unique treatment. We can see this today in the way that every Christian testimony dramatically differs from every other. The Lord communicates to people in a way which is tailored specifically to each individual.

God is a God of individuality. Every snowflake, tree, mountain and star are uniquely different. We differ as individuals from each other. Our physical features, i.e. our hand and finger prints, voice prints, eyes and ears, and our personalities, intellect, character traits, even our smells, are unique to us. Every individual is a unique person, and therefore deserves unique treatment.

We need therefore to resist the temptation to push people through a spiritual sausage machine. Potential converts, we feel, have to go through the ABC of conversion, yet often the biblical examples break our patterns. For example, Jesus tells Levi to leave everything and 'Follow me' (Mt 9:9). To another man he says, 'Go home to your family and tell them how much the Lord has done for you' (Mk 5:19). When talking to two women, who had both been involved in adultery, he talks to one about repentance but to the other about worship (Jn 8:11; 4:21-24). Often our focus in evangelism is merely to convey information about the gospel, whereas our emphasis should be to draw people into a relationship with the Lord. The key in evangelism is for people to discover the reality of knowing Jesus. It is not just a mental assent to Christian doctrines or to nutshell gospel presentations.

After all, we cannot learn a technique or set process to enable us to relate to a friend. Friendship is living and interactive with a give-and-take process of mutual appreciation and commitment. The key to salvation is a real introduction to Jesus – to know him as a personal, genuine friend. Jesus emphasises this in Matthew 7 verse 23 when he quotes his Father as saying, 'I never knew you. Away from me, you evildoers!' Of course, there are important facts which we must understand and believe with regard to the gospel, but we must never confuse *knowing about* Jesus with actually *knowing* him.

In his evangelism, Jesus did more than just provide people with information. He gave them the opportunity to experience the Father. With powerful supernatural activity they could touch the reality of the things Jesus was teaching about. In fact, as he shared, he expected the Father to be involved, revealing the truth to those around him who were listening. In this way, their relationship with the Father was established through personal contact with the Son.

PRINCIPLE 43

Jesus presented the toughest of terms

Luke 14:33

Often we shy away from presenting any kind of challenge to potential converts for fear of driving them away. Interestingly, Jesus didn't pull any of his punches, in fact he seemed to go out of his way to make it as difficult as possible for people to accept his message. He never said to people, 'Come to me and be happy and blessed.' On the contrary, he stressed the harsh consequences of absolute commitment.

Jesus says that every disciple must forsake everything, deny himself and take up his cross in order to follow him (Mt 10:38). Another time he says, 'Foxes have holes and birds of the air have nests, but the Son of Man has nowhere to lay his head' (Mt 8:20). Another man is not allowed to bury his father; he is told he must put his commitment to Jesus before his family ties (Mt 8:22). 'He who loves father or mother more than me is not worthy of me' (Lk 14:26, NASB). A rich man is told to go and sell everything he has and give it to the poor before he can become a disciple (Mt 19:21). 'No one can be my disciple who does not give up all his own possessions' (Lk 14:33, NASB). Jesus tells the crowd on one occasion that they are only seeking him because he fed them (Jn 6:26). Sinners are told to 'Go and sin no more' (Jn 8:11). Jesus told potential followers, 'All men will hate you because of me' (Mt 10:22), because he himself was the subject of abuse. 'If the head of the house has been called Beelzebub, how much more the members of his household!' (Mt 10:25). Converts should expect even their families to turn against them. 'A man's enemies will be the members of his own household' (Mt 10:36). There would be inevitable persecution. 'They will deliver you up and scourge you' (Mt 10:17, NASB). 'Anyone who kills you will think he is offering a service to God' (Jn 16:2).

With a catalogue of warnings like these, you can understand why Jesus encourages would-be disciples to sit down and first count the cost. If you start, are you prepared to see it through? Work out if you have what it takes to build the tower before you begin. Decide before you put your hands on the plough whether you are going to stay with it. Be sure that you are not stony ground where the seed withers as soon as persecution or affliction comes.

Before you throw this book down in despair, let me say that the compensations are of course well worth the sacrifice. Jesus shows that great joy and peace are ours in the heat of opposition (Mt 5:12). Great joy is ours in discovering the treasure in the field (Mt 13:44). We also have another comforter in the Holy Spirit, who is at our side to carry us through (Jn 14:26). Jesus also takes our heavy loads and gives us a burden that is light and a yoke that is easy (Mt 11:28–30). We will also have great reward in heaven (Mt 25:21). We will receive one hundredfold both now and in the life to come (Lk 18:30).

More often than not, we try to make it as easy as possible for our converts. Is this perhaps the reason why the gospel's appeal is so weak? We have watered it down. The appeal of the gospel should present a radical alternative to a 'normal' lifestyle. Jesus presents the gospel as an absolute priority, a radical change of everything. So often, we present it as a nice extra activity to fill in our leisure time.

I can remember my first reactions when I realised the radical implications of Jesus' message. I was so excited because here was a radical, life-changing challenge. The Gospels were talking about something which was utterly life-transforming. Jesus demanded total commitment and that meant every aspect of life: ambitions, lifestyle, personality, character. I was really drawn to this, precisely because it was so demanding. Christianity was not church once a week. It was a total alternative to the way that the world lives. It was the very toughness of this commitment which caught my imagination and set my spirit on fire. I think, however, that we have largely lost this incentive in our challenge to non-Christians.

In fact, the only people who have been successful by preaching such a radical message of total commitment are the cults. If the Christian church doesn't profile this kind of challenge, we will continually pick up people whose commitment is weak. I wonder, do we have an anaemic church because we have a seemingly anaemic gospel?

PRINCIPLE 44

Jesus uses the art of conversation

John 4:1–7

Are there any features which characterise Jesus' evangelistic encounters which we can make our own? Is there anything that we can consciously adopt as part of our approach which is borrowed from his? I think there are many. Firstly, there is his style of language and conversation. He deliberately used certain rhetorical or literary techniques to convey his message. His teaching style was very distinctive and particularly effective.

As Christians, we need to learn again the art of conversation. We are living in a society where this skill has been largely lost. It is no longer normal in our culture for people to talk to strangers as they travel on a train or wait at the bus stop. Perhaps this is because, in a television age, people are so used to sitting passively watching without participating. Perhaps we have learnt to be so private that we want to remain anonymous and uninvolved with others, or perhaps life has become so complex that we don't have the emotional energy or desire to be open to others. Whatever the reason, as Christians, we need to be able to bridge the gap and pioneer conversation wherever we go.

Going into a café, sitting down next to someone and

opening up a conversation about the gospel would be the modern equivalent of what Jesus was doing with the woman at the well. As he sits there, although he is tired from his journey, there is nevertheless no slacking in his zeal for evangelism. As the Samaritan woman arrives to draw water, he asks her for a drink and then uses the conversation to explain the meaning of 'living water' (Jn 4:1–7). Not only does she come to believe, but many in her village do so too.

I was amused when I heard of the approach that one of our church members had developed in trying to make an evangelistic opportunity out of nothing. He would go up to people in the hospital where he worked and ask, 'Tell me, has anyone ever tried to convert you?' When they said 'No', he would say, 'Do you mind if I have a go?' But if they answered 'Yes', he would ask, 'Do you mind me asking how they got on?' Being totally bold and up-front about our faith has a certain appeal to the unchurched and it demonstrates our sense of pride in what we believe.

PRINCIPLE 45

Jesus uses dialogue not monologue

As we watch Jesus in action with the woman at the well, we learn that evangelism is dialogue not monologue. She speaks almost as much as Jesus does in this conversation. She speaks about 167 words and Jesus 202 words, depending on the version of the Bible. Listening and responding is one of the keys to conversation. Jesus engaged people where they were. He would listen to them and answer their questions. He was also a master at using questions. We can learn much from the way he shared in the cut and thrust of real life situations.

0   100

The diagram shows various people in their process of getting to know God. If they were at '0' on this scale they would have no concept or understanding of God whatsoever. I think it is fair to say that there is no one at this point, because everyone has an awareness of God's existence and his character. When a person reaches '100' it is the point at which he is converted. So every non-Christian is somewhere on this line. Our task in evangelism is to discover where they are and seek to move them in the direction towards '100'. It would be wrong to try and lead someone from say '25' to the point of conversion, as they would not yet be ready. We just pick them up at '25' and bring them along the scale to, say, '35'. The next time you meet, perhaps you can move them along to '50'. Every contact we have with non-Christians is positive and draws them ever nearer to Christ. It is those who have reached '85' or '90' who are ready to make a response to the Lord. These are the fruit that are ripe for picking. The purpose, then, of dialogue is to discover where people are on this scale. We need to be able to gauge how much they understand and how quickly they perceive truth as we are sharing.

Principle 46

Jesus gives individual attention

A breakdown of all Jesus' ministry situations shows us that he spent approximately one third of his time with individuals and two thirds with groups. This shows that a good percentage of his involvement was on a personal level. He could have spent all his time preaching to vast crowds, but he   didn't stand aloof, or set himself apart from individual needs. He engaged people on a one-to-one level. Jesus gives us a wonderful model of availability, of being prepared to get alongside individuals, prepared to take time to converse even with complete strangers.

PRINCIPLE 47

Jesus uses questions

Jesus is constantly using questions in his conversations with people. He asks 252 questions throughout the pages of the Gospels. He would ask questions:

- To diagnose;
- To draw out;
- To dialogue;
- To distance;
- To divert.

1. To diagnose: When Jesus asks, 'Do you believe that I am able to do this?' (Mt 9:28), he is ascertaining what level of faith this blind man has. When the man replies, 'Yes, Lord,' Jesus heals him saying, 'Be it done unto you according to your faith.' There are many examples of how Jesus used questions to diagnose where his hearers were. 'Don't you believe that I am in the Father, and that the Father is in me?' (Jn 14:10). 'Whoever lives and believes in me will never die. Do you believe this?' (Jn 11:26). 'Who do people say the Son of Man is?' (Mt 16:13). 'Who do you say I am?' (Mt 16:15). 'Have you understood all these things?' (Mt 13:51).

Evangelism Explosion is an excellent presentation of the gospel. It demonstrates the importance of questions and uses two diagnostic questions to ascertain whether a contact is truly born again or not. The first question is: 'If you were to die tonight, would you be absolutely certain that you would go to heaven?' and the other question is: 'If you did die and stood at the gates of heaven and were asked why they should let you in, what would you say?' Most non-Christians would answer the first question with an uncertain response. Maybe they would say something like: 'I hope so', or 'I don't know', or 'Perhaps', or 'Nobody could know that for certain!' To the second question it is only a born again Christian who trusts in Christ for salvation. Everybody else gives a typical 'good works' answer.

2. To draw out: We see that Jesus also used questions to draw both people and subjects out into the open. An example of the former is when he asked the crowd who had touched him, because healing power had gone out from him, (Lk 8:45). The woman with the healed haemorrhage was drawn out into the open to be commended for her faith.

Jesus was a master at provoking people to think more deeply. Questions make you think for yourself. There is a catalogue of such questions. 'Consider the ravens: They do not sow or reap, they have no storeroom or barn; yet God feeds them. And how much more valuable you are than birds! (Lk 12:24. 'What good will it be for a man if he gains the whole world, yet forfeits his soul?' (Mt 16:26). 'If a man owns a hundred sheep, and one of them wanders away, will he not leave the ninety-nine on the hills and go to look for the one that wandered off?' (Mt 18:12; Lk 15:4). 'Which of these three do you think was a neighbour to the man who fell into the hands of robbers?' (Lk 10:36).

3. To dialogue: Jesus' dialogue with the adulterous woman is incredibly short. 'Woman, where are they? Has no-one condemned you?' (Jn 8:4–10). This is such a striking example because he had refused to be drawn into conversation with this woman's accusers. He just stooped and wrote with his finger in the ground. Yet, although the dialogue is so brief, it results in a completely changed life.

Classic conversations, like the one with Nicodemus in John 3, seem to get under way through asking questions. There are five questions asked back and forth to tease out the answers as to what it means to be born again.

4. To distance: We are all used to this particular way that people use questions. Often non-Christians will ask this kind of question, not because they are looking for answers, but to hold us at arm's length. They use questions as red herrings to keep us away from perhaps the real issues going on in their lives.

There are a few instances of Jesus using questions in a similar manner in order to avoid getting into a fruitless debate. When the Pharisees come to him for no other reason than to argue and test him, Jesus answers their request for a sign with the question: 'Why does this generation ask for a miraculous sign?' (Mk 8:12). He perhaps hopes they will discover the truth that it is an evil generation that seeks for signs, but anyway, no sign will be given.

Here are just a few similar examples: 'Why do you break the command of God for the sake of your tradition? (Mt 15:3–6); 'Doesn't each of you on the Sabbath untie his ox or donkey from the stall and lead it out to give it water?' (Lk 13:15); 'Then should not this woman, a daughter of Abraham, whom Satan has kept bound for eighteen long years, be set free on the Sabbath day?' (Lk 13:16); 'Has not Moses given you the law? And yet not one of you keeps the law' (Jn 7:19); and then he goes on in the same verse to ask: 'Why are you trying to kill me?'

5. To divert: Jesus' opponents often used questions to try and trap him but Jesus would come back and confound them with questions of his own. Mark chapters 11–12 gives us four such examples, where the opposing questions being asked cover a whole range of subjects: legal, political, theological and devotional.

The first question comes in chapter 11 verse 28 and is about his authority. Jesus 'pulls the rug out' from under their questioning by asking a question of his own: 'John's baptism – was it from heaven, or from men?' (v 30). Because they were afraid to answer his question, Jesus was excused from having to answer their question. The second question is in chapter 12 verse 14, and is about whether or not it is lawful to pay tax to Caesar. With incredible wisdom Jesus sends for a coin and asks: 'Whose portrait is this?' and then goes on to encourage them to give to Caesar what is Caesar's but to God what is God's. The third question is about who will be married to whom when we get to heaven (12:23). Once again Jesus replies with a question: 'Are you not in error because you do not know the Scriptures or the power of God?' He then goes on to give us insights into heaven which would be unknowable to anyone unless they had actually been there.

The fourth and final question was asked by one of the scribes who heard how wisely he had answered every other question. 'Of all the commandments, which is the most important?' he asked (12:28). This time Jesus answers with a plain statement not a question. 'Love the Lord your God with all your heart and with all your soul and with all your mind and with all your strength . . . Love your neighbour as yourself.' This brought all the questioning to an end. 'From then on no-one dared ask [Jesus] any more questions' (v 34). Jesus, however, continues to ask all kinds of probing questions.

PRINCIPLE 48

Jesus uses words of knowledge

In Luke 2 verses 40–47 we read of Jesus as a child growing in wisdom. He was obviously keen to learn, as we find him, as a twelve-year-old, sitting in the midst of the teachers in the temple, asking questions and listening to their teaching. 'Everyone who heard him was amazed at his understanding and his answers' (v 47). But there are many occasions where Jesus used knowledge that was not learned in the conventional sense but received supernatually. I can find twenty-nine occasions when Jesus used a gift of knowledge in his dealings with people. It certainly kept him one step ahead of the game and he used this to meet the needs of those around him and to open doors into people's lives. We should certainly desire from the Lord similar gifts for our evangelism. We will look at this in more detail, particularly as it operated in the early church, in the chapter 'Manifestations of the Miraculous'. But here we will look at the evangelistic impact that 'words of knowledge' had in Jesus' ministry.

When the Bible says that '[Jesus] knew all men . . . and what was in a man' (Jn 2:24–25), I am not sure whether this was natural knowledge or supernatural. However, it affected his dealings with people. There are numerous occasions when he knew what people were thinking and this affected the direction of his conversations. I have included a few such examples below:

Words of Knowledge about What People Were Thinking

- Jesus knew that they wished to question him, Jn 16:19.
- Jesus knew what they were thinking, Lk 6:8; Mt 12:25.
- Jesus knew that they had not understood him, Mt 16:8.
- Jesus was aware that the disciples were indignant, Mt 26:10.
- Jesus knew they were discussing who would be the greatest, Lk 9:47.

These insights enabled Jesus to answer questions that were not being asked but which were nevertheless in people's hearts.

Other words of knowledge were more visual and were used more overtly in evangelism, for example, when Jesus meets Nathaniel and tells him: 'I saw you under the fig tree before Philip called you' (Jn 1:48). This was enough to create faith in Nathaniel. It almost seems as though Jesus is surprised that he believed so easily, 'Do you believe? You shall see greater things than these.' The woman at the well is amazed when Jesus says, 'You have had five husbands.' 'Come, see a man who told me everything I ever did. Could this be the Christ?' she tells her friends (Jn 4:18, 29).

One of the plainest statements which Jesus made regarding his authority to forgive sins comes in Mark 2 verses 5–12. Jesus was aware in his spirit that they were reasoning within themselves that it was blasphemy for him to forgive the paralytic's sins. 'Which is easier,' asked Jesus, 'to say your sins are forgiven or to say arise take up your bed and walk?' The crowd were amazed and glorified God because they had never seen anything like this before.

When the disciples had spent a fruitless night fishing Jesus told them, 'Let down your nets for a catch' (Lk 5:4) and they enclosed a great shoal of fish, so much that their nets began to break. As a result Peter fell on his knees pleading,

'Depart from me for I am a sinful man.' 'No,' says Jesus. 'From now on you are going to catch men just like this!'

Jesus also often used words of knowledge alongside his miracles, with obvious evangelistic impact. Here are just a few illustrations:

Words of Knowledge and Miracles

- Healing the son of the official at Capernaum: 'You may go. Your son will live' Jn 4:50.
- Feeding the 5,000: 'He already had in mind what he was going to do' Jn 6:6.
- Healing the paralysed man: 'Why are you thinking these things in your hearts?' Lk 5:22; Mt 9:4.
- Raising of Lazarus: 'This sickness will not end in death' Jn 11:4, 11, 14.
- Raising Jairus' daughter: 'She will be healed.' Lk 8:50
- Miraculous catch of fish: 'Throw your net on the right side of the boat and you will find some' Jn 21:6.

Space prevents us from looking at all the other occasions, for example when Jesus perceived that the people wanted to make him king (John 6:15); or when he told Peter about the coin in the fish's mouth (Mt 17:27); or when he gave detailed instructions about finding the colt and what they should say to its owner (Lk 19:30); or when he gave the amazing directions as to how to find the upper room for the Passover, by following a man carrying a pitcher (Lk 22:10 etc).

PRINCIPLE 49

Jesus uses picture language
(Matthew 13:34–35)

Jesus communicated through pictures, parables, figures of speech and analogies. In fact, he said he would not communicate in any other way. His stories, with striking, thought-provoking metaphors, poured forth in a constant stream. We are told, by experts, that this is the most powerful form of communication. Pictures fire up our imagination and, once the creative side of our brain has grasped the image, it will be remembered. Words that create pictures in our minds leave a lasting impression. We know that the brain is divided into two lobes, left and right. The left lobe controls our logical thinking, dealing with mathematical problems and analysing information. The right lobe is the creative side of the brain with which we fantasise, imagine and dream. It is interesting that the Holy Spirit's communication with us often uses our power to be able to see pictures in our imagination. He speaks into our imagination through visions, dreams and some prophecies.

This is exactly what Jesus does when he communicates. He doesn't just give us a list of spiritual statements. He speaks of the yeast used in bread-making, of vineyards where workers toiled, of wedding customs and ceremonies as they were celebrated in his time and of many other familiar and simple situations. He wrapped truth up with stories so that we see the truth in the context of narrative. Surveys on the mission field confirm the effectiveness of this method. Where missionaries confined themselves to teaching doctrinal principles in the form of unadorned statements of truth, such as: 'You must be born again'; 'Believe and you will receive eternal life'; 'You must repent and turn from sin'; or 'You can receive forgiveness', these and other similar statements had much less impact than when they were taught by telling simple Bible stories. Jesus took time to wrap each principle up in a graphic illustration. For example, he would tell the story of the prodigal son to convey forgiveness; or he would evoke the Old Testament picture of Moses lifting up a brass serpent in the wilderness to illustrate believing to receive life; or he would use the story of the Good Samaritan to make the point of loving your neighbour.

Interestingly, the whole Bible is picture language. It is like a photograph album, every page of which triggers the imagination. It is not a book of rules but a series of narratives in which we can see certain spiritual laws worked out in real-life situations. Every story creates a corresponding picture in our minds. I think that we, too, when we evangelise, should take time to tell a few stories. Imagine knocking on someone's door and saying, 'Excuse me, can I tell you a story?'

It would be relevant at this stage to comment on the place of art in evangelism. Every work of art inevitably conveys the character and nature of the artist. I am reminded of a young man who asked me, 'Why doesn't God write "I love you" on the underside of every leaf?' It appeared to be a reasonable question. Since God obviously wants to communicate his love to us, it follows that this was indeed a possible way of doing so. After some reflection, the young man answered his own question by observing that God's love, which is his character, is indeed portrayed in every aspect of his creation. We touch the very nature of God as we draw near to the nature of creation. God says, 'I love you' through the beauty and creativity of everything he has made for us.

Our evangelisation should likewise contain and display the creativity of God which is within us. In the Old Testament there are many instances of people using art forms such as poetry, dance, song and music. People also used art in the form of wood- and stone-carving, as well as metal work, for the purpose of glorifying God. Examples of this are seen in the building of the Tabernacle and the temple. Modern-day institutional churches give a prominent place to icons and statues, while the evangelical churches dismiss them as idolatry. It is nonetheless worthwhile to consider the place of the artist in evangelism. Icons and statues should not be venerated, but could such concrete visual images perhaps be used as an effective means of conveying the nature and spirit of God?

PRINCIPLE 50

Jesus uses parables

(Matthew 13:10–13)

While picture language is without doubt the most effective way to communicate any message, interestingly Jesus gives the opposite reason for speaking in parables. He used these analogies and metaphors to keep the message a mystery from those who didn't want to be part of the kingdom. 'The knowledge of the secrets of the kingdom of heaven has been given to you, but not to them' (Mt 13:11). 'This is why I speak to them in parables: "Though seeing, they do not see; though hearing, they do not hear or understand" ' (v 13).

We learn here some important insights. Jesus communicated his messages expecting the hearers to be granted understanding. The point to his preaching remained hidden unless revelation was given by the Father. This is a wonderful demonstration of communication by faith. The process only worked successfully if the Father was involved in giving the true meaning behind the pictures. Jesus expected his followers to be in touch with the Father to such an extent that his teaching would be clearly understood. Those outside the kingdom, however, would be left in the dark.

Often we present truth too easily, serving up the secrets of the kingdom on a plate. Jesus would hide the meaning, let people puzzle over it, and wait for the spiritually discerning to receive understanding from heaven. How often, for example, when we present a drama on the street, do we jump in with an immediate explanation. Perhaps there is wisdom in outsiders not understanding too much, because they can too easily become innoculated against the reality of what we want them to grasp.

The figure opposite gives an overview of some of the pictures Jesus presented to his hearers. As there are no parables in John's Gospel, I have included a list of the figurative images which we find in his Gospel instead. Jesus

Examples of Figurative Language in John's Gospel Jn 16:25

Light Jn 1:4–5
Temple Jn 2:19
New Birth Jn 3:7
Wind Jn 3:8
Water Jn 4:14
Food Jn 4:32
Harvest Jn 4:35
Wages Jn 4:36
Lamp Jn 5:35
Bread of Life Jn 6:35
Thirst Jn 7:37
Slave Jn 8:35; 15:20
Gate/Door Jn 10:7
Shepherd Jn 10:11
Sheep Jn 10:16
Day and Night Jn 11:9–10
Grain of Wheat Jn 12:24
Washing Jn 13:10
Children Jn 13:33
Mansions/Rooms Jn 14:2
The Way Jn 14:6
Orphans Jn 14:18
Vine Jn 15:1
Branches Jn 15:5
Labour/Birth Jn 16:21
Kingdom Jn 18:36

Parables in the Gospels

The Sower Mt 13:5ff; Mk 4:3ff; Lk 8:5ff
The Tares Mt 13:24ff
The Mustard Seed Mt 13:31f; Mk 4:31f; Lk 13:18
The Leaven Mt 13:33; Lk 13:21
The Hidden Treasure Mt 13:44
The Pearl Mt 13:45f
The Drag Net Mt 13:47ff
The Unmerciful Servant Mt 18:23ff
The Labourers in the Vineyard Mt 20:1ff
The Two Sons Mt 21:28ff
The Vineyard Mt 21:33ff; Mk 12:1ff; Lk 20:9ff
The Wedding Feast Mt 22:1ff
The Ten Virgins Mt 25:1ff
The Talents Mt 25:14ff
The Seed Mk 4:26ff
The Two Debtors Lk 7:41ff
The Good Samaritan Lk 10:25ff
The Importunate Friend Lk 11:5ff
The Rich Fool Lk 12:16ff
The Barren Fig Tree Lk 13:6ff
The Great Dinner Lk 14:16ff
The Lost Sheep Mt 18:12ff; Lk 15:4ff
The Lost Coin Lk 15:8ff
The Prodigal Son Lk 15:11ff
The Shrewd Manager Lk 16:1ff
The Rich Man and Lazarus Lk 16:19ff
The Unprofitable Servants Lk 17:7ff
The Persistant Widow Lk 18:1ff
The Pharisee and the Tax Collector Lk 18:10ff
The Ten Minas' Lk 19:12ff

tells thirty parables in Matthew, Mark and Luke and gives us twenty-six analogies in John. All of these are rich with spiritual insights for the discerning hearer and are perfect examples of how we can best communicate our message. If we find it difficult to come up with our own illustrations, we couldn't do better than re-use some of his.

PRINCIPLE 51

Jesus uses 'miracle language'

While picture language defines graphically the kingdom of God, 'miracle language' demonstrates it practically. It's one thing to talk about God's love, even using analogies, but it's another thing to prove it. There are thirty-five different miracles described for us in the Gospels. They authenticated Jesus' claims. 'At least believe on the evidence of the miracles themselves' (Jn 14:11). Jesus would say; 'If I drive out demons by the Spirit of God, then the kingdom of God has come upon you' (Mt 12:28).

Because there is a whole chapter devoted to the miraculous a little later, we will be brief here, but it is important to observe the major part miracles played in Jesus' ministry. His miracles have been defined as the signs of the kingdom, demonstrating that the power of God was around. These miracles were expressing God's heart for the world, as well as his ultimate plan for mankind, a world where there would be no tears, no pain, no suffering. Here is a God who cares for the individual – body, soul and spirit, and who is 100 per cent committed to undoing the works of the evil one. This is no less his heartbeat today than it was then, and I am sure we should never question whether it is God's heart to heal. This is displayed so clearly as Jesus healed all those who came to him for healing, sometimes in vast numbers.

I invite you to join me in a quick tour through Matthew's Gospel looking at some of the statements regarding Jesus and his healing ministry:

Jesus went throughout Galilee, teaching in their synagogues, preaching the good news of the kingdom, and healing every disease and sickness among the people. News about him spread all over Syria, and people brought to him all who were ill with various diseases, those suffering severe pain, the demon-possessed, those having seizures, and the paralysed, and he healed them. Large crowds . . . followed him. (Mt 4:23–25)

When evening came, many who were demon-possessed were brought to him, and he drove out the spirits with a word and healed all the sick.
This was to fulfil what was spoken through the prophet Isaiah: 'He took up our infirmities and carried our diseases.' (Mt 8:16–17)

Jesus went through all the towns and villages, teaching in their synagogues, preaching the good news of the kingdom and healing every disease and sickness. When he saw the crowds. (Mt 9:35–36)

Jesus replied, 'Go back and report to John what you hear and see: The blind receive sight, the lame walk, those who have leprosy are cured, the deaf hear, the dead are raised, and the good news is preached to the poor. (Mt 11:4–5)

Aware of this, Jesus withdrew from that place. Many followed him, and he healed all their sick. (Mt 12:15)

When Jesus landed and saw a large crowd, he had compassion on them and healed their sick. (Mt 14:14)

And when the men of that place recognised Jesus, they sent word to all the surrounding country. People brought all their sick to him and begged him to let the sick just touch the edge of his cloak, and all who touched him were healed. (Mt 14:35–36)	Great crowds came to him, bringing the lame, the blind, the crippled, the mute and many others, and laid them at his feet; and he healed them. The people were amazed when they saw the mute speaking, the crippled made well, the lame walking and the blind seeing. And they praised the God of Israel. (Mt 15:30–31)
Large crowds followed him, and he healed them there. (Mt 19:2)	The blind and the lame came to him at the temple, and he healed them. (Mt 21:14)

These miracles were not only proof of the message but they also accredited the messenger. When John the Baptist sent disciples to ask, 'Are you the one who was to come, or should we expect someone else?' Jesus answered, 'Go back and report to John what you have seen and heard: The blind receive sight . . . the deaf hear, the dead are raised, and the good news is preached to the poor' (Lk 7:18–23). That was enough for John. The Lord continued this same work through the early church and desires to do the same today.

PRINCIPLE 52

Jesus uses social action

When people went to John the Baptist and asked him how they should live their lives, he gave them special social instructions, such as to be content with their wages or if they had two coats, to give one away to someone who needed it.

These were acts of prophetic repentance, the performance of which would prove to themselves and to others that they really meant business with God. What an excellent way of proving our faith – by going out and serving society in some way.

Jesus introduced his own ministry as that of preaching the gospel to the poor and releasing the captives, recovering the sight of the blind and setting free those that are downtrodden. 'Today this scripture is fulfilled in your hearing' (Lk 4:21). He was declaring, right at the beginning of his ministry years, that his mission was to the poor, the needy, the vulnerable, the damaged. His social agenda is summed up in passages like Matthew 25 verses 35–45 where he identifies with the hungry, the thirsty, the strangers, the naked, the sick, and those in prison.

In defining who our neighbour is, Jesus tells the story of the Good Samaritan and then twists the tale to tell us to go and do the same. He answers the question 'Who is my neighbour?' with another: 'Whose neighbour are you?' (Lk 10:29–37). We need to be actively pursuing a good neighbour policy with every stranger we meet. I guess this includes our actual neighbours too! This parable also highlights a particularly relevant form of social action in today's society: the relief of victims of crime. The Good Samaritan not only cares for the man who is injured and robbed, but also pays the bill for others to care for him too.

There are so many other areas we could examine. For example, we will look a little later at the way Jesus recommends kindness, not just to the victims of crime but also to the criminals when he suggests we give our coat when someone takes our jacket. He shows favour to the thief as he dies on the cross. He shows the importance of campaigning for social justice with those in authority (Mt 23). He is clear in his teaching about family and the importance and permanence of marriage (Mt 19:9). Some of these things will be developed later in the chapter entitled 'The Ministry of the Merciful'.

PRINCIPLE 53

Jesus is motivated by compassion

I often wonder how pure our motives are when we go out in evangelism or when we pray for revival. Is it the spiritual exercise of witnessing or praying that makes us feel better, because we have done our duty? Or is it the results that are important, seeing our church growing or our ministry successful? Or are we motivated by an overwhelming care for each individual.

I can remember in my youth listening, over and over again, to the words of a song sung by an Australian evangelist.

> Give me a passion for souls, Lord
>   Fill all my being with love
> Give me a passion for souls, Lord
>   Direct my life from above.

These words were etched onto my heart and seemed to affect the way that I looked at people. I would sit on a train intensely caring for those around me. I was never much good at getting beyond that and actually expressing that care in words, but nevertheless a foundation was being laid in me that, over the coming years, was going to motivate me into evangelism and social action.

'God so loved the world that he gave his only begotten son.' That little word 'so' seems to define the kind of love that is motivated enough to give. We can love people but do we 'so love' them that action ensues. This conjures up in my mind the picture of a steam engine with a pressure gauge,

where the pressure has to reach a certain level before it begins to move. Jesus so loved the multitudes that he had to heal them, feed them, lead them, teach them and die for them.

Jesus healed people because he loved them, not in order to gain fame and glory. His healings were a pure demonstration of love. There were times when he would strictly forbid those who had been healed to say anything about it. This seems strange. Why not exploit such happenings to their fullest evangelistic advantage? It is true that his miracles drew large crowds, as they also did in the days of the early church, but on these occasions, Jesus displayed the absolute purity of motive in his heart as he healed people, asking them to say nothing about their healing. He showed that it was an expression of love for each individual and that he cared primarily about relieving their suffering. His agenda was not a selfish one. He didn't heal to get glory for himself, he healed to put a hurting life right. It was enough for him that a blind man could now see. Even if no one ever heard about it, he would doubtless have still done it, because he cared for that individual. This reveals Jesus' underlying motive which was to see each individual blessed. We need to make sure our motives are of the same purity as we ask the Lord to demonstrate his love to the world, miraculously, through us.

PRINCIPLE 54

Jesus uses hospitality

We see Jesus communicating his message in the temple courts, on the hillsides, in the streets or from a fishing boat. However, during the course of his ministry we see Jesus on many occasions also using the home. In fact the first disciples were won through hospitality. Two of John the Baptist's disciples were following Jesus and asked him where he was staying. Jesus replied, 'Come and see.' They went and saw and stayed there that day (Jn 1:39). Andrew, one of them, then went and found his brother Simon Peter and told him,

'We have found the Messiah.'

Mark's Gospel recounts ten different times where people's houses become the base for kingdom activity.

Homes in Mark's Gospel	
1:29	Healed a mother-in-law
2:1	Paralytic healed
2:15	Levi's repentance party
3:20	Discussion with scribes
5:38	Girl raised from dead
7:17	Discussion over parables
7:24	Demon cast out of girl
9:28	Disciples questioning
9:33	Discussion with disciples
10:10	Blesses children and discusses marriage

Some people might question the wisdom of starting a ministry by getting your mother-in-law healed! However, Levi's repentance party was a great idea. Twice Mark uses the expression that Jesus was 'at home' or 'came home'. In fact, it is the house where he is described as being 'at home' whose roof was broken up to let the paralytic in. I have always wondered what the owner felt about that. As this was where Jesus was staying, the inconvenience undoubtedly would have been borne by Jesus, and I am sure it was his carpentry skills which repaired the roof at the end of the day.

In Luke's Gospel we see that Jesus had no qualms about inviting himself to the house of Zacchaeus (Lk 19:5). How about that as an evangelistic strategy? I guess that is not far off what Jesus is encouraging the disciples to do when he says 'Whatever town or village you enter, search for some worthy person there and stay at his house until you leave' (Mt 10:11). Although Zacchaeus would not have been described as worthy, quite the opposite, nevertheless, as a result of Jesus' visit, not only does salvation come to his house but the poor are benefited and the victims of his extortion are recompensed.

PRINCIPLE 55

Jesus uses the context of a shared meal

The various 'Process Evangelism' courses being advertised at the moment which include a meal, like the Alpha course, have discovered the value of sharing the gospel in the context of shared food. In my present church, once every six weeks we have lunch together after the service on Sunday. These Sundays have become our best attended services. It was presumably because Jesus ate and drank so often like this that he was accused of being a glutton and a wine bibber. He was also criticised for eating with sinners. But all this was an integral part of his evangelistic strategy. Not only did he share the good news during meals, he also communicated powerfully through his rather novel food preparation, or should I say food creation. Turning water into wine to keep a wedding party going says a great deal to me about the character of God. On more than one occasion he fed crowds of people with next to nothing. These miracles created a dramatic talking point, but he really wanted the crowd to grasp the fact that he was the true Bread of Heaven.

Jesus must have shocked his disciples on the day when he said, 'Unless you eat my flesh and drink my blood you have no part with me'. The offence, of course, was removed when they understood the institution of Communion. It is significant, however, that Jesus used ordinary elements of daily food, bread and wine, for us to remember him by. In fact he develops this analogy to say that we should feed on him, that he himself is our food, just as he would say that his food was to do the will of him who sent him (Jn 6:53–57; Jn 4:34).

Feasting and fasting played an important part in Jesus' teaching. Many of his parables feature food, for example the picture of the kingdom as a banquet to which outsiders should be invited. Maybe the modern saying 'The way to a man's heart is through his stomach' is not far from Jesus' emphasis. The informal atmosphere of the mealtime provided the context for many theological discussions. What better model could we have for learning to reach people?

Sharing questions and answers comes naturally as we share food and drink together.

PRINCIPLE 56

Jesus encourages the use of money in evangelism

Luke 16:9–11

Luke 16 verses 9–11 tells the story of the shrewd manager (or unjust steward) who squandered his master's possessions. On losing his job, he calls together his master's debtors and writes off a large proportion of their debts with the aim of making friends with them. Jesus applies this parable by saying that the steward was a shrewd man and that we too should make friends with 'the mammon of unrighteousness'. I believe there is a spiritual principle here. Jesus even says that if we are faithful in this, if we use money on non-Christians, God will entrust to us true riches. This is a complicated parable but Jesus' application is simple – use money to make friends with non-Christians. In fact, he even gives the impression that those we seek to bless with money will welcome us into heaven (v 9). If investing money in non-Christians sees them converted, it makes sense to do it as much as possible.

This means that we should not think twice about taking someone out for a meal or buying a round of drinks for everyone, or paying for non-Christians when we play them at sport. Neither should we hesitate to take on someone's debts. We should pay for anything that we feel blesses individuals. If you use money like this, friends are never too far away. I know we often feel guilty about this sort of spending and probably even justify our lack of generosity by the idea that in this way we are being good spiritual stewards. This parable, however, seems to indicate that the Lord observes our generosity with unrighteous mammon before entrusting to us the true riches of the kingdom.

Some years ago, the wife of a non-Christian came to see

me one Sunday morning and informed me that her husband was drinking very heavily, actually spending all their social security benefit on alcohol, and that the family were going hungry. She asked if I would go and see him. The next Tuesday evening we sat chatting together for about forty-five minutes. Then I asked him outright, 'You've not always drunk so heavily, what's the problem? Why are you getting so drunk?' He shared how he had bought a new television set on hire purchase. Unfortunately, he was unable to get insurance because he lived in a high risk area and the TV was stolen on the very first night. He was now having to pay for something he did not have. That, to him, was so painful that, instead of paying off the bill, he spent his money on getting drunk to try to numb the pain. 'Well,' I said, 'the answer is simple. We will pay for the TV as a church.' His eyes suddenly lit up and he sat up in his chair. 'If we pay for this, you obviously won't need to go out drinking will you?' I asked. He replied instantly, 'No, if you would pay this I will definitely stop drinking.' The next Sunday we had a 'whip-round' as a church and paid the outstanding £300.

Four days later, I went back to see him and he had stopped drinking. When I said to him, 'Now you have stopped drinking you must have a little spare cash, mustn't you?' he began looking at me very nervously, thinking that he would now have to pay the church back. 'Listen,' I reassured him, 'don't worry about the money, we have paid that for you. But now you have a little extra money, why don't you invest it in your family?' I pointed to the carpetless floor and suggested that a carpet off-cut would make it a lot more comfortable for his toddlers. I walked around the house with him. 'Why don't you put some shelves on the wall here and sort out some of these bits and pieces?' and 'Why don't you paint this wall here?' We actually went off to the DIY store together and bought something to get started with.

Well, to cut a long story short, he turned up to church about three weeks after this. I think he began to feel good about himself, probably for the first time in his married life. A month or two later he became a Christian. The wonderful thing was that when he became a Christian he started going round to other people's houses and would say, 'Why don't you put a carpet on this floor?' and 'Why don't you paint this wall?' But then he would say, 'You probably can't afford it or perhaps you don't have the time, so I will do it for you.' It cost us £300 to see him saved, but even if he hadn't been converted, it would have been worth the investment just to have removed the hurt from that family. As it turned out, he was learning what it meant to be a disciple even before he came to church and he gave back far more than he ever received once he started following Jesus.

PRINCIPLE 57

Jesus is described as the friend of sinners

Jesus gained the nickname 'friend of sinners'. I often wonder what nickname non-Christians give to us. They enjoy jesting at our expense and their terminology usually centres around the religious. We are often perceived as the 'friends of the church' rather than 'friends of sinners'. We are often seen as being weird or freaky. But Jesus' nickname represents a challenge for us to get involved and be identified with those who are not so holy. Sinners saw Jesus as approachable, as a friend and not a critical judge. We must, therefore, accept others as Christ has accepted us. Jesus doesn't leave us as he found us, but accepts us as we are, warts and all. It is very important for non-Christians to feel accepted as they are.

PRINCIPLE 58

Jesus only followed up those who followed

There is today a heavy emphasis put on follow-up, and rightly so. Being keen on sport, I have always been taught that follow-through is essential to maximise any impact on the ball, whatever the ball game. I have always used this analogy to encourage churches to think about their follow-through strategy to maximise their evangelistic impact. Yet, strangely, Jesus doesn't do conventional follow-up. Only on one occasion did he go looking for someone who had responded to him. That was the blind man, who was being persecuted by the synagogue because of his healing (Jn 9). Jesus went and found him, not only to encourage him but also to reveal his own true identity to him. As a general principle, however, Jesus did not chase up his contacts.

Maybe there is a danger that, through our follow-up programmes, we breed self-orientated converts who wait to be followed up. Jesus turns this right round and demands that they 'follow him up'. 'Anyone who does not take his cross and follow me is not worthy of me' (Mt 10:38). The disciple must make the running. It is his job to pursue the Christian faith. In Jesus' day many did follow, sometimes for miles, sometimes without food, sometimes for days at a time, eager to hear, keen to understand and enthusiastic to receive. Jesus gave them follow-up teaching as they were following him.

Follow-up is essential. In fact, most of the New Testament is follow-up material. However, the critical emphasis is that we follow up those who are following us. When I first became serious about Christianity, I found in my heart a great deal of energy to pursue Jesus. I couldn't put the Bible down. I couldn't learn enough quickly enough. I am disappointed when our converts need to be dragged to church or need to be force-fed the Word. Jesus expected people to follow. Do we waste too much time trying to make disciples of those who are not really interested? Should we maximise our use of time by actually putting those people off and going for those who are really receptive?

CHAPTER 5

THE MORALS OF THE MESSENGER

'Christians don't smoke, don't drink and don't go to wild parties.' I have always been disappointed that this is the world's classic definition of Christianity. The shame is that these impressions are all negative. I would much rather be known for all the radical, good things that we do, than for the few things which we don't do. As we look at 'the morals of the messenger' I am not so interested in defining the immorality which we shouldn't do. It goes without saying that if we behave immorally, we are going to negate everything we stand for and thus nullify our evangelistic impact on the world. No, here we are going to outline the positive morals: the radical, productive code of conduct which is not so much the overcoming of sin, but the constructive demonstration of doing and being what is most Christlike.

Jesus shows evangelism to be a constant performance of the gospel by the sort of people we are and the way that we live. If there is a credibility gap between the message and the lifestyle, the world will definitely read the lifestyle. Sadly, too many non-Christians have their hypocrite stories about Christians, which they feel justify them in not looking into the faith any further. Jesus gives us a blueprint for building a radically different kind of behaviour, which should impress the world, just as Jesus himself did. We are going to use some of the thoughts in Jesus' first sermon as a basis for this chapter. The Sermon on the Mount is his 'get your life right' material. It starts with the *Beatitudes* which show us the 'beautiful attitudes' which we need to have in order to be a powerful visual aid to the community.

PRINCIPLE 59

God uses the weak

Matthew 5:3

Often we feel that the evangelist has to be a rather brash, confident go-getter with a slick overpowering personality, a man's man, with the kind of strength of attributes that non-Christians can look up to and be impressed by. We naturally feel that a good-looking person, well presented, makes the best public relations representative. The problem is that not many of us fit this description. It was prophesied of Jesus that 'He had no beauty or majesty to attract us to him, nothing in his appearance that we should desire him' (Is 53:2). Personally I am grateful that the Lord has chosen to use the weak, the base and the foolish. The sort of people he uses are: the humble, the selfless, those lacking natural confidence, the least, the insignificant, those with low self-esteem. Yes, Jesus begins his sermon on the mount by revealing that the kingdom is given to the poor in spirit (Mt 5:3).

The meek shall inherit the earth (Mt 5:5)

This word 'meek' has been translated as 'gentle', 'selfless', 'yielding' and even 'weak'. I actually think these first three definitions are qualities of strength not weakness. They are, however, not the kind of qualities you would expect to enable anybody to inherit the earth. The world would say that it is the forceful, determined 'go getters' who will take the earth. Those with the strongest drive, the most powerful, the most confident, will accomplish the task of monopolising and dominating the world. Jesus shows a completely different spirit. It is the generous, the humble, the self-giving, who will ultimately win the world. The church maybe seems so weak. Who would have believed from its humble beginnings that it would have outlived the Roman Empire? Yet it is this seeming weakness that is its strength. The church carries the same heart as its Creator, who embodies total selflessness. God created a world in order to give it away to those whom he created. Yet it is the selfishness of the devil, who seeks to grab everything for himself, which unfortunately is mimmicked by the world. Christ died in humility, in selflessness, in service for others, in obedience to his Father, as a sacrifice for sin. This is the spirit that wins the world!

It used to be a frustration to me that whenever the church gave a general appeal for volunteers for evangelism, it was always the oddballs who turned up. I used to wish that I had the confidence to ask those with the highest cringe factor to stay behind and pray while the more respectable went out. But through the years I have come to appreciate that these are the very people whom the Lord uses. If the world is won by the meek, then let us use them, and perhaps in some ways we need to become like them, while nevertheless trying to eliminate as much of the unnecessary cringe factor as possible.

The majority of people are not confident; many struggle in the area of low self-esteem. What could be more appealing than to meet those of a similar nature, and to discover how much they are blessed and used by God. Certainly, God cares for those who are poor in spirit. As we evangelise, it is these 'meek-spirited souls' who attract heaven's attention. I am sure too that the world is attracted to the meekness of the Christian spirit.

PRINCIPLE 60

We are salt, light and a city

Matthew 5:13

Evangelism is not just a formula of words to say. Neither is it a series of meetings. The world needs the infallible proof of changed lives. We are not even merely bringing light into the world. We *are* the light for the world. Jesus causes his light to shine through our hearts (2 Cor 4:6).

Evangelism is simply living out the principles of Christianity in our daily lives as we rub shoulders with non-

Christians. Jesus says: 'You are the salt of the earth. But if the salt loses its saltiness, how can it be made salty again? It is no longer good for anything, except to be thrown out and trampled by men. You are the light of the world. A city on a hill cannot be hidden' (Mt 5:13). There are three pictures here: salt, light and a city. These pictures define our role in evangelism.

We should be like salt, which acts like an antiseptic stopping corruption, combatting negative spiritual infections in society and seeking to preserve it from moral decay. Or we should be like seasoning which savours and brings out the taste. We should bring out the best, not only in each other, but also in the world, drawing out all the good savours and flavours of life. Isn't it interesting when people who swear in our hearing apologise to us? Who told them that what they were doing was wrong? Then, like salt we should be creating a thirst in those around us. When people hunger and thirst for righteousness they will be satisfied (Mt 5:6). Or perhaps we should be acting like a fertiliser, providing a seed bed for people to grow into the things of God. These things are the salty dynamic of why the church exists.

Jesus tells us that a city on a hill cannot be hidden. So whether we evangelise or not, the world is still going to see the church. It is impossible to hide a city during the day. It is perhaps a little easier at night, and maybe we are living in a society which is in spiritual darkness. But a city at night becomes even more dramatically visible, when all its lights are shining, than the city of the day.

Where the darkness has been darkest, the light will shine brighter by contrast. The more ungodly the environment into which we are evangelising, the brighter our witness becomes. On a dark night, a pilot flying at 30,000 feet can see a match struck on the ground. It only takes a little glimmer of light to affect a dark place. 'The people living in darkness have seen a great light; on those living in the land of the shadow of death a light has dawned' (Mt 4:16 quoting Is 9:2). Light always overcomes darkness. Darkness never consumes the light; in the same way truth always cuts through deception. The fact that light can affect darkness, but darkness cannot affect light, is an important emphasis in what we are doing in evangelism. You don't have to gather up the darkness and throw it out of a room, you just switch on the light and the darkness disperses. What kind of implications does that have in the area of spiritual warfare? Does the putting on of the light mean that the evil forces are automatically dispersed?

Jesus refers to not letting salt lose its savour and not hiding a candle away. Both the salt and light are described as losing their potential, but he affirms that a city is permanently there for all to see. I puzzle as to why Jesus used the salt and light analogies in the way that he did. Salt, scientifically, can't lose its savour, unless it becomes contaminated. Salt only loses its flavour when we add all kinds of other impurities to it. It is OK to add salt to the world, but it is not OK to add worldliness to the salt. As for the image of the candle, since it can be blown out so easily, why didn't Jesus say, 'Don't let your candle go out'? Instead he said, 'Don't put it in the cellar or under a bucket. Wouldn't it have been more sensible to suggest that we shouldn't hide the salt in the cellar (or even in the salt-cellar)? The impression given is that it is not easy to lose the savour or to let the candle burn out. So, as long as we are burning, we just have to be careful not to hide this flame or contaminate our savour.

I have always felt that the verses about the salt and the light are the heart of the Sermon on the Mount. The salt seems to refer back to the verses about attitudes, described in the beatitudes. The rest of the teaching goes on to develop what it surely means to be light to the world. Certainly, many of the following principles are evangelistic and explain how we can be very different in nature and lifestyle from non-Christians. As we live by these morals we will shine like beacons and, interestingly, Jesus describes how to place the light to be best seen. In other words, he defines various real-life scenarios into which we bring light.

PRINCIPLE 61

God uses our actions and reactions

Matthew 5:38ff

Jesus outlines thirty-four practical principles in the Sermon on the Mount which are all an exact antithesis of the way people naturally behave. In fact, they are so radical that even many Christians think that they are impossible to live out in practice. However, they provide us with actions and reactions modelled on the behaviour of Jesus, and which the Holy Spirit produces in us when we sincerely desire to be like Jesus. I will only select and explore a few of these to make the point, and leave you to discover the rest for yourself.

PRINCIPLE 62

Turn the other cheek

Matthew 5:38

Jesus seems to take it for granted that we are all going to get hurt in the course of life. 'If someone strikes you on the right cheek, turn to him the other also' (Mt 5:38). When we are hurt or insulted we should react like Jesus did, which means that we ought not to retaliate, nor even resist, but turn to receive more of the same. We need, then, to be able to absorb the hurt. Just as a shock absorber in a car has to soak up the energy of the bumps in the road, so we must be shock absorbers in society. Somehow we have to cope with hurts and bitternesses, without carrying them around with us. Through the Holy Spirit we must take hurts and absorb their destructive energy thus rendering them ineffective. The illustration of snooker balls is very helpful. When they hit each other, hardly any energy is lost on impact. They continue to ricochet around the table. When one hits another they both get knocked off course. We need to demonstrate the exact opposite of this behaviour. We should be like snooker balls made out of Blu-tack, which absorb energy and refuse to transmit violence. In this way we don't get deflected and we remove all the sting from their attack. To react in a right way when everybody around you is reacting wrongly is what this evangelistic principle is all about. Literally, when someone tries to punch your lights out, they discover just how much your light still shines.

Jesus makes it clear that we will be opposed for our faith. I have been attacked physically eleven times during the course of my ministry. Three times I have been threatened with knives; once, rather oddly, someone tried to stab me in the forehead. On another occasion I was completely knocked out by an enraged youth, which at least afforded me a few moments of relaxation in a busy schedule! However, on all eleven occasions, l can honestly say that I have found, in the heat of the moment, that the Holy Spirit has absorbed the attack. Our natural reaction may be to want to get back at our aggressor, but we need to make Jesus our example. When they hit him round the head, having blindfolded him, jokingly asking him to prophesy who hit him, or when they plucked the beard out of his face, or whipped his back, or put nails through his hands and feet, he did not react, or retaliate like others would have done. He, instead, breathed out total forgiveness.

Of course, humanly speaking, the principles of the Sermon on the Mount are far beyond our own ability to live up to, but if we at least agree with these principles in theory, we will find that God can then live them in us practically. He will absorb the aggression, thus enabling us to pray for those who assault us. We will be able to 'bless those who curse [us], pray for those who ill-treat [us]' (Lk 6:28). Jesus teaches us that it is precisely on these occasions that we can 'rejoice and be exceedingly glad'. Luke's account even says that we can 'rejoice in that day and leap for joy' (Lk 6:23).

PRINCIPLE 63

Give to those who steal from you

Luke 6:29–30

'If someone takes your cloak, do not stop him from taking your tunic . . . if anyone takes what belongs to you, do not demand it back' (Lk 6:29–30).

Nowhere is the spirit of Jesus more clearly exhibited than in these statements. It is where the best in the kingdom of God meets the worst in the kingdom of the world. It is a challenging strategy for evangelism.

In the early days of our marriage, Sallie and I studied together the Sermon on the Mount and we often puzzled over Jesus' more radical statements. It hardly seemed wise to us to give more to someone who steals from you, and yet Jesus says that the person who puts into practice this code of behaviour is like a wise man building his house on a rock. The sermon finishes by saying that it is a wise man who hears these sayings and does them (Mt 7:24–27). At that time, we had eighteen homeless teenagers living with us. Of course, some of them were a little lightfingered. Within the first few weeks of our marriage, a lot of our wedding presents disappeared and other valuables went missing. My mother-in-law got into the habit of giving me the same Christmas present for several years running, because it would invariably have been stolen by the time the festive season came round again.

Sallie and I decided that if we found out who had taken something, we would then go and give them more. I hope they realised that we were much more excited about the spiritual kingdom of God than about the material possessions of the physical world around us. Some of them started asking questions and even getting up early in the morning to study the Bible with us to discover what Jesus had to say about life. We quickly discovered the wisdom in what Jesus was saying. These words of his actually changed lives. Some of these young men were completely turned around from being totally selfish go-getters to become genuinely kind disciples of Jesus. When someone is converted from a life of crime, society is blessed. The abuse against all their future victims is now removed. Sins are not just forgiven they are more significantly prevented from happening.

I remember a long conversation with a psychiatrist in Sweden, one very cold afternoon, as we debated together the wisdom in some of these statements of Jesus. Many criminals are aware that they are parasites on society. At a deep psychological level they actually welcome punishment. The law and the penal system give them a sense of security. They often hate themselves and feel that they are worthy to be hated by the community. But Jesus came in order to show seemingly worthless people that they were actually valuable and worth sacrificing for.

These principles suggest that we should treat people differently from the way that the world would do. No non-Christian would give extra to someone who has just stolen from them. Jesus gives us a way to literally shock people with grace. Our merciful and kind attitudes speak volumes which could not be put into words. This is communication of the highest order. Incidentally, I am also persuaded that these principles are good for us too, because they free our hearts from the care of material things. We know where we stand, pretty quickly, by whether or not we are prepared to obey Jesus in these commands.

One day, a young man came to tell me that his best friend had just run off with his girlfriend. He was obviously very hurt by this, but also said, 'What's more, he has also run off with the trousers of my new suit.' As we prayed about it, he suddenly said, 'I've got it! I know what I should do. Instead of asking for my girlfriend and my trousers back, I shall simply give him the jacket of the suit as well.' In the process of giving more to his (former) friend, he found that he also lost all the hurt and bitterness from his heart. His outward actions had overcome his own inward attitudes and given him victory. When we give to those who steal from us, we are affirming that it is not they who are taking, it is we who are giving.

Matthew 5 verse 40 reads: 'If someone wants to sue you and take your tunic, let him have your cloak as well.' A businessman running his own company came to see me one day with a dilemma. He was being swindled out of a lot of money by a business partner. He asked me what I thought he should do. I said that he probably wouldn't want to hear what I had to say. He replied, 'No, I think I know what you are going to say, but I just need to hear you say it.' Well, I read him Matthew 5 verse 40 and then asked, 'Do you think God is blessing your business?' to which he replied, 'Yes, God is really blessing what I am doing.' I told him that God's blessing was ultimately the most important thing. Consequently, anything which further attracted God's blessing would definitely be worthwhile doing. Even a financial loss would be worth it if it attracted the Holy Spirit to his business dealings. Then I said that I thought he should not only let the partner have what he was after but also write a cheque and give him more. Well, he did what I suggested and the Lord richly blessed his business that year as a result. In fact his abundance was such that he set up a trust fund so that he could tithe his business profits for the poor.

This is a powerful form of evangelism. We need to treat people with love and respect, no matter what their history. Yes, of course we need laws, law courts and a police force. The law of the land is part of the law that hopefully leads people to Christ. But when sinners encounter Christians, they should experience a taste of grace. We exercise mercy because we have received great mercy. No wonder the crowds were often amazed at Jesus' teaching. This is flying in the face of all worldly logic and yet in practice, it proves to be so astutely right. It is through our attitudes that non-Christians hopefully learn about God's grace, love, mercy, forbearance and forgiveness.

PRINCIPLE 64

Go the second mile

Matthew 5:41

Jesus applies to his followers a Roman law which dictated that a soldier could force someone to carry his bags for one mile. No doubt this was a common occurrence in occupied Palestine. A person would have had to carry these bags whether he was a Christian or a non-Christian. Jesus points out, however, that a disciple could use this as an opportunity for evangelism. By carrying their bags twice as far, he would demonstrate a radically different attitude from other people. I can imagine the early Christians walking alongside Roman soldiers just waiting to be asked to carry their luggage. They would carry it willingly and joyfully, not muttering under their breath about oppression and the imposition of this military occupation. They were now not carrying the bags for the Romans but for Jesus.

This injunction is about being willing to go 'over the top' in the way that we behave. At work, for example, do we just do what is required or do we go beyond our duties. This becomes an excellent demonstration of the Christian attitude. A non-Christian has absolutely no incentive to do more than he is asked, but a Christian is expressing his love for the Lord in going twice as far. Even if our service is never noticed or acknowledged by our bosses, it is nevertheless noticed by the Lord and thus becomes a high form of worship.

To go the second mile doesn't necessarily mean putting in twice as much time. You could just run twice as fast in the same time. I think that Christians should be able to work twice as hard as non-Christians, partly because it is such fun to use everyday activities to embody and express our faith. But also because we can run on the energy which God supplies: 'Those who hope in the LORD will renew their strength. They will soar on wings like eagles; they will run and not grow weary, they will walk and not be faint' (Is 40:31).

PRINCIPLE 65

Give to everyone who asks . . . lend expecting nothing back

Luke 6:30–35

Unfortunately these verses are sometimes used by Christians in order to sponge off fellow church members. I don't think that we should ever use them as a basis for abusing one another in the church. We should never borrow anything which we do not intend to give back. The whole thrust of the Sermon on the Mount is evangelistic, and consequently these two principles deal with our financial dealings with non-Christians. We need to get excited about giving to unbelievers. Again, this is a privilege and an opportunity to graphically demonstrate the gospel. We want the world to understand God's generosity, how freely he gives, so we should freely give too.

A friend of mine became a Christian, but his fiancée did not. She was the most lovely person, but even after they were married, she would not have anything to do with church. He found the first three years of his marriage very difficult. She seemed totally out of reach of the gospel. Then one day when they were going on holiday I offered them my car. She was astonished. She could not believe that anyone would spontaneously lend their car and she became a Christian as a result. Later, the husband said that he felt that her conversion was the real beginning of their marriage, and that that holiday with the borrowed car was their real honeymoon. Sometimes you can fail to reach people through argument whereas a simple demonstration of the gospel will break through the barriers to create faith.

A man walked into one of our church plants in Peckham one Sunday morning and asked the person on the door for some money to pay his electricity bill. The man on the door was very wise and pointed to me preaching at the front of the church. 'That's the man you need to see,' he said, 'but wait until he has finished talking.' The man sat at the back of the hall throughout my sermon and then, the moment I had finished, he limped up to me dragging his right leg and repeated his request. This time he said the money was for groceries. I read to him the passage from Acts where it says, 'Silver or gold I do not have, but what I have I give you. In the name of Jesus Christ of Nazareth, walk' (Acts 3:6). I read the whole passage, then I explained that I couldn't say that to him, as I did have some silver. Actually I had about £7 in my pocket which I gladly gave to him. But I suggested that we should also pray for his leg, like Peter had done for the lame beggar at the Beautiful Gate. I closed my eyes to pray for him and almost as soon as I began, I could hear him asserting, 'I don't believe it, I don't believe it.' Thinking he must be very hardened in unbelief, I kept on praying until eventually I opened my eyes to find that he was staring at his healed leg in disbelief, waving it about and saying, 'I don't believe it!' He then sat for a whole hour while we explained the gospel to him. We gave him a copy of Matthew's Gospel and suggested that he should read through it to see whether he was prepared to follow Jesus. Unfortunately, I haven't seen him since, so I don't know whether he committed his life to Christ. But I do know that he touched the kingdom of God that morning in a way that he would remember for the rest of his life. He could never deny the goodness or the power of God.

When we give to everyone who asks, as Luke's Gospel challenges us to do, we have a way of blessing people spiritually through material things. If a non-Christian walked up to me on the street and asked me for my watch, I would count it a privilege to give it to him. I would explain exactly why I was giving it and I would ask if I could pray with him. I know that my apparently crazy action would have an impact that words cannot make. (On second thoughts, I would probably take him to a shop and buy him a watch, as mine has sentimental value.)

We planted a church in Soho some years ago, and people often used to accost me on the streets and ask for money. I used to be confused by this at first as I did not know how to react. I would of course ask what they wanted it for, and their reasons always seemed legitimate, like wanting to buy a sandwich. But I was often suspicious because I could sometimes smell drink on their breath, or detect the obvious effects of drugs. I would argue that my giving to them would only further damage them. What was the point of giving to them if it was going to lead them into destroying themselves? I would then feel somehow justified in not giving them any money.

Part of the reason I didn't give to them was that I didn't like the way that they spent the money, but the major problem was that I didn't like to part with it. The Lord had to challenge me and he gave me a novel solution. Nowadays, if people ask me for money, I will give it to them but I will usually ask if I can pray with them first. People who ask you for money on the streets are usually going to spend it on some vice or other: prostitutes, drugs, gambling or drink. I will offer them money, but as I do, I will pray for them that God's grace and power will give them the opportunity to get out of the trap they are in. On the other hand, if you have the time, the best thing is of course to take them to a café and buy them a meal. This then gives you plenty of time to talk to them. They are open to what you say as you share the gospel because you have blessed them with your kindness.

A friend and I were once in Amsterdam when a man asked me for money on the street. I offered to give him some but on the condition that we could pray for him first. He was very unwilling but I just reached out my hand and placed it on his shoulder. As I began praying he burst into tears. 'I used to be a Christian,' he said. He had sunk into a life of drugs, but his encounter with us had filled him with a new resolution to put his life straight. 'I know of a Christian hostel and I will use this money to go there tonight,' he told us.

The word for 'gift' in Greek, is 'charis', which is exactly the same word as for 'grace'. I don't have any doubt that giving releases grace into people's lives. We are saved by *grace* and this is a *gift* from God (*charis* is used for both words here, Eph 2:8). We are also healed and set free by grace. The more we give, the more grace is available to non-Christians. In this way, we can turn material things into a blessing. If we hang on to material possessions we are in effect closing heaven, whereas if we give generously we are opening up heaven for those we give to. We are instructed to give to everyone who asks, although we don't necessarily have to give what they are asking for. Peter and John gave the lame man the ability to walk, when he was asking for money. (He asked for alms and got legs!) The whole of discipleship is about giving and blessing.

PRINCIPLE 66

Love your enemies

Matthew 5:43

In Romans 5 we read that a person might just give his life for a very good friend. Jesus, however, gave his life for us while we were yet unlovable sinners. We had rejected God, but he still thought we were worth dying for. In the same way, Jesus calls us to love the unlovable. 'You have heard that it was said, "Love your neighbour and hate your enemy." But I tell you: Love your enemies and pray for those who persecute you, that you may be sons of your Father in heaven' (Mt 5:43). In verse 46, Jesus goes on to say that if you love those who love you there is no reward because even the tax-gatherers do the same. What then makes us different from them? The answer is that we love the unlovable, even our enemies.

The Lord taught me this lesson in a very graphic way. A previously homeless young man, who came to live with us in Lewisham, turned out to be totally objectionable. His language was foul, abusive and blue. He was, we later discovered, regularly mugging elderly people. On just one court appearance, he was charged with stealing thirty-eight cars. My stomach would turn over when he came into the room. He opposed everything we, as an extended family, stood for, and we eventually came to the conclusion that he would have to go. I spent the whole day phoning hostels and reception centres, but he had already been thrown out of them all, and none were willing to have him back. I could not bring myself to put him back on the street, but I could hardly bear the thought of him staying with us any longer.

By the end of the day I was totally frustrated. That night as I prayed, I confessed to the Lord that I had nothing but hatred for this young man. But in so doing I suddenly felt the Holy Spirit begin to pray through me. I was so surprised by what I was praying that I fell to my knees. I instantaneously became aware of God's love for him. I didn't understand how he could love him; but even though he was unlovable, I knew God really loved him. I prayed that the Lord would love him through me. By the time I got up off my knees, I had such an intense love burning in me, that my attitudes were instantly, completely changed. I fasted for the next seven days for him. I couldn't spend enough time with him. It was not long before he became a Christian and his life changed so radically that his probation officer said that it was just as if he had 'turned from darkness to light'. But the real miracle was that God changed me. He showed me that human love was inadequate in this kind of situation (in fact in any kind of situation), and that I needed to love with 'agape' love. I needed Jesus' love in my life.

When Jesus says he wants us to love our enemies, he is saying that there is a supernatural love available to us which non-Christians do not have access to. It makes us like light in darkness, able to love where people will not love us back. Our love is our most effective evangelistic tool. We are loving with God's love, which is not dependent on the person we are loving. Neither is God's love dependent on us, but only on him. He wants our hearts to be so filled with his love that we can love a broken and unlovable world, thus releasing his heavenly heart.

PRINCIPLE 67

Be perfect

Matthew 5:48

I love the way this is put in at the end of Matthew 5 almost casually as if it is an afterthought. By the way, be perfect. Of course this is as impossible as all the previous injunctions. Only God can do these things. I don't consider these as the commandments of the New Testament. They are just an expression of the nature of Jesus. Only Jesus can do these things. Only he can consistently react and behave in these ways, but by faith he can do these things through us. I see these precepts as an expression of our worship. We love Jesus so much that we want to be like him. We ask Jesus to live out these things in us, so that we can effectively BE Jesus in society. 'I no longer live, but Christ lives in me. The life I live in the body, I live by faith in the Son of God, who loved me and gave himself for me' (Gal 2:20).

CHAPTER 6

THE MINISTRY OF
THE MERCIFUL

A West Indian teenager knocked on our door one evening and asked, quite out of the blue, if he could start studying the Bible with us. He had eaten meals in our home on many occasions as he was a friend of some of the lads who lived with us. After just a few of these Bible studies, he became a Christian. On the day that we baptised him I asked him what exactly had made him ask for those studies on that first night. 'I am not going to tell you,' he said. 'If I tell you, you will laugh.' He then went on to reveal, 'It was the way you passed the salt to one another. I could see that you did it with love.' Personally, I haven't got a clue how to pass the salt with love, so I am not sure what exactly he saw. Nevertheless, it was so clear to him that he used to go home and try passing things to his family members with love. The more he tried, the more he discovered he couldn't do it. He eventually came to the conclusion that we had something that he didn't have. That was the cause of his enquiry into the Christian faith. Even the simplest of actions can be an extremely powerful demonstration of the gospel.

The gospel, as shared through our actions, is a major theme in the New Testament, which repeatedly emphasises that practical social care is the genuine outworking of our faith. In fact, there follow twelve different areas of Christianity which find their expression through serving the poor or needy.

PRINCIPLE 68

Repentance and social action

Repentance today carries fairly theoretical, mind-orientated overtones, emphasising a change of mind towards sin or the gospel. I love the way that John the Baptist encouraged the multitudes to prove their repentance by practical life change, for example, 'The man with two tunics should share with him who has none, and the one who has food should do the same' (Lk 3:11). John's challenge was, 'Produce fruit in keeping with repentance' (Lk 3:8). What a great way to express a new found faith in God. We can show our sincerity towards the Lord by our loving actions towards our fellow man.

Zacchaeus was a wonderful example of someone living out these genuine principles of repentance. He was prepared to deal with the root cause of all that was wrong in his life. Greed and selfishness had made riches the centre of his existence, at the expense of his fellow compatriots. In the process of his repentance he didn't just demonstrate a change of heart for the poor, but actively gave half his goods to serve them. He also recompensed those whom he had mistreated and cheated, restoring fourfold what he had taken from them (Lk 19:1-10). Presumably he also, from then on, ceased to oppress people and restricted himself to collecting no more than that which he was ordered to do. Zacchaeus spontaneously recognized that his own freedom, forgiveness and salvation demanded a corresponding release and relief for those around him. His repentance evoked a social consciousness and corresponding actions.

PRINCIPLE 69

Salvation and social action

Social action is described as one of the reasons for our salvation. We are saved *for* good works, even though we are not saved *by* works (Eph 2:8–10). Titus describes the church as being a people redeemed for God's possession who are zealous for good works (Tit 2:14). These works are so important that we shall be judged by them. Paul tells us that the quality of each man's work will become evident, for the day will reveal it. 'The fire will test the quality of each man's work' (1 Cor 3:12–14). It is particularly challenging that the Lord is not only looking for 'the service' to the needy but for *quality* in this work. The Lord 'will give to each person according to what he has done' (Rom 2:6–7), 'therefore persevere in good deeds'. These 'good deeds in Christ' are a recurring thought in the letters to the churches in Revelation where the warning, 'I know your deeds', occurs seven times (Rev 2:2, 19; 3:1, 8, 15).

The teaching Jesus gives us regarding the separation of the sheep from the goats (Mt 25:31–46) occurs in the context of God judging the nations. As someone has said, 'This is not the damnation of the saved, but the salvation of the damned.' The key factor in the salvation of these sheep is their willingness to provide for the hungry, thirsty or naked, or to visit the prisoners or the sick. If this is the challenge for nations, it has to be true too for individuals. It shows that God judges us according to how we deal with those less fortunate than ourselves.

Although, strictly speaking, Jesus is talking about how the non-Christians will be judged by their kindness towards the Christian brothers, nevertheless, if this is the standard which is expected of non-Christian behaviour, how much more compassionate should Christians be towards their poor and suffering non-Christians brothers.

If we heard that Jesus himself was sick, or hungry, or left out on the street, would we go to him? Of course, we would be glad to pay for any medical care he needed. We would be more than happy to give him our own bed. Interestingly, Jesus doesn't say that service to these poor is a substitute for serving him. He states that it *is* serving him. 'As much as you've done it to one of the least of these you have done it to me.' Although we are saved through faith not works and salvation is a gift not earned, nevertheless, the linking in this passage between our actions of concern and inheriting the kingdom is undeniable.

PRINCIPLE 70

Faith and social action

James 2:15–17

'Suppose a brother or sister is without clothes and daily food. If one of you says to him, "Go, I wish you well; keep warm and well fed," but does nothing about his physical needs, what good is it?' No one had deeper insight into true Christianity than James, the half brother of Jesus. He watched Jesus closely for thirty or so years and clearly knew what his agenda really was. James' emphasis throughout his letter is extremely practical. He starts by defining pure religion as social action, 'Religion that God our Father accepts as pure and faultless is this: to look after orphans and widows in their distress' (Jas 1:27). Then he defines faith in terms of the action it produces (2:15–17), and he even explains wisdom in the terminology of expressing mercy and good deeds (3:17).

More and more the church is coming alive to the fact that we have to express our faith with actions not just words. James clearly states, 'Show me your faith without deeds, and *I will show you my faith by what I do*' (2:18, my emphasis). The world has grown tired of words because so many promises are unfulfilled: too many marriage vows are broken, numerous political mandates are negated, countless sales pitches disappoint us, and even the media betray us with sensationalist mis-reporting. Yes, words have become more and more untrustworthy, but the old adage 'actions speak louder than words' proves the point.

Jesus recounts stories which instruct us to actively demonstrate our faith in ways other than just supernatural healing. The Good Samaritan is an excellent example of helping someone through common sense and practical social action (Lk 10:30–37). Interestingly, the Old Testament Law required: 'If you see your brother's donkey or his ox fallen on the road, do not ignore it. Help him to get it to its feet' (Deut 22:4). The example of the priest and the Levite passing by, in Jesus' story, condemns much of our social unresponsiveness today. Being neighbourly demands action, with both short- and long-term care, just as the Good Samaritan gave the emergency help needed, as well as paying for the on-going hotel bills. Prayer for healing was not the issue here, at least, not at this point. He is contrasting the inactive faith of the priest and the Levite with the genuine love of this Samaritan.

On other occasions Jesus encouraged us to invite the crippled, the lame and the blind for a meal (Lk 14:12–14, 21). Don't invite your relatives or your rich neighbours who, in turn, can invite you back, because then you are repaid. When you invite those who cannot return the favour you will be blessed and you will be repaid at the resurrection. This demonstrates another aspect of our faith: trusting in the rewards promised by the Father from both the present and eternal points of view.

He also enjoins us to 'let [our] light shine before men, that they may see [our] good deeds and praise [our] Father in heaven' (Mt 5:16). However, he then goes on to say, 'Be careful not to do your "acts of righteousness" before men to be seen by them' (Mt 6:1). So therefore some deeds must be done in secret. This is particularly relevant when giving to the poor. 'Beware of practising your righteousness before men to be noticed of them.' We must not blow our own trumpet. We don't even let our right hand know what our left hand is doing. It is significant that we don't have a timetable of Jesus' fast days. Neither do we have a record of how much he gave to charity, and we only have glimpses here and there of his prayer life. Doing some of our deeds in secret keeps our motives in check. We need not only to get our outward actions of service right, but also the hidden motivation of our hearts (as will be developed in the next principle).

The chart on the next page is not meant to be an

exhaustive list of practical expressions for our faith. Actually, it is just a list of social projects that I have personally been involved in, or aware of, in the course of my ministry:

Social Projects

1. Unemployment/job clubs
2. Nursery school/Pre-school
3. Hostel for teenagers
4. Down and outs – nightshelter/Drop ins
5. Soup runs
6. Dacorum Rent Aid (help with deposit/rent)
7. Crash pad (emergency accommodation)
8. Charity shops
9. Advice centres
10. Telephone helplines
11. Pregnancy counselling
12. Greenlight project (rehab, red light area)
13. AIDS Hospice
14. Radio Cracker (sponsored for Third World)
15. Jesus action (offer of help to all)
16. 'The Happening' youth project
17. MIND clubs (mental illness)
18. Hospital voluntary work
19. Prison visiting
20. After school clubs
21. Handiperson's scheme
22. Borrow it scheme
23. Fostering and adoption
24. Poverty fund
25. Prayer for healing
26. Third World projects
27. Clothing barrels
28. Child sponsorship
29. Relief projects

PRINCIPLE 71

Love and social action

1 Corinthians 13:1-3

In 1 Corinthians 13 verses 1-3 we are told that, even if we were to give all our possessions to feed the poor, unless we have love we are nothing and have gained nothing. Even if we give our bodies to be burned, it profits us nothing without love. (I must remember this in the moment of martyrdom!) Every area of service to others is sacrificial. It entails the use of time, money, energy and perhaps even the losing of life itself. But compassion has to be the motivation for it all. Paul was so intensely motivated by love that he said he could wish himself accursed for the sake of his fellow Israelites (Rom 9:1-3). Jesus defined this kind of love and graphically demonstrated it, 'Greater love has no-one than this, that he lay down his life for his friends' (Jn 15:13).

John in his epistle picks up this theme again:

This is how we know what love is: Jesus Christ laid down his life for us. And we ought to lay down our lives for our brothers. If anyone has material possessions and sees his brother in need but has no pity on him, how can the love of God be in him? Dear children, let us not love with words or tongue but *with actions* and in truth.

(1 Jn 3:16-18, my emphasis)

Again Jesus is applying the OT Law: 'If there is a poor man among your brothers . . . do not be hard-hearted or tight-fisted towards your poor brother' (Deut 15:7).

The Father is good to the just and the unjust. He causes the sun to rise on the good and the evil (Mt 5:43-48). Our loving actions should also be indiscriminate. Like the Father, we are to love even our enemies. 'If your enemy is hungry, feed him; if he is thirsty, give him something to drink' (Rom 12:20). James highlights discrimination by saying, 'As believers . . . don't show favouritism' (Jas 2:1). Through his picture of how people respond when a rich man and a poor man turn up to the same meeting (Jas 2:1–8), he draws an interesting conclusion. It is not just a sin to treat the poor with disrespect, but it is a sin to respect and show favour to the rich man. God is impartial in how he serves and love demands that we be the same.

PRINCIPLE 72

Prayer and social action

Offering prayer for the sick is one of the most obvious services the church can undertake for the community. People are impressed by the care demonstrated when we get alongside those who are suffering. We minister with our prayers to lift the worries and burdens from the shoulders of those weighed down by sickness. From time to time we have offered prayer on the street and arranged special healing services. In Canada recently we distributed leaflets informing people that there would be prayer for healing on the High Street at 3.00 pm that afternoon. We started praying for those in our own team who needed a touch from the Lord but it wasn't long before non-Christians were asking for prayer too. Those prayed for were blessed and those standing around watching were learning something important about the caring ministry of the church.

Obviously, much of the Lord's service to the sick and infirm was supernatural. (See chapter 'The Manifestation of the Miraculous'.) Our strategy is also to bring healing to those suffering physically around us. Just as the medical world is committed to finding medical remedies when confronted by diseases with no known cures, we too should be seeking answers as to how to break through with supernatural healing even when perhaps we haven't seen breakthroughs in the past.

On one occasion a lady informed us that she had a physical problem for which the doctors had no solution. We had prayed for her a few times which always seemed to make a difference, sometimes for as long as a week, but then the symptoms seemed to return. Eventually, about a dozen of us agreed to lock ourselves in the church on a Friday evening and stay there fasting and praying until we saw the necessary breakthrough. We weren't sure whether we would ever leave the church again but in fact we saw the supernatural healing at midnight of the first day.

An angry young woman came out for prayer at the end of a service one Sunday night. She was really furious and asserted that God simply didn't answer prayers. It turned out that she had foolishly been to see a fortune-teller. (I say foolishly because she was a Christian and should have known better. She thought it was a joke.) The astrologer had made some frightening predictions about her life which were all rapidly coming true. From the day she went there, she felt a sort of demonic presence sitting on her head. She had prayed frantically every day for six months for this presence to leave her and for the curses to be broken, but she had received no reply.

We simply said to her that it was good that she hadn't yet had those prayers answered because she had a very important lesson to learn – she needed her brothers and sisters in the church. She was not supposed to cope with this on her own. In a simple one-sentence prayer, we commanded the presence to leave and the spell to be broken. Both of these requests were instantly granted. Six months later, she saw me again and reported she had been completely free from all the effects ever since. This is such a simple dynamic; 'Confess your sins to each other and pray for each other so that you may be healed' (Jas 5:16).

PRINCIPLE 73

Spiritual warfare and social action

Spiritual warfare has clear implications regarding our social action. We have from time to time invited people in the community to come with anything, and everything, that they have felt spiritually bound by to a 'releasing service'. Just as those who practised magic in Ephesus brought their books and burned them in the streets (50,000 pieces of silver's worth, Acts 19:19), we have had 'sin barbeques'. People would bring pornography, videos, charms, amulets, satanic or cultish literature, cigarettes etc. and destroy them publicly as a step to freedom. We want the world not only to understand the dangers of entrapment in these things but to see that Jesus is the key to freedom.

I was driving home from church one Sunday with my family when we drove past some youths stealing from a builder's yard. I had driven past them and got to the end of the road before I actually realised what they were doing. So I reversed my car and pulled up beside a shopping trolley which they were stacking high with materials. As I got out of my car, three of the youths ran away, but two of them were trapped behind the wire fence of the yard. I walked up to them. I have to be honest, I felt absolute fear and trepidation, and I hadn't a clue what I was doing or what I was going to say. However, trying to sound confident, I stammered, 'Errrr excuse me,' then out of my mouth came this seemingly crazy statement: 'Are you aware that what you are doing right now is allowing evil spirits to come and have a crack at your lives.' I think that this sentence took me as much by surprise as it did them. They looked at me rather puzzled and said, 'Could you say that again?' I repeated the statement that, by our actions, we either open the door for God to bless us, or for demons to come and put the boot in. To my further surprise, these two then shouted for their friends, who had disappeared up a tower block, to come back. When they arrived on the scene, I was asked to, 'Tell them what you just told us.'

After a little discussion, the ringleader said to me, 'What do you want us to do then?' I replied that I thought that it was really up to them what they wanted to do. They looked at me and then started taking things off the trolley and passing them over the fence. Those on the inside returned them to the piles from which they had come. They returned everything except for four things left on the trolley. The ringleader turned to me and asked nicely, 'Is it OK if we keep these four things.' I said, 'It is entirely up to you.' At which he replied, 'Yes, you're right,' and promptly picked them up and put them back over the fence too.

This was a bizarre situation with a wonderful outcome, which made me aware of how responsive even tough youths can become when they understand the dangers of negative spiritual powers. How little the world understands of the pitfalls, bondages and destruction which the devil wreaks on unsuspecting individuals. The church has a part to play in prevention as well as cure.

Jesus was sent to proclaim release to the captives. Later, he says of us 'as the Father sent me so send I you' (Jn 17:18). So we, too, are sent to proclaim freedom to those who are bound up, whether this is by their pasts, or their habits, or by demonic activity. When Jesus makes people free then they are really free (Jn 8:36) from all the yokes that bound them. There is no clearer passage than Isaiah 58 verses 6-9 in helping us to understand the process of breaking the yokes of bondage. There seems to be a fivefold process described here in these verses.

Isaiah 58:6–9

1. Loosen bonds of wickedness
2. Undo the yoke
3. Let the opressed go free
4. Break every yoke
5. Remove the yoke from the midst

It becomes a privilege to fight for the freedom of others. It seems a little ironic that the battle is won, not so much by fighting but by fasting. It is by our fasting that bonds and yokes are broken. We can then let the oppressed walk free. Like the angel freeing Peter from his chains and leading him out of prison (on two separate occasions), we need to walk people free with a sense of ease (Acts 5:19; 12:7f). The terminology of breaking the yoke and removing it from our midst is a graphic way of ruining the mechanisms of sin which formerly destroyed people's lives.

PRINCIPLE 74

Bible reading and social action

James encourages us to be doers of the Word and not just hearers (Jas 1:22). Action is the ideal response to any Bible reading. The chart on the opposite page covers a few of the areas biblically defined as deserving of our care and service. The Lord recorded his heart on paper for us so that we can pick up and run with his agendas. As individuals, we can't do everything on a list like this, but by mobilising as many members of the church as we can, to serve in maybe one or two areas each, we can perhaps make a caring impact on many of them.

There are many pictures and laws regarding the poor in the Old Testament. For example, what is called the 'right of redemption', where a family member could, on behalf of a dispossessed relative, buy back property lost through extreme poverty (Lev 25:24–30); or the law of 'gleaning' which allowed the poor to pick up grain left in the fields, including all the edges and corners of the crops which had to be left purposely by the harvesters (Lev 19:9–10). Another law prevented farmers from shaking their olives trees more than once or from picking the grapes off their vines more than once. Everything which grew after that was available for the poor to pick (Deut 24:19–22).

These, and so many other verses, show the Lord to be on the side of the underdog. He champions the cause of the disadvantaged. He supports and provides for the weak and the vulnerable. The biblical challenge to us all is to respond to God's call for action: to serve the categories of people often left forgotten by the world but clearly the focus of a God who cares for the whole of society.

Biblical Categories Deserving Our Care

1. Foreigners Dt 14:29; 24:19–21
2. Orphans Dt 14:29; 24:19–21
3. Widows Dt 14:28; 24:19–21
4. Poor Dt 15:4, 7–11
5. Church workers Dt 16:10–14; 26:12–13
6. Strangers Dt 16:10-14; 26:12-13
7. Deaf Lev 19:14
8. Blind Lev 19:14
9. Weak Ps 82:1–4
10. Needy Ps 82:1–4
11. Hungry Mt 25:35–36
12. Thirsty Mt 25:35–36
13. Naked Mt 25:35–36
14. Sick Mt 25:35–36
15. Imprisoned Mt 25:35–36
16. Diseased Mt 10:1
17. Sick Mt 10
18. Dead Mt 10:8
19. Lepers Mt 10:8
20. Demonised Mt 10:8
21. Oppressed Is 58:6–7
22. Homeless Is 58:6–7
23. Family Is 58:6–7
24. Elderly Lev 19:32
25. Debtors Lev 25:10
26. Exhausted Is 35:3–5
27. Anxious Is 35:3–5
28. Dumb Is 35:3–5
29. Burdened animals Ex 23:4ff; 10–11

PRINCIPLE 75

Worship and social action

Jesus made the observation that 'those who show mercy will receive mercy'. We obtain leniency from the Lord when we exercise pity for the needy. When Jesus said, 'I desire mercy and not sacrifice,' he was referring to one of two things. Either he meant that he prefers to show mercy himself, rather than to receive our sacrifices, which remarkably he does, without expecting anything in return. Or he was saying that he desires that we exercise this mercy and that we show forbearance to fellow individuals rather than offer sacrifices to God. Thus our care for others is seen as a genuine substitute for worshipping the Lord. I have puzzled for some time over this twice-repeated phrase of Jesus, which seems so important that he prefaces it with the expression, 'Go and learn what this means'. Amazingly, he doesn't even say, 'I desire mercy and sacrifice.' It seems that the Lord prefers that we serve the poor instead of serving him in sacrifice. The Lord looks for a ministry of mercy from each of us and this becomes a crucial part of our lifestyle in evangelism and of our worship towards God.

Paul defines a clear example of a merciful ministry when he describes the role of the older widows (1 Tim 5:9–10). The list of qualifications is incredibly socially-minded. If they had shown care to others then they would definitely be cared for themselves. They had to:

- Have a reputation for good works;
- Have brought up children;
- Have shown hospitality to strangers;
- Have washed the feet of the saints;
- Have assisted those in distress;
- Have devoted themselves to every good work.

Widows who by their actions had fulfilled the criteria on this list were to be taken into the care of the church. This not only shows how high the standards were among the original disciples, but also the way in which caring for the needy had become a real test of where a person stood spiritually. Worship is showing, by our actions, that we think the Lord is 'worth it'. We love him enough to do the things that he says. Are we prepared to obey him by serving in areas which perhaps don't come naturally to us? 'Whatever you did for one of the least of these . . . you did for me' (Mt 25:40). We don't have idols in our churches because the images we serve are those of our fellow man – made in the image of God. We show our adoration for God by serving his image.

PRINCIPLE 76

Giving and social action

Giving is a thorny subject to talk or write about. 'Giving' and 'evangelism' are probably the two subjects least likely to attract large audiences at optional seminars. Interestingly, there is no pressure or compulsion to give in the New Testament. Not even the tithe is really given to us as a strict mandate. As the story of Ananias and Sapphira points out, all our resources are our own, and we are able to do with them what we choose. 'Didn't it belong to you before it was sold? And after it was sold wasn't the money at your disposal?' (Acts 5:3). There are, however, many encouragements and examples of generosity in the New Testament and none more powerful than that of Jesus himself. 'Though he was rich, yet for your sakes he became poor, so that you through his poverty might become rich' (2 Cor 8:9). All our giving to some extent makes us poorer, but there are not many who are prepared to make themselves totally poor for the sake of helping the poor to become better off.

The Law required that every third year the people of Israel should tithe all their produce and bring it into the town as a resource to feed the strangers, the orphans and the widows (Deut 14:28–29). If they did this, the Lord promised to bless them in all the work which they put their hands to. This 'pay back' of the Lord blessing them as a result of how they served the poor is a major emphasis in the Old Testament. 'If a man shuts his ears to the cry of the poor, he too will cry out and not be answered' (Prov 21:13). 'If you spend yourselves on behalf of the hungry and satisfy the needs of the oppressed, then your light will rise in the darkness, and your night will become like the noonday. The LORD will guide you always; he will satisfy your needs' (Is 58:10–11). This emphasis is clearly continued in the New Testament: Jesus is quoted as saying, 'It is more blessed to give than to receive' (Acts 20:35). I emphasise, the intention here is not what some call 'prosperity doctrine', if we receive more back from the Lord it is in order that we have more to give. This is a high 'turnover doctrine'.

Another Old Testament aspect of helping the poor was the cancellation of debt. At the Jubilee, all debts were wiped out. Most loans in fact were borrowed against the year of Jubilee which meant that they would be paid off by the fiftieth year. However, if someone was unable to pay off their debt because of extreme poverty, their debts were to be forgiven anyway (Lev 25:28).

Members of the early church began selling property and possessions, and sharing the proceeds with anyone who had need (Acts 2:45). By Acts 4 verse 38 we are told that there was not a needy person among them. They sold lands or houses and brought the money and laid it at the feet of the apostles, who would then distribute it to those in need. This presents a clear challenge to the church today in a society which is built on credit, where people often get into financial difficulty. Particularly when working among the poor, it presents a tremendous objective to be able to say that there is not a needy person among us. In our church, we have worked on the principle of laying aside 20 per cent of all church income for the poor. We call this a Poverty or Compassion Fund. We are also often called upon to help people with debt counselling in order to try to get their lives back onto an even keel.

Giving was obviously so much a feature of the lifestyle of the apostolic band that when Judas went out, actually to betray the Lord, everyone else presumed that he had gone out to give something to the poor (Jn 13:29). Jesus had instilled into his followers that they were to sell their possessions and give to the poor (Lk 12:33). We are not all told to sell everything, like the rich man in Matthew 19 verse 21, but we are all asked to forsake everything and to give something as a demonstration of this fact. Jesus had a wonderfully cryptic message for the Pharisees: 'Give what is inside the dish to the poor, and everything will be clean for you' (Lk 11:41).

PRINCIPLE 77

Work and social action

The principle of gleaning (Lev 19:9–10) gives us an important key to dealing with the poor. The grain, the olives or the grapes were not harvested and then given to the poor (Deut 24:19–22). The poor had to go into the fields and reap for themselves. This meant that it was not just a handout, they had to work for it. We are currently seeking to help a drug addict in his process of coming off drugs and crime. He is doing all sorts of little jobs around the fellowship, from mending bikes to cutting hedges, in an effort to apply his mind to something positive. We also overpay him for his time to help pay for his rather expensive treatment.

The book of Proverbs underlines the fact that laziness leads to poverty (Prov 13:4; 14:23; 19:15), but also asserts that wealth is created by work (Prov 10:4–5). We need to do all we can to encourage people into employment. For years Ichthus and other evangelical churches in Peckham have together run an excellent, award-winning programme for the long-term unemployed. It is hard work trying to motivate those who have become paralysed by hopelessness. The PECAN (Peckham Evangelical Churches Action Network) team knock on 20,000 doors a year to root out the most demotivated in the community and through personal friendship seek to motivate, retrain and educate them in the most basic of life skills. They are taught how to wash, to clean and to cook, as well as how to apply for a job, how to deal with an interview, and how to put together a CV. Once they have reached this stage, the team work alongside them as they apply for several jobs every day until eventually someone agrees to employ them. This programme has one of the highest success rates in the country.

PRINCIPLE 78

Church and social action

Hebrews 10 verse 24 exhorts us to be positively competitive in the church: 'to outdo one another with good works' (NASB). This means being eager to gain the status of servant to all, and to work harder at it than anyone else. Church exists to provoke one another into good works, 'especially [towards] those who are of the household of faith'. We practise on church members so that we will be excellent at our tasks in serving the world. Paul says, 'Let us not become weary in doing good' (Gal 6:9–10).

Jubilee Principles
Leviticus 25

1. Jubilee meant returning property vv 15, 23
2. Jubilee meant forgiving debts vv 10, 28
3. Jubilee meant setting slaves free vv 40–41
4. Jubilee meant restoration of the family v 10
5. Jubilee meant time to seek the Lord v 4
6. Jubilee meant triple blessings! v 21
7. Sound ram's horn throughout the land v 9

We have been involved in planting two churches over the last four years, both of which have had an emphasis on Jubilee (Lev 25:8–55). (The chart above highlights some of the principles of Jubilee.) In our most recent church plant, which is called 'The 418 Project', we have sought to bring the Jubilee principles right up to date. Our name comes from Jesus' application of Jubilee in Luke 4 verse 18, hence the 418 Project. Jesus seemed to use the Jubilee concept as his mission statement, quoting from Isaiah 61, and we use it as our mission statement too. We call the church a 'project' rather than a 'church' to show that we exist to serve society as a team together, not just to be an inward-looking religious group.

Luke 4 verse 18 describes the mandate of Jesus from a social perspective, and Jesus seems to make himself the fulfilment of this Jubilee. Hence he states, 'Today this scripture is fulfilled in your hearing' (v 21). The fourfold mandate implies:

- Good news to the poor;
- Release for the trapped;
- Sight to the blind (or caring for the sick);
- Freedom for the mistreated.

I have commented on each of these points elsewhere in the chapter, but the fourth area should be mentioned here. Jesus brought liberty to 'the downtrodden', 'the bruised' or, as we have described it here, 'the mistreated'. 'A bruised reed he will not break, and a smouldering wick he will not snuff out' (Mt 12:20).

There are so many potential areas where people can get bruised, and so many circumstances where individuals get mistreated, such as being victims of crime, or bereavement, or illness, or accident or natural disaster. There are also the abused, the exploited, the oppressed, the discriminated against, the dominated. All these experiences hurt, and sometimes they totally crush us. I am so glad that God cares enough about the mistreated to get involved and that he encourages us to do the same. Unfortunately we live in a very cruel world, where often it is the innocent who suffer.

When Jesus quotes his mandate in Luke 4 verse 18 he doesn't finish the verse as it is in Isaiah 61, because there it goes on to say, 'To proclaim the year of the LORD's favour and *the day of vengeance of our God*' (my emphasis). It is

The Mistreated

1. Victims of crime
2. Abuse in the family
3. Exploitation at work
4. Oppression by authorities
5. Oppression by demons
6. Discrimination by society
7. Debtors
8. Bullying at school
9. Racism
10. Persecution
11. Bereavements
12. Illnesses
13. Accidents
14. Natural disasters

comforting to know that the tables are eventually turned, in the after-life for example, as the story of the rich man and Lazarus teaches us (Lk 16:25). 'In your lifetime you received your good things, while Lazarus received bad things, but now he is comforted here and you are in agony.' There is divine justice and God will release his vengeance in a coming day. However, it looks to me as if God's vengeance is not quite what we would expect, as the ensuing verses describe blessings not judgement. Instead of giving us what we deserve, he blesses us with: comfort, or a garland, or gladness and/or a double portion etc. as the chart overleaf describes.

If this is God's kind of vengeance, bringing blessing to those who have suffered, we need to offer the same relief to those around us who are hurting. If you look at the last words of each line in the same chart, they often sum up the sufferings of those we seek to care for. Sometimes people's lives go up in smoke and all that is left are ashes and mourning. At times life weighs us down to the point of leaving us with a spirit of heaviness. At other times we may experience

---

**<u>Proclaim the favourable year of the Lord and
the day of vengeance of our God</u>**
Isaiah 61:1–7

- Comfort those who **mourn**
- Garland *instead of* **ashes**
- Gladness *instead of* **mourning**
- Praise *instead of* **fainting**
- Rebuild the ancient **ruins**
- Double portion *instead of* **shame**
- Joy *instead of* **humiliation**

---

the humiliation and shame of total ruin. But notice that there
are five 'instead ofs' in these verses. In each of these cases,
there is a corresponding wonderful 'instead of'. God offers
society blessings which bring freedom and healing from the
hurts of life, a consolation instead of a curse.

PRINCIPLE 79

Jesus and the cup of cold water

Matthew 10:42

'And if anyone gives even a cup of cold water to one of these
little ones because he is my disciple, I tell you the truth, he
will certainly not lose his reward.' It is difficult to know
whether the cup of cold water is being given to the disciple,
or being given by the disciple to someone else. Either way,
this illustration is exciting. Perhaps it is ambiguous in order
to allow for both senses in the text. If this is Jesus saying that
any act of kindness towards a Christian is valued so highly
by God that he rewards the benefactor, it underlines the
benefit of sending the disciples out without money and
supplies (Mt 10:9–10). Anybody serving them along their

way would be wonderfully blessed by God. 'Truly they would not go without their reward.'

If the gift of this cup of cold water is going from the disciple to a non-Christian, the insight Jesus gives us is just as exciting. The Lord watches the tiniest areas of our social action and will reward us for every caring act for others. Such acts are soon forgotten by us, but not by the Lord. He remembers each seemingly insignificant service and not only remembers it but will reward each one. It seems remarkable that Matthew 10 begins with encouraging us to raise the dead but finishes by saying, in effect, 'Oh by the way don't forget to make people cups of tea'. It is interesting that Jesus says he will reward us for giving away a cup of cold water but mentions no rewards for raising the dead. Does this perhaps show God's value system when it comes to serving the world?

CHAPTER 7

THE MANIFESTATION OF THE MIRACULOUS

I can remember the debates we used to have with organisations working with the universities and colleges regarding the manifestations of the charismatic movement. I once turned up to speak at a certain London college only to be met at the door by the leader of the Christian group who said: 'Would you mind not being charismatic tonight, please.' I replied, 'I am sorry, I don't really understand what you mean.' They had asked me to speak on Mary Magdalene, about whom there are only a couple of verses in the New Testament. One says she ministered to the Lord out of her own resources and the other that she had had seven demons cast out of her. 'Would these verses be regarded as being charismatic?' I asked. 'If so I had better not speak this evening.' I did speak and I think they were happy with what I had to say, and the leader apologised to me afterwards. There seemed a deeper issue at stake here than just whether something was charismatic or not. Were young Christians being taught to disregard or, even worse, to disobey Jesus? It is Jesus who commands us to cast out demons and to heal the sick. The manifestation of the miraculous is part and parcel of being a disciple of Jesus. How can we say that we love the Lord if we don't do the things that he says (Mt 28:20; Jn 14:15).

Manifestation of the Miraculous in the Gospels

In total there are thirty-four recorded instances of super-natural manifestations in the ministry of Jesus. If we look at

Matthew's Gospel there are twenty-eight miracles and fifty-two other incidents recorded in his narrative. Thirty-five per cent, therefore, of Matthew's material describes the kingdom of God coming in power with signs and wonders. The chart opposite separates Jesus' manifestations out into three different categories: healings, miracles and deliverances from demons. These proved his Messiahship by the fulfilment of Old Testament scriptures (e.g. Is 53:4; 32:3–4; 35:5–6; cf Acts 2:22 etc.). That is why Jesus could say, 'The very work . . . that I am doing, testifies that the Father has sent me' (Jn 5:36). 'Believe me . . . or at least believe on the evidence of the miracles themselves' (Jn 14:11). Certainly this was proof enough for John the Baptist, who believed when he heard the report that the blind had received their sight and the lame walked, the lepers were being cleansed, the deaf were hearing and the dead had been raised (Mt 11:5). John in his Gospel reminds us that Jesus did many more than just these thirty-five miracles: 'Jesus did many other miraculous signs in the presence of his disciples, which are not recorded in this book. But these are written that you may believe that Jesus is the Christ, the Son of God, and that by believing you may have life in his name' (Jn 20:30–31).

These miracles also proved that the kingdom of God had come: 'If I drive out demons by the finger of God, then the kingdom of God has come to you' (Lk 11:20). It is not surprising, then, that we see miracles happening which only God could do, like the raising of the dead, or the cleansing of lepers, or the controlling of the elements, or the creating of huge feasts out of small snacks, or the turning of water into wine. Only God can forgive sins, yet Jesus proved he had this authority by healing the paralysed man (Mk 2:5–12).

So these miraculous manifestations proved who Jesus was, both as Messiah and in his Divinity. They also prove to us something else very significant – that he cares about people and that he wants to deal with the problem of suffering in the world. These miracles are a clear demonstration of God's love for mankind. Jesus shows this love, not just for the Jews, but he heals the Gentiles too, even those considered as the Jews' enemies. In fact, Jesus healed everybody who came to him for healing. No one who asked went away with the suffering that they had brought to him. He healed every kind of sickness and every kind of disease (Mt 9:35).

Healings

1. Noble's son
2. Lame man (Bethesda)
3. Peter's mother-in-law
4. Leper
5. Paralytic
6. Man (withered hand)
7. Centurion's servant
8. Widow's son
9. Blind and dumb
10. Woman (haemorrhage)
11. Jairus' daughter
12. Two blind men
13. Dumb demoniac
14. Deaf mute
15. Blind man
16. Man born blind
17. Crippled woman
18. Man with dropsy
19. Lazarus (raised)
20. Blind Bartimaeus
21. Malchus (ear)

Miracles

1. Water into wine
2. Catch of fish
3. Stilling storm
4. Feeding 5,000
5. Walking on water
6. Feeding 4,000
7. Tribute money
8. Cursing fig tree
9. Second catch of fish

Demon/Deliverance

1. Demoniac
2. Two demoniacs
3. Syrophoenician's daughter
4. Boy possessed

This ministry was having a dramatic, evangelistic impact. Josephus, the Jewish historian, recorded that the whole country was going after this man. 'News of this spread through all that region' (Mt 9:26, 31). 'They were going through the cities and the villages gathering together all those who were ill or demon possessed' (e.g. Mk 1:32). At times the crowds were such that Jesus couldn't enter into the cities: 'As a result, Jesus could no longer enter a town openly but stayed outside in lonely places. Yet the people still came to him from everywhere' (Mk 1:45).

PRINCIPLE 80

Don't look for signs in themselves

Matthew 12:39

A wicked generation looks for a sign

Although miracles affirmed who Jesus was, he said it is a wicked generation which puts God to the test. Jesus refused to use signs to prove himself to those who had no faith. Signs and wonders confirm, strengthen and build up the faith of someone who wants to believe but they cannot destroy the unbelief of someone who has chosen to disbelieve. For this reason there are occasions where Jesus couldn't do many miracles, because of the people's unbelief (Mt 13:58). Today we need to be wary of this kind of sign seeking. We must seek the giver not the gifts. We pray for miracles to bless the needy, not to get personal glory. The devil is aware of our appetite for signs and wonders, and is happy to oblige if he can deceive us in the process. A wrong desire for signs becomes a sign in itself, indicating an evil heart.

PRINCIPLE 81

Beware of false Christs

Matthew 24:24

Jesus warned us not to rush here and there when something new happens. 'So if anyone tells you, "There he is, out in the desert," do not go out; or, "Here he is, in the inner rooms," do not believe it.' He then adds this stinging sentence, 'Wherever there is a carcass, there the vultures will gather' (Mt 24:26–28).

As the kingdom of God breaks into this world with signs and wonders, and in the power of the Holy Spirit (as Paul described in Romans 15:1–19), it is not surprising that the devil would seek to counterfeit it. This counterfeit would of course be meaningless if there wasn't the genuine article. There would be no point in having a counterfeit £20 note if there wasn't a real one. 'False Christs and false prophets will appear and perform great signs and miracles to deceive . . .' (Mt 24:24). So, while we should be careful, we must not, however, throw the baby out with the bath water. The manifestation of the miraculous is as much part of our evangelistic strategy today as it was for the Lord, and for the early church.

PRINCIPLE 82

Use signs and wonders

Matthew 10:1, 7–8

Everything demonstrated by Jesus was passed in turn to his followers (eg Mt 10:1): '[He] gave them authority to drive out evil spirits and to heal every disease and sickness.' He instructed them to go and preach, but then added a little rider, '[and by the way] heal the sick, raise the dead, cleanse those who have leprosy, drive out demons' (vv 7–8). These commands now become ours, as we too seek to follow in his footsteps.

The writer to the Hebrews records that, 'God was also bearing witness with them, both by signs and wonders and by various miracles and by gifts of the Holy Spirit according to his own will' (Heb 2:4, NASB). It is interesting to notice that God was bearing witness *'with'* them not *'to'* them, indicating that this was a sign to the world not to the Christians. These are similar words to those which finish Mark's Gospel: 'Then the disciples went out and preached everywhere, and the Lord worked with them and confirmed his word by the signs that accompanied it' (Mk 16:20). This is what Jesus had promised a few verses earlier in the same chapter: 'These signs will accompany those who believe: In my name they will drive out demons; they will speak in new tongues . . . they will place their hands on sick people, and they will get well (vv 17–18).

The chart on the opposite page outlines ten different supernatural signs which Jesus said were available to those who believed. The verses listed are references in the book of Acts. We discover that there are twenty-three occurrences of these manifestations recorded as happening in the early church. It is encouraging to see that what Jesus had been doing in the Gospels, he now continued to do through the first generation of the saints.

Evangelistic miracles

My real exercise in looking at these miracles in Acts was to try and discover whether these were happening in the context of evangelism or in the church. I was enthused to discover that the vast majority of these miracles are in an evangelistic setting. In fact sixteen out of the twenty-three are evangelistic miracles. These are underlined in the chart and on each of these occasions somebody was saved. Indeed, some of them resulted in multitudes getting saved. This proves that the early church grew very fast as a result of supernatural miracles. The dynamic which drew large crowds to Jesus also operated in the early church in the same way.

PRINCIPLE 83

It is easier to see non-Christians healed than Christians

Acts17–23

Because in Acts there are far more miracles happening on the street than in the church, we have to conclude that it is easier to see non-Christians healed than Christians. If you want to see the Lord's loving power at work, reach out and pray for a few non-churchgoers. We know God wants to show his love to them.

23 Miracles in Acts

Restoring sight	9:18	13:11		
Casting out demons	5:16	8:7	16:16	19:12
Healing sick	4:30	6:8	5:14	14:3
	-	-	19:12	28:9
Cleansing lepers	-	-	-	-
Restoring hearing	-	-	-	-
Taking up snakes	28:4	-	-	-
Raising the dead	9:40	20:9	5:1	-12:23
Lame walking	3:2	8:7	14:10	-
Drinking poison	-	-	-	-
Speaking in tongues	2:4	10:46	19:6	-

Observations on the chart: Principles 84-89 expand upon the chart.

PRINCIPLE 84

Sometimes miracles are a negative use of power

Acts 13:11

1) Negative miracles

The first miracle which the Apostle Paul did, although placed on the chart under the category 'the blind seeing', was actually when he caused a sighted person to go blind (Acts 13:11). Elymas, on the island of Cyprus, was seeking to turn the proconsul away from the faith. Paul, fixing his gaze upon him, said, 'You are a child of the devil and an enemy of everything that is right! You are full of all kinds of deceit and trickery. Will you never stop perverting the right ways of the

Lord? Now the hand of the Lord is against you. You are going to be blind, and for a time you will be unable to see the light of the sun' (13:10–11). This negative miracle of discipline had an evangelistic impact and the proconsul became a Christian as a result.

There are other similar examples such as Ananias and Sapphira dropping down dead, which had the obvious effect that no one else dared to be associated with them (Acts 5:1–14). But the next verse says, 'Nevertheless, more and more men and women believed in the Lord and were added to their number' (vv 13–14). When King Herod was struck down and died because of his self-glorying (Acts 12:21–24), the result was that the Word of God continued to grow and to be multiplied. Before we start getting ideas about zapping our enemies in this way we need to remember the Lord's response to James and John, when they wanted to call down fire from heaven to consume those who did not receive Jesus (Lk 9:54–56). He rebuked them and said, 'You do not know what kind of spirit you are of, for the Son of Man did not come to destroy men's lives, but to save them.'

PRINCIPLE 85

Miracles meet the need

2) Missing miracles
There are no accounts in the Acts of the Apostles of lepers being cleansed, or of the deaf hearing, or of those who had drunk poison not being harmed. It is of course entirely possible that many had drunk poison, but because they were not harmed it remained undiscovered. As to why Luke reports no healing of the deaf or of the lepers, we don't know the answer. It was perhaps that Jesus had already healed them all! Or perhaps Luke wasn't around when it happened, and because he didn't personally witness these particular healings, he didn't record them.

All healings are the result of specific needs being met. We have to have our eyes open, to be alert to the areas of suffering in people's lives around us. As we dare to get involved in these situations and pray, the door is opened to release God's supernatural power. Where we are prepared to take initiative, the Lord can bless people and relieve their afflictions. If we don't do this, the miracles will still be missing today!

PRINCIPLE 86

Miracles protect us in the task

Luke 10:19

3) Taking up snakes

We saw earlier that Jesus didn't use miracles to glorify himself, he healed people out of love for them as individuals. Taking up snakes was not some miracle, like a trick that we hold up our sleeve, to prove ourselves to non-believers. It is not a sign, like the signs given to Moses to show to Pharaoh. This sign was saying we would be protected in the course of life. We would not be harmed if we accidentally stood on a serpent or a scorpion (Lk 10:19).

These are verses of encouragement, as we go out as sheep in the midst of wolves, that nothing can harm us unless, of course, the Father allows it. Paul wasn't looking for snakes, in Acts 28 verse 4, to prove a point. It was accidental when he picked up a viper among the twigs for the fire. It probably hurt when it bit him, but he suffered no harm.

We should never use these verses as an excuse to tempt the Lord, as some extreme sections of Christianity have done. Having accidentally picked up a viper years ago I am pleased to report that it didn't bite me, but I wouldn't want to do that again. I was in India two years ago where a villager had caught a rattlesnake, which he was proud to show me. He suggested that I hold it while he took a photograph of me with my camera. Although I didn't speak his language, I think he understood how emphatic my 'NO' was.

I was waiting for a plane on one occasion in Pakistan and was left stranded for six hours between flights, unfortunately forced to wait outside the airport as it closed down for the night. I sat on a bench on the perimeter of the airport behind a policeman on duty, thinking I would be safe there. The policeman, however, didn't seem to put off the mosquitoes, and I spent a couple of hours shooing them away. On the flight earlier that day, I had been reading Mark 11 about faith moving mountains, and so I fervently asked the Lord to remove these little pests, which seemed easier than moving the mountains. Eventually, however, I got so tired that I just gave up and offered myself to them. 'Go on then have a good meal,' I said, as I closed my eyes. Although they feasted on me for the rest of that night, I was amazed to find the next morning that I didn't have a single bite on my body. Perhaps this is a case of drinking poison and it didn't harm me. I can't vouch for the effect on the mosquitoes however!

PRINCIPLE 87

Tongues can be used in evangelism

1 Corinthians 14:21–23

4) Speaking in Tongues

There seems to be a conflicting message about tongues and evangelism in 1 Corinthians 14 verses 21–23. It starts by saying that tongues are a sign to unbelievers, but then goes on to say that if a stranger comes in and we are speaking in tongues, he will think that we are mad (v 14). Quoting from Isaiah 28 verse 11, Paul is applying the prophecy that God would speak to his people through foreign tongues, because they were no longer understanding him and had become as unbelievers. The sign of speaking in tongues, therefore, served as a warning that they needed to return to God. Interestingly, though, the first use of speaking in tongues in the New Testament is actually in evangelism where the hearers were understanding the message (Acts 2:11). The cosmopolitan crowds which had gathered in Jerusalem were saying, 'We hear them in our own tongues speaking of the mighty deeds of God.' This was certainly supernatural evangelism and resulted in 3,000 people being saved.

It is great to hear, in our day, of similar reports of the use of tongues to communicate the gospel in languages never learnt. However, we have also felt that there is a wisdom in Paul's warning not to appear too mad when unbelievers are coming into our meetings. It is perhaps better to exercise the gift of tongues as worship or in prayer in our more 'in house' times together.

PRINCIPLE 88

Spiritual gifts in evangelism

1 Corinthians 12:8–11

5) Spiritual gifts and healing

These verses speak of healings which can be released through any of the members of the church. Some have taught that such manifestations are only wrought by the hands of the apostles. Experiences like Philip's in Samaria put paid to that argument (Acts 8:6–7), as do the encouragements in this passage for us all to seek these gifts (1 Cor 12:31; 14:1). The Spirit distributes gifts as the Christians seek to receive them. Healing, for example, is received by faith on behalf of a sick person. This means that the Christian becomes nothing more than a channel through whom the healing is imparted. Interestingly, there is no reference to people being called 'healers' in the New Testament. Each individual healing is a gift, we have no power to perform these things. Now, as then, healing is in the hands of Jesus.

It is wonderful, and never ceases to amaze me, how stringing together a few words in a sentence, in the name of Jesus, can permanently turn someone's health for the better.

What a privilege to be able to bless the world in this way. As we seek to give, we will receive from the Lord for them. This is why Jesus said, 'Freely you have received, freely give' (Mt 10:7). We need to think particularly about the use of all these gifts in the context of evangelism. We have mentioned already the use of tongues, miracles, discernment of spirits and healings, and we will go on to explore the use of some of the 'word' gifts like 'words of knowledge'. These, too, are an essential tool in our evangelistic outreach.

PRINCIPLE 89

Words of knowledge in evangelism

Acts 9:10–15; 10:4–8

6) Words of knowledge in evangelism

We have already looked in some detail at the way Jesus used words of knowledge in his evangelism (see chapter 'The Model of the Master'). Here we will examine the way the early church saw people saved through the use of this gift. We will look at two or three examples from the book of Acts; firstly in the conversion of the Apostle Paul, and secondly in the conversion of Cornelius, the first real breakthrough into the Gentile world.

Conversion of Paul

The actual manifestation of the brilliant light in Paul's vision and the subsequent conversation with the Lord were dramatic ways to get this hardened persecutor into repentance. But, to me, some of the most exciting, supernatural revelations were those received by Ananias concerning Saul of Tarsus, as Paul was then known. Imagine sitting having a quiet time with the Lord, when he suddenly gives you an eightfold revelation. Ananias received details like: names of people, the place where to find them, how the person was going to be healed, the kind of ministry they would be involved in after they had been converted. This is not, 'I think there might be somebody here, who maybe has something like a headache.' This was an amazingly specific word of knowledge which caused a significant breakthrough in evangelism.

The chart below outlines all the instructions given to Ananias. All these were fulfilled either immediately or over the coming years. Wouldn't it be great if the Lord could lead us directly to specific individuals who need to get saved? Philip was responding to a word of prophecy when he was led by the angel of the Lord into the desert at Gaza to meet the Ethiopian eunuch, the first African convert (Acts 8:26–40). The Lord said, 'Go' and he went. He didn't, however, know why or to whom he was going. Ananias, on the other hand, knew exactly whom he was going to meet. In fact he had heard many things about this persecutor, and that he had come to Damascus to do the church harm. Despite all this, the word of knowledge was so clear that all his fears were dealt with, and a new evangelist, apostle, church planter and prolific writer was born, or rather born again.

Ananias' Words of Knowledge
Acts 9:10-15

1. Go to the street called Straight
2. Enquire at the house of Judas
3. Ask for a man called Saul from Tarsus
4. He is praying
5. He has seen you coming, Ananias
6. Lay hands on him and he will receive his sight
7. He will evangelise the Gentiles
8. He will witness to kings and the sons of Israel

Conversion of Cornelius

Cornelius' experience (Acts 10) is even more remarkable, not only because of the vision given to Peter to help break his preconceived ideas about the Gentiles, but also because the amazing 'words of knowledge' given to Cornelius are given to a non-Christian. Cornelius is a religious man but quite clearly not yet saved. Interestingly, both the Ethiopian eunuch and Saul were religious people in their own ways. However, here the Lord speaks directly to the unconverted party, so clearly and specifically that he was able get the help he needed to get saved.

This fourfold word of knowledge, outlined in the chart below, turned out to be absolutely correct. On this basis, Cornelius was able to send for Peter, and the door opened for the gospel to the Gentile world.

Cornelius' Words of Knowledge
Acts 10:4–8

1. Dispatch some men to Joppa
2. Send for a man named Simon called Peter
3. He is staying with a tanner named Simon
4. His house is by the sea

The most striking example of a word of knowledge like this, in my personal experience, was during the days when I was working with a missionary in the South of France. A man, a professional racing driver, drove all the way from England to Marseille with his wife. He felt that God had told them that they should go to this particular village, and to a particular house, and that they should wait there. It was the house where I was living, which happened to be in the middle of nowhere. They turned up at our house just after we had left for a conference in Spain which lasted for four days.

When we returned, there was an extremely sporty car parked in the drive. Out climbed this very stiff, angry Brit. He slammed the car door and exclaimed, 'I haven't got a clue what I am doing here. We've been sitting in this car for four days.' He calmed down considerably when he discovered that we spoke English, and even more when he found out that we were Christians, because he had felt that God had told him to come to this place. As you might expect, he committed his life to Christ and we spent some great days of fellowship together. Stories like this and the biblical accounts of Saul or the Ethiopian eunuch or Cornelius all point out how concerned the Lord is to reap the harvest. He gives what revelations are necessary to put people in contact together so that salvation can be shared and grasped.

PRINCIPLE 90

Preach the gospel to *all creation*

Mark 16:15

'Go into all the world and preach the good news to *all creation*' (my emphasis). The healing we bring is to the whole of creation. It is not surprising that Mark defines it as affecting demons, serpents and the physical state of people's bodies. Could this be the answer to the anxious longing of creation described in Romans 8 verse 19? Could these be the days where the sons of God are revealed? Could it be now that creation can be set free from its slavery to corruption, and be brought into the freedom of the glory of the children of God (v 21)? I know these verses look forward to the days of the Lord's return, but is there a way that in miniature we bring the Lord's return through our hearts and that in so doing we bring Jesus back to his creation?

I remember on one occasion teaching at a houseparty in Sussex. Between the teaching sessions, I went out to spend some time in prayer as I walked around the lakes at the centre. As I was strolling through the woods, I felt keenly aware of the nature around me, to the point where I felt that the trees were actually glad that I was there. It made me start reflecting on verses like Romans 8 verse 19 and Isaiah 55 verse 12. As I was meditating, suddenly a fish popped up out of the water in the middle of the lake. I must admit that I have not done this before, nor since, but I shouted out to the fish and said, 'Come and enjoy the presence of Jesus.' To my amazement, it swam straight to my feet and not just that fish, but many, if not all the fish in the lake. They came right to where I stood and rolled over one another at my feet.

Later that day, when the teaching sessions had finished, I ran all the way back to that lake, because I supposed the lake to have so many fish that it was always seething with them wherever you stood. However, I found not a single fish. It was to me a little miracle to say that creation really enjoys us bringing Jesus back to it. We carry the presence of the Creator everywhere we go. Surely this makes sense of verses like Isaiah 55 verse 12: 'You shall go out with joy and be led forth with peace and the mountains will break forth into shouts of joy before you and all the trees of the field will clap their hands.' We are here to exert the pressure of God's kingdom into the world. We pray, 'Let your kingdom come, let your will be done on earth as it is in heaven.' Wherever the reign of Jesus comes we should expect there to be a manifestation of the miraculous.

Jesus and Words of Knowledge

1. Nathanael, I saw you under the fig tree Jn 1:48
2. You have had five husbands Jn 4:18
3. Go your way, your son lives Jn 4:50
4. Let down your nets for a catch Lk 5:4
5. From now on you will catch men Lk 5:10
6. Why are you reasoning in your hearts? Lk 5:22; Mt 9:4
7. He knew what they were thinking Lk 6:8; Mt 12:25
8. Jesus knew they were discussing among themselves about there beingno bread Mt 16:8
9. Disciples indignant why perfume not sold – Jesus knew this Mt 26:10
10. Jesus aware in his spirit that they were reasoning, blasphemy Mk 2:8
11. Jesus knew who did not believe Jn 6:64
12. Jesus knew who was going to betray him Jn 13:11
13. Jesus knew all men and what was in men Jn 2:24-25
14. Jesus said this knowing what he was going to do. Feeding 5,000 Jn 6:6
15. Perceiving they wanted to make him king he departed Jn 6:15
16. One of you is a devil Jn 6:70
17. Why do you seek to kill me? Jn 7:19
18. This sickness is not unto death Jn 11:4
19. Lazarus has fallen asleep Jn 11:11; 14
20. One of you will betray me Jn 13:21
21. Jesus knew that they wished to question him Jn 16:19
22. Jairus' daughter had died. Jesus says she will be well Lk 8:50
23. Knowing what they were thinking, who should be the greatest Lk 9:47
24. Jesus knew that the Pharisees plotted against him Mt 12:14-15
25. He perceived their cunning Lk 20:23
26. Cast net on the right side, you will find a catch Jn 21:6
27. Go into the village and find a colt . . . say the Master has need of it Lk 19:30
28. You will find a man carrying a pitcher, follow him Lk 22:10
29. This night you will betray me three times Mt 26:34

CHAPTER 8

THE MAXIMISING
OF THE MESSAGE

PRINCIPLE 91

Jesus gives us the message

Matthew 10:7

The message which Jesus entrusts to us is both vast and complex, but also essentially simple and succinct. It is simply profound as well as being profoundly simple. Here we will try and examine both sides of this coin in order to grasp the elementary, pithy punchiness of the gospel while at the same time understanding what it means to proclaim Christ fully.

On the one hand, the message is vast. Years ago, I heard a talk given to the National Evangelists' Conference, entitled 'What is the minimum a person needs to know to become a Christian?'. The subject seemed a little basic for the few hundred evangelists present; after all, this was our bread and butter. The answer given, however, provoked us all. The answer to the question was: 'The sum total of all the material recorded in the four Gospels.' I have forgotten who the speaker was, but his sermon has lived with me ever since. Sure enough, Jesus instructs us to make disciples, 'Teaching them to observe everything I have commanded.'

On the other hand, the message Jesus taught us is essentially simple: 'Preach this message: "The kingdom of heaven is near" '(Mt 10:7). Whether we proclaim this one sentence, or expound the whole of Jesus' teaching, the fact is that the message is given to us by the Lord. Just as Jesus would say, 'My teaching is not my own. It comes from him who sent me' (Jn 7:16), so we too now pass on the propositions entrusted to us.

The message is given to us whether it is received prophetically or biblically. Jesus says in John 16 verses 12–15 that he had more to say to his disciples than they were able to bear at that time. The Holy Spirit would from generation to generation keep receiving truth from Jesus and disclosing it to them. So, part of the message is pre-recorded, and part is prophetic. The following points will explore some of the prophetic ways in which Jesus communicates his message through us. He says, 'I will give you words and wisdom that none of your adversaries will be able to resist or contradict' (Lk 21:15).

PRINCIPLE 92

The message is positive – heaven not hellfire!

Matthew 10:7 (Luke 10:9, 11)

Heaven is at hand

Jesus presents us with a brief, positive message to pass on to the world: 'Heaven is at hand.' We are not told to threaten people with a 'turn or burn', a 'hell is nigh' theology. The gospel, by definition, is good news not bad news. In essence, the message is that heaven is so close that you can reach out and touch it. It is within everyone's grasp. That is the literal sense of something being 'at hand'. As I type this, my keyboard is at hand, as is the phone, my pens and notebook. They are all close enough for me to reach out and take them. I don't have to move. They are all within my grasp where I am right now. Jesus is declaring that heaven is available like this, to all, not just in the future but here and now. God's healing, love and joy are so close that we can reach out and take them.

Our task in evangelism is, then, to bring heaven near to people. Paul quotes in Romans 10 verses 6–8 from Deuteronomy 30 verses 11–14:

> Now what I am commanding you today is not too difficult for you or beyond your reach. It is not up in heaven, so that you have to ask, 'Who will ascend into heaven to get it and proclaim it to us so that we may obey it?' Nor is it beyond the sea, so that you have to ask, 'Who will cross the sea to get it and proclaim it to us so that we may obey it?' No, the word is very near you; it is in your mouth and in your heart so that you may obey it.

Our message echoes the words of the Lord's prayer: 'Let your kingdom come, let your will be done on earth as it is in heaven.' As you read this, heaven is so close to you. This is what Jesus asks me to say to you. If you need a touch from heaven, reach out, receive. It is within your grasp.

Overlap of the ages

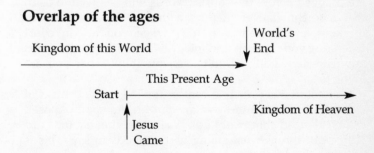

Paul described us as living in the overlap of the ages. We are those upon whom the ends of the ages have come (1 Cor 10:11). We are living in heaven and at the same time in the world. Soon the world will pass away and then we shall experience heaven in all its fullness. The kingdom of heaven began to be released on earth 2,000 years ago in Jesus. The

165

Gospel writers often mixed their terminology of 'The kingdom of God' with 'The kingdom of heaven' and these phrases seem interchangeable. 'Heal the sick who are there and tell them, "The kingdom of God is near you" ' (Lk 10:9, 11). This is our privilege; to be the channels through whom God's kingdom invades the earth.

PRINCIPLE 93

The message is prophetic

Matthew 10:19–20

He speaks through us

We are also given a promise by Jesus that he will give us the words to say, especially when we are in a difficult situation. 'Do not become anxious about how or what you will speak; for it shall be given you in that hour what you are to speak.' In fact, the context of this quotation is persecution, when we are dragged before the courts. Words will be given to us in that moment. If ever there is a time to be clear in your thinking and presentation it is when you are in court defending your honour and integrity. Jesus calmly dismisses our fears by saying, 'Don't even pre-think what you are going to say.'

I am sure this principle can be applied to the context of evangelism. Many times we are put on the spot, opposed and challenged about our faith. We can be sure that the Lord will speak through us, giving us the words to say. This is living evangelism. People cannot come to Christ unless the Father draws them. We must be willing to be used by the Father so that he can speak through us to non-Christians. He uses *us* so that he can speak to *them*. If we are too bound by evangelistic, pre-learned programmes, we are in danger of missing the privilege of being this channel.

He speaks to us – Matthew 10:27

Interestingly, it is not just in the heat of the moment that the Lord will give us what to say. Jesus further instructs us: 'What I tell you in the dark, speak in the daylight; what is whispered in your ear, proclaim from the roofs.' On occasions, the Lord will whisper to us in advance what we need to say.

Once a month in Ichthus we used to have a large evangelistic open-air which was preceded by a day of fasting and a half night of prayer. The reason for this was partly so that we could hear from heaven what message we should take out onto the streets the following day. There have been occasions when there have been so many words of knowledge that we have not known what to do. We used to write any names of people, or ailments which we felt the Lord wanted to deal with on a big board. The next day we would take the board onto the streets and ask anyone who spotted their name or condition to come and talk to us, as we had a message from God for them.

One day, the Lord showed us that we would meet a person called James who had damaged his right knee in a sporting accident. When one of the team came across a man called James on the street the next day, he was amazed to find that the team member knew of his sports injury. It was explained to him that God had said that we would meet him and that he would be healed. James agreed to be prayed for and was healed immediately. He was so excited that he brought his whole family to church the next Sunday to get us to pray for them too.

The great evangelist Smith Wigglesworth used to get many of his sermons in dreams. This has occasionally happened to me. Is this what Jesus meant when he said, 'What I tell you in darkness, speak in the light?' Once, I was even given a three-point sermon, with visual aids in a dream. The following morning, I made up the visuals and gave this sermon at an open-air meeting. It was actually the first time I had ever used visual aids on the street. As I explained the first illustration, a woman walking past was completely transfixed. She said later that the three pictures completely described her life. I shared with her how the Lord had given me those points during the night in a dream, that they were especially for her and that this proved how much God cared for her. She burst into tears as I prayed for her. She was healed emotionally, physically and spiritually, and became a Christian there and then. Five days later, she phoned me to say that her life had been totally transformed.

Peter's Message

One of the ways we can understand the content of the message is to observe the early evangelists in action. The chart on the next page highlights some of the common denominators in the first four evangelistic sermons of Peter. A little later we will do the same with Paul. Here there are six themes, which seem to sum up Peter's message. We will only comment on them briefly.

1) Jesus' death

PRINCIPLE 94

We preach Christ crucified

A quick scan through these sermons shows a development in the message from that of the Gospels. It is not that the foundations laid by Jesus are now no longer relevant, quite the opposite. The message of Jesus is essential to understanding the heart of Christianity. Peter clearly emphasises this in his second sermon: 'You must listen to everything [Jesus] tells you' (Acts 3:22). The message now develops to include the death and resurrection of Jesus, and to explain that forgiveness is being offered as a result of his sacrifice.

2) Forgiveness

Principle 95

We offer God's forgiveness

Peter proclaims forgiveness of sins for all those who believe in Jesus. He says that our sins will be wiped out when we repent, and that the Lord's desire is to turn us from our wicked ways. Interestingly, Acts 2 verse 38 links this forgiveness to the action of baptism.

3) Resurrection

Principle 96

We proclaim a living Saviour

The resurrection was of course the touchstone that completely changed the previously disillusioned disciples into radical, death-defying preachers of the gospel, bold enough to look those who had condemned Jesus straight in the eye and proclaim, 'You disowned him.' 'You rejected him.' 'You crucified him.' 'But God raised him from the dead.' Of this fact they were absolutely convinced, because Jesus had shown himself alive to them with 'many convincing proofs' (Acts 1:3).

4) Witnesses

Principle 97

We share our personal testimony

It was his own personal experience which became very much part of Peter's message. In the same way, we would

	Acts 2:22–36	Acts 3:12–26	Acts 4:8–12	Acts 10:34-44
Jesus Exalted	Jesus attested by miracles, wonders and signs v 22. Highly exalted v 33. Made Lord & Christ v 36.	Glorified his servant Jesus v 13. Raised up prophet hear him in every-thing he says v 22. Holy and Righteous One v 14.	Healed in the name of Jesus v 10. Become the corner-stone v 11. Salvation in no other name/ must be saved v 12.	Peace through Jesus. He is Lord of all v 36. God anointed him with Holy spirit and power, doing good and heal-ing all v 38. Judge of all v 42.
Jesus Crucified	Delivered up. Nailed to the cross. Put to death v 23.	You disowned him v 14. Put to death the Prince of life v 15. Christ should suffer v 18.	Whom you crucified v 10. Rejected by you v 11.	They put him to death by hang-ing him on a cross v 39.
Jesus Raised	God raised him v 24. Did not abandon or allow to decay v 27. Resur-rected v 31. God raised again v 32.	God raised up his servant v 26.	God raised him from the dead v 10.	God raised him up on the third day v 40.
Jesus Predicted	David says vv 25-28. Joel says vv 16–21.	Likewise all the prophets vv 18, 21–2. From Sam-uel & successors v 24. Covenant to Abraham v 25.		Of him all the prophets bear witness v 43.
Jesus Forgives	Be baptised in the name of Jesus for the forgiveness of your sins v 38.	Repent that your sins may be wiped out v 19 Turning every-one from your wicked ways v 26.		Everyone who believes in him receives forgiveness for sins v 43.
Jesus' Witnesses	To which we are all witnes-ses v 32.	To which we are witnesses v 15.		Became visible to us as witnesses. Ordered to preach & testify vv 40–41.

encourage personal testimony to be part of our sharing the gospel today. The enthusiasm of John overflows as he writes in his first epistle: 'That . . . which we have heard, which we have seen with our eyes, which we have looked at and our hands have touched – this we proclaim concerning the Word of Life . . . We proclaim to you what we have seen and heard' (1 Jn 1:1–3)..

It is our first-hand experience of the Lord which gives authenticity to our message. Otherwise, our communication becomes a passing on of mere historical facts; '. . . they observed the confidence of Peter and John and understood that they were uneducated and untrained men. They were marvelling and took note that they had been with Jesus' (Acts 4:13). The gathered assembly could not deny that these men had experienced something that had changed them, and the fact that they had seen a noteworthy miracle was apparent to everybody in Jerusalem (v 16).

5) Jesus Exalted

PRINCIPLE 98

We make much of Jesus

The descriptions of Jesus throughout these short sermons are wonderful. He was attested, glorified, anointed and appointed by God. His miracles, wonders, signs, healings and good deeds, proved his status. He is described as the Lord, the Christ, the Prophet, the Prince of Life, the Holy and Righteous One, the Cornerstone and the Judge of the living and the dead. Our task, as we communicate, is to make much of Jesus.

As Peter exalts the Lord, the crowds are 'cut to the heart' and thousands become Christians. 'Salvation is found in no-one else, for there is no other name under heaven given to men by which we must be saved' (Acts 4:12). There is no doubting the effectiveness of his message. I calculate that he only preached for about forty-five seconds on the Day of Pentecost and 3,000 people got saved. He didn't preach long in his last sermon either, because the Holy Spirit fell and finished the meeting rather abruptly so that they could get on with the baptisms.

6) Jesus predicted

PRINCIPLE 99

We prove Jesus is the Christ

The last observation to be made on Peter's preaching is that he more often than not referred back to the Old Testament prophets as a confirmation and affirmation of Jesus. He refers to 'all the prophets' twice and he names in person Abraham, Moses, Samuel, David and Joel, who all stand as prophetic attestation of Jesus of Nazareth. This was of course an obvious strategy in seeking to win the Jews, by showing that Jesus was the fulfilment of all the Old Testament prophecies. Maybe nowadays people are not so familiar with these historical characters. Nevertheless, their prophetic support for Jesus makes him totally unique in history. No other human being has had so much material predicting his coming for thousands of years before he came.

So we see that in his preaching Peter starts by exalting Jesus as the Lord and Christ. He finishes with the personal experience of witnessing his power. Between these two he expounds the prophecies about the Messiah and explains the forgiveness available through believing in Jesus' death and resurrection.

Paul's Message

Paul, like Peter, also makes an interesting study. It is sometimes difficult to get a whole picture of how he used to present the gospel, because often his sermons were cut short as he entered yet another round of persecution. He seemed to have a group of antagonists who followed wherever he went and who stirred up opposition before he could get his message out. However, we have a few good examples of finished sermons and many supporting comments from the epistles, where he wrote what he saw as important in the communication of the gospel.

There are some interesting paradoxes when we look at Paul. For example, he would say of himself, 'My message and my preaching were not with wise and persuasive words, but with a demonstration of the Spirit's power' (1 Cor 2:1-5). And yet the book of Acts uses words to describe his evangelistic conversations like 'reasoning', 'explaining', 'giving evidence', 'testifying', 'conversing', 'persuading', 'powerfully refuting' and 'debating' (Acts 17:2-3, 17-18; 18:4-5, 19; 19:8-9). Although he was utterly dependent on the Spirit, he certainly used his intellectual abilities to lay out a logical platform from which faith could take off. Faith needs convincing. Once a person is convinced, faith rises automatically. Our task is to convince people of the truth of Jesus. Peter and Paul both used the Old Testament Scriptures to build faith, by convincing their hearers through using the Messianic prophecies. Today, we need to use apologetics (the reasons for our faith) to inspire belief in our hearers.

Paul's Gospel

Paul declared that he wanted to know nothing among them except two things: '(1) Christ and (2) him crucified' (1 Cor 2:2). This puts together the two elements which we have examined so far. Firstly we have the presentation of the historical Jesus, getting people to follow the Jesus of the Gospels and to observe everything that he commanded. Secondly we have the presentation of the saving work of Christ in his death.

Paul further emphasises this second area when he writes to the Romans and the Corinthians:

- 'I am not ashamed of the gospel, because it is the power of God for the salvation of everyone who believes' (Rom 1:16).

- 'For the message of the cross is foolishness to those who are perishing, but to us who are being saved it is the power of God' (1 Cor 1:18).
- 'Christ died for our sins according to the Scriptures, that he was buried, that he was raised on the third day according to the Scriptures' (1 Cor 15:3–4).

PRINCIPLE 100

We preach the gospel fully

Paul also talks of preaching the gospel fully. He preached the gospel everywhere from Jerusalem to Yugoslavia, before launching out further into Europe. He also preached a full gospel of *works* and *wonders* as well as *words*. But I have included, in the chart below, some of the other expressions which show the richness of the message which we preach. These all deserve individual meditation which I trust will

---

Fully Preached the Gospel   Romans 15:19

1. Preach the kingdom of God Lk 9:60; 16:16; Mt 28:18
2. Preach the Good News Lk 4:18; 9:6; Mk 16:15
3. Preach the kingdom of heaven at hand Mt 10:7
4. Preach repentance and forgiveness Lk 24:47
5. Preach the riches of Christ Eph 3:8; Col 1:28
6. Preach righteousness Ps 40:9
7. Preach the whole purpose of God Acts 20:27
8. Preach the faith Gal 1:23
9. Preach the Word 2 Tim 4:2; 1 Thess 1:8
10. Preach the mystery of Christ Col 4:3
11. Preach peace Eph 6:15; Mt 5:9; 2 Cor 5:20
12. Preach Jesus Christ as Lord 2 Cor 4:5
13. Preach ourselves your servants 2 Cor 4:5
14. Preach the message Acts 2:4; 1 Cor 15:3–4
15. Preach the cross 1 Cor 1:23

---

provoke some further thoughts as you read them.

The next chart overleaf seeks to trace, as we did with Peter, some of the points of interest in the evangelistic sermons of Paul. I have selected these sermons because they are complete talks not cut short by the interruptions of the crowd. They are not so easy to categorize as Peter's sermons, although there are some similarities between them.

1) Like Peter, Paul emphasises the themes of Jesus' death, resurrection, forgiveness and judgement.

PRINCIPLE 101

We relate to where people are

2) Paul was an expert at relating his remarks to his audience. To the Jews he became a Jew, and to the Gentiles he became a Gentile. These sermons demonstrate how he tailors his comments to his hearers. For example, he acknowledges King Agrippa's expertise on all customs, or he relates in a masterly way to the religious superstitions of the Athenians, even quoting their poets. He addresses the crowd in the Hebrew language, having been talking to the soldiers in Greek outside the barracks at Jerusalem. He also gives a wonderfully concise and vivid recap of Jewish history as he evangelises in the synagogue of Pisidia. We could learn much from studying Paul about how we should seek to contexualise our message and to start from where our hearers are. This is truly building bridges, getting ourselves onto their wavelength.

PRINCIPLE 102

We explain how our life has changed

3) Paul also uses his personal testimony to relate to his

Paul's Evangelistic Sermons

Acts 13:16–41

History of the Jewish people vv 16–22.

God brought a Saviour to Israel, Jesus v 23.

John proclaimed baptism of re-pentance to all Israel vv 24–25.

To us the word of this salvation is sent out v 26.

Rulers not regognising the prophets con-demned him. Putting him to death Took down from the cross and laid in a tomb vv 27–29.

But God raised him from the dead v 30.

Appeared to those from Galilee v 31.

The very ones who are now witnesses v 31.

Preach to you the good news of the promise made to the fathers vv 32–37.

Through him for-giveness of sins is proclaim-ed v 38. Through him all are freed from all things e.g. Law of Moses v 39.

You will never believe even if someone des-cribed it to you v 41.

17:22–31

Observe religious Examine objects of worship, one with inscription Unknown God vv 22–23.

God made all things He gave life and breath to all things vv 24–25. He made all nations v 26.

That they should seek God, not far from each of us v 27. In him live and move and have our being v 28.

As your poets say – we are his offspring v 28. Therefore God can't be in image of gold, silver or stone v 29.

God demands all men every-where to repent v 30.

He has fixed a day when he will judge the world through a Man appointed, having furn-ished proof by raising him from the dead v 31.

22:1–21

Addressed them in Hebrew v 2.

Testimony of being Jew, zealous, persecuting the Way vv 3–5.

Light on the road to Damascus vv 610. I am Jesus v 8. What shall we do Lord. Blinded vv 10–11.

Ananias prophesies vv 12–15.

Now be baptised wash away your sins v 16.

Lord appeared to Paul in trance in Jerusalem vv1718.

I imprisoned and beat Christians and consented to Stephen's death vv 19–20.

Go I will send you far away to the Gentiles v 21.

26:1–29

Fortunate to give defence to Agrip-pa expert in all customs vv 2–3.

They know me I lived a Pharisee v 5.

On trial for hope of promise to fathers vv 6–7.

Why is resurrection so incredible? v 8.

I persecuted Christians vv 9-11.

Light on road etc I am Jesus whom you are persecut-ing vv 12–16.

Sending to Gen-tiles. To open their eyes. Turn from darkness. From the power of Satan. To receive forgiveness & an inheritance by faith in me vv 17-18.

I state nothing but what Moses & prophets said would take place v 22.

Christ should suffer & by resur-rection proclaim light v 23.

King do you believe the prophets? v 27.

I would that all that hear me be as I am except for these chains v 29.

hearers. There is nothing like admitting to your persecutors who are holding you captive that you too once persecuted Christians, and sought to have them imprisoned and even gave consent to them being put to death. Paul explained how radically his life was turned around on the road to Damascus and how he couldn't do anything other than to obey the vision he had received.

Principle 103

We make the introduction between man and God

4) Paul not only described God as the Creator of all things, sustaining all things with the breath which he gives to all, but he also had a powerful way of bringing this God close for his hearers. 'God did this so that men would seek him and perhaps reach out for him and find him, though he is not far from each one of us. For in him we live and move and have our being' (Acts 17:27–28). Our task is to make the introduction between man and God. Intimacy with the Lord is the successful outcome of our message when it is well communicated.

Principle 104

We challenge people to change their lifestyle

5) Paul also emphasises the need for repentance, not only by pointing his hearers back to the baptism which John proclaimed, the baptism of repentance for all Israel, but also by developing the idea. He says, 'In the past God overlooked such ignorance, but now he commands all people everywhere to repent' (Acts 17:30). Paul's constant challenge

was to see his converts changing their lifestyle. He wanted to see them putting off the old and putting on the new.

PRINCIPLE 105

We proclaim freedom from all things

6) Across these four sermons, there are many references to our being set free. The first sermon reminds us that 'Through Jesus the forgiveness of sins is proclaimed to you. Through him everyone who believes is justified from everything you could not be justified from by the law of Moses' (Acts 13:38f). In the third sermon, Paul uses baptism as a visual demonstration of washing away sins (Acts 22:16). The last sermon describes our mandate, 'To open their eyes and turn them from darkness to light, and from the power of Satan to God, so that they may receive forgiveness of sins and a place among those who are sanctified by faith in [Jesus]' (Acts 26:18).

PRINCIPLE 106

We feel so secure that we want everybody to be like us

7) The last point made by Paul in his last sermon sums up the kind of motivation we should have. 'Short time or long – I pray God that not only you [Agrippa] but all who are listening to me today may become what I am, except for these chains' (Acts 26:29). We need to feel so secure and fulfilled in our faith that we could wish others to be completely like us.

We lead people to Christ

Having gained some understanding of the message which we seek to communicate, we will look at the actual process of how we bring someone out of the kingdom of darkness into the kingdom of God. We often call this 'leading someone to Christ'. I think the Great Commission (Mt 28:19) paints a wider picture. We should lead people to the Father and the Holy Spirit as well.

Three steps in conversion

Jesus gives us in Matthew 28 verse 19 three keys to understanding what is required when becoming a Christian. He says that people need to be baptised into the Father, the Son and the Holy Spirit. This shows us in a nutshell that to be committed as a Christian means to be immersed in, wrapped up with, committed to the three Persons of the Godhead.

Total commitment to the total Godhead Mt 28:19

1. Commitment to the Father – Repenting
2. Commitment to the Son – Responding
3. Commitment to the Holy Spirit – Receiving

For many years now, this three-point plan has been my vehicle in seeking to lead people into the experience of New Testament conversion. It gives us an excellent basis for explaining the necessary steps to be taken in becoming a convert.

PRINCIPLE 107

We lead people to the Father

1. Commitment to the Father – repenting

Firstly, the potential convert has to be prepared to commit himself to the Father. Jesus states that it is only those who do the will of the Father who will enter the kingdom of heaven

(Mt 7:21). I have often challenged a person to speak out to the Father as they become a Christian and say, 'Father, I want to live your way in your world.' That presupposes changing from the way we have been living. Repentance is the biblical term that sums up this practical challenge of the gospel. God commands all men everywhere to repent (Acts 17:30). This is not because God is gratuitously bossy, but because he knows that this is in our best interest and he wants to save us from self-destruction.

PRINCIPLE 108

We lead people to Christ

2. Commitment to the Son – responding

Secondly, the convert has to make a commitment to Jesus. As we have seen, Paul preached 'Christ and him crucified' (1 Cor 2:2). The 'and' here is important. We preach not just about the cross, but about Jesus Christ in his entirety. Often in the past the gospel has become too narrow, the field of focus has been solely the cross. We have neglected to challenge our converts with the lifestyle, teaching and works of our Lord. The Great Commission concludes with the challenge, 'Teaching them to obey everything that I have commanded you' (Mt 28:20). I have often, out of interest, asked Christians if they know how many commands Jesus gave to us. It concerns me that I have not yet met a Christian who could tell me. Most churches have responded by quoting two commands, whereas in fact I can find almost 300. Why has this teaching been so neglected by the church, when actually this is the most basic part of making disciples? After all, how can we lead people into calling Jesus 'Lord' without a total commitment to the things that he says? (Lk 6:46).

By making this observation we don't want in any way to belittle the importance of preaching about Christ's death.

The cross is at the heart of the gospel. Nobody has at any time got into the kingdom any other way, and everybody ultimately has to be led to the foot of the cross. This is the power that brings about salvation.

PRINCIPLE 109

We lead people to the Holy Spirit

3. Commitment to the Holy Spirit – receiving

Thirdly, converts have to make a commitment to receive the Holy Spirit into their life. They must open up fully to his influence. It has amazed me how much literature which has been written to help lead people into the kingdom seems to miss out this crucial element of conversion. We need to see converts empowered by the Spirit from the very first day. For me personally it took six years to take all three of these steps. I was not helped to understand this total commitment and I felt cheated out of the fullness of New Testament Christianity for many years. We owe it to our converts to help them into both the understanding and the experience of a total commitment to the total Godhead.

Baptism – picture or tool for conversion?

We have already alluded to the position and importance of baptism. We cannot really say we have examined the area of conversion without looking at this picture. The threefold thread above of repenting, responding and receiving is taken from the Great Commission, 'Go therefore and make disciples of all nations . . . *baptising* them in the name: i. of the Father, ii. of the Son and iii. of the Holy Spirit.' These, interestingly, are related to the act of baptism. They are found again in Acts 2 verse 38, where Peter tells the crowd, who are asking what they must do to be saved, that they must: i. Repent, ii. *Be baptised* for the forgiveness of sins and iii. Receive the Holy Spirit.

I am positive that in the early church they used to lead people to faith through baptism. In fact, in Acts we have no illustration of anyone being led to Christ any other way. All of them were baptised immediately, seemingly as a way of bringing them to salvation. This perhaps seems controversial and I personally understand why we have laid a slightly different emphasis on the meaning or purpose of baptism. I do however feel that this was an extremely helpful piece of picture language to help converts understand the processes which they go through in order to receive salvation.

Baptism seems to mark the point where people are added to the church (Acts 2:41). The Ethiopian eunuch asked to be baptised even before Philip knew whether he was believing what he was saying (Acts 8:36–37). The Philippian jailer and his family were baptised in the middle of the night (Acts 16:33). Paul was encouraged to rise up, be baptised and wash away his sins (Acts 22:16). Baptism is the outward sign of an inward spiritual truth. It is a perfect picture of how someone is saved. If this is so, it must be possible to put the outward and inward experiences together. We could receive the inward reality by faith at the same time that we express the outward action. Of course there are obvious dangers in implying that we are saved through a physical act and perhaps that is why we have tended to concentrate on the faith aspect rather than on the ritual.

PRINCIPLE 110

We baptise people in the name of the Father, Son and Holy Spirit

However, Jesus draws the faith and the ritual together in Mark 16 verse 16: 'Whoever believes and is baptised will be saved, but whoever does not believe will be condemned.' He is of course underlining the importance of the belief, but he nevertheless connects it here with baptism. I personally am sorry that we have lost this evangelistic tool, but probably our modern equivalent of leading people into conversion through prayer can be seen as a viable alternative. But perhaps we can still use the picture of baptism as a clear illustration in explaining the various steps to be taken in the course of conversion.

PRINCIPLE 111

We make disciples not just converts

In the Great Commission our mandate was to make disciples of all nations. How do we know when we have made a disciple? The answer is simple, we just need to teach them to observe everything that Christ commanded. For example, in the same breath, Jesus tells us all to baptise people in the name of the Father, the Son and the Holy Spirit. Baptising people was a part of basic discipleship for all, not the responsibility of church leaders alone.

Discipleship Model

If we are all supposed to be baptising converts, it is also our responsibility to make disciples out of them. So our task doesn't end when we have evangelised someone. We must go on to establish these young Christians as disciples. The mission is not completed until we have equipped these new believers into becoming disciplers themselves so that they are able now to continue the cycle by evangelising and establishing the next generation of converts.

CHAPTER 9

THE MEASURE OF THE MAN

What about those who have never heard about Christ? This is a question which is asked so often. The answer is of course simple: 'Salvation is found in no-one else, for there is no other name under heaven given to men by which we must be saved' (Acts 4:12). Interestingly though, Jesus shows us that he is able to read whether people would have repented if they had had more light. 'Woe to you, Korazin! Woe to you, Bethsaida! If the miracles that were performed in you had been performed in Tyre and Sidon, they would have repented long ago in sackcloth and ashes' (Mt 11:21–23). He then proceeded to declare that Sodom would have remained in existence if it had seen the miracles which had occurred in Capernaum. Ultimately, the Lord alone is able to make true and righteous judgements and he hints that he is able to assess how people would have responded given different circumstances. Are there, therefore, certain ways in which God measures our attitudes and reactions in life so that he can make these spiritual judgements? The answer seems to be 'yes'. The following are a few statements which reveal that our acceptance of Christ can be perceived by our receiving of something, or someone, else.

PRINCIPLE 112

Receiving a child = receiving Christ

Luke 9:48, 18:16–17

When the disciples were arguing as to which of them was going to be the greatest (Lk 9:46–48), Jesus took a child, stood him by his side and said, 'Whoever receives this child in my name receives me' (NASB) This statement gives us a remarkable insight into how Jesus interprets our heart attitudes towards others. The Lord is equating our receiving of a child to receiving him. He reads the way that we relate to a young child and sees in it our sensitivity and openness to the kingdom. Maybe the opposite is also true, if we are uncaring spiritually, then we are also likely to be uncaring towards little children.

It is significant that the last verse in the Old Testament speaks of the hearts of the fathers being restored to their children and the hearts of the children to their fathers. Is this one of the keys for opening the doors and ushering in the kingdom? It is not surprising that Jesus rebukes the disciples for preventing the children from coming to him. 'Let the little children come to me, and do not hinder them, for the kingdom of God belongs to such as these' (Lk 18:16–17). God values them so highly that he suggests that anyone who causes a child who believes in him to stumble would be better off being thrown into the sea with a millstone hung around his neck (Mt 18:6–10). There are not many verses which reveal Jesus as being anti-healing but here he suggests that we should cut off hands and feet rather than become a stumbling block. His reason is because the angels of little children always behold the face of the Father in heaven – so be careful!

Yes, God views children so highly that he says, 'Therefore, whoever humbles himself like this child is the greatest in the kingdom of heaven' (Mt 18:4). We not only need to be accepting of little children, we actually need to become like them. You cannot enter into the kingdom unless you accept it like a little child (Lk 18:17). Crazily, the next verse shows a certain ruler asking, 'What shall I do to inherit eternal life?' as if he had totally ignored what Jesus had just been saying. It takes humility to accept this message. Hence, it is hard for the rich, the proud, the wise and the noble to accept the simplicity of God's salvation. The process of entrance into the kingdom is by being born again, so the illustration of becoming like a little child is very appropriate.

PRINCIPLE 113

Babes receive revelation

Luke 10:21

Jesus 'rejoiced greatly' that the gospel was not perceived through human wisdom or earthly intelligence. He says, 'I praise you, Father, Lord of heaven and earth, because you have hidden these things from the wise and learned, and revealed them to little children. Yes, Father, for this was your good pleasure.' The gospel is revealed from above, and the Father chooses to reveal it to ordinary people, to the simple, the base, the ignoble – the 'babes'. We, of course, get as excited by this same principle as Jesus does, particularly as we qualified for the kingdom by finding ourselves in one of these categories.

We understand from this that there are certain types of people who receive revelation and this surely provides us with a strategy for evangelism. It makes sense to work with, as a priority, the kinds of people with whom the Father is pleased to work. Consequently, we need to identify the individuals most likely to receive revelation. Potentially no one is left out from being able to attain to the qualities of these categories. It is possible for all to humble themselves to become like little children in every sense that Jesus meant it. If, however, Jesus had demanded that maturity was the basic requirement, some would be permanently disqualified. It is, for example, possible for the rich to make themselves poor, but not quite so easy for the poor to become rich. On this basis, we have always made it our objective to work into the poorer estates, and have always found a receptivity there.

PRINCIPLE 114

Serving the poor = serving Christ

Matthew 25:40f

We have already examined this area in the chapter 'The Ministry of the Merciful' (in the section on 'Salvation and Social Action'). It is, nevertheless, important to observe again that the Lord reads a far deeper agenda into the world's disposition towards the poor than we would imagine. Serving the poor is the same thing as serving Jesus himself. During their lifetime the Lord is able to gather a vast amount of data about non-Christians based on their care and attention for the poor. This is such a clear measure that, using this information, he is able to separate those he calls sheep from those he calls goats.

PRINCIPLE 115

Forgive everybody to be forgiven

Matthew 6:12, 14

The Lord also measures to what extent we forgive other people in order to qualify for his forgiveness. Jesus makes it very clear that if you will not forgive others then neither will your heavenly Father forgive you. The Lord's prayer teaches us to ask the Lord to forgive us as we forgive others. The one is dependent upon the other. What better way of breaking from the past, of releasing damaging hurts, of freeing ourselves from the bitternesses of life? As a person becomes a Christian, God forgives him a great debt but only if he, for his part, will forgive all his little debtors.

I recall an evangelistic meeting where a crippled lady very noisily stomped out during the appeal. The callipers on her legs and her crutches made such a noise that she drew everyone's attention to her protest. On her way out she tossed her head back in unbelief at a banner on the wall which read 'Jesus My Hope'. I met her on the street later that night and asked if she was all right. She curtly replied, 'Yes.' I said, 'You're not, are you? What's the problem?' She then lifted her finger and pointed at me and said, 'You are! You have stopped me from becoming a Christian tonight.' Then she quoted these words of Jesus that unless you will forgive others you will not be forgiven. She went on to explain how she had been sexually abused over and over again because of her disabilities and how people had taken advantage of her. 'I will never forgive them for doing that,' she said.

For a moment she left me speechless, then I said, 'I know this is extremely difficult, but if you don't forgive them, who is it hurting? It is not hurting them because they are long gone. It is really hurting you. I know this is hard, but if you can't forgive, why not ask Jesus to help you? Would you pray with me?' 'No I will not,' she said, as she began to turn away. 'Listen,' I said, 'I really believe in prayer and I am going to get some others praying for you too. If Jesus does help you to forgive, come back to the church and we will show you how you can become a Christian.' 'You can do what you like,' she said as she began walking away. 'But one thing I can promise you; I shall never come back to this church ever again.'

Well, we did pray for her and the next night she was sitting in the audience in the church, and when it came to the appeal she came forward and received God's forgiveness. She was also freed from some spirits of bitterness in the process.

PRINCIPLE 116

Accepting a Christian = accepting Christ

Matthew 10:40–41

Jesus applies exactly the same principle to the attitudes people hold towards believers. If someone accepts us it is equivalent to accepting Jesus. Everyone has an instant response to us when they discover we are Christians, which is either negative or positive. At the time of writing this I had just spent a week in the north of France, in an area where so much activity went on in the last World War. During the course of the many conversations around that topic I began to see a clear analogy with what Jesus was saying.

During the war many Allies escaped from prisoner-of-war camps. In their attempt to flee from enemy territory, they would often try to get in touch with the French resistance movement. You would have to be extremely careful who you talked to, because every person had an allegiance either to the Nazis or to the Allies. The moment they discovered who you were, you would get an instant response from them. They would either be sympathetic with you or they would be totally against you. Even if someone wasn't actively working with the resistance, once they knew which side you were on, you would quickly ascertain where their sympathies lay.

In the same way, people today, when they hear of our Christian faith, respond either positively or negatively. If they react to us with a certain amount of sympathy, it reveals where their heart lies with regard to the Lord. This is one of the most exciting principles in evangelism, because when someone befriends us, it is tantamount to being friendly to the Lord. Openness towards us shows an openness towards Jesus. Receiving us is identical, it seems, to receiving the Lord.

Because of this dynamic, the Lord rewards all those who are positively inclined towards us. He says, 'If they receive a prophet . . . they will receive a prophet's reward.' 'If they reckon us righteous . . . they will receive a righteous person's reward.' God is so thrilled at their acceptance of us that even if they give us just a cup of cold water, he says, 'They shall in no way go without a reward.'

PRINCIPLE 117

Rejecting Christians = rejecting Christ

Matthew 10:14–16

The converse also happens to be true. To reject a Christian seems to indicate a complete rejection of Jesus. To hear the words of Jesus regarding this shows that he has an enormous sense of pride over his disciples. To see them rejected is more hurtful to God than the sins of Sodom and Gomorrah. He says that it will be more tolerable for those cities in the day of judgment than for the person who rejects us, or the city where we are unwelcome. We are assured of God's closest attention in the process of evangelism. He watches the response of every non-Christian. To shut us out is to shut God out and this is severe in its consequences. We can understand why Jesus goes on to say, 'Be as shrewd as snakes and as innocent as doves' (Mt 10:16). We need to do everything in our power to make sure that we don't put people off. With love and grace we must seek to win people over to accepting both us and our message.

PRINCIPLE 118

Men of peace receive peace

Luke 10:6

Jesus said, 'When you enter a house, first say, "Peace to this house." If a man of peace is there, your peace will rest on him; if not, it will return to you' (Lk 10:6). 'Men of peace' is one of the phrases Jesus uses to describe people who are open to the kingdom of God. He also uses the expression 'worthy person', and refers to some people's hearts as 'good ground' and still others as being 'ripe for harvest'. All these expressions prove a receptivity to the blessings, or the people, of the kingdom. Bless a man of peace with peace and it rests on him, but if he is not a man of peace it rebounds off him back to us. It is interesting that we get the blessing which was intended for them, if they are not receptive. This is one of the reasons why we can always walk away from a rebuff feeling blessed.

PRINCIPLE 119

To him who has shall more be given

Matthew 13:12

Jesus often repeated the phrase, 'He who has ears to hear, let him hear.' There are those who seem to be able to receive more readily than others, and once that process has begun, it seems easier for it to continue. 'To him who has shall more be given and he shall have an abundance' (NASB). Our challenge, as we look at society, is to provide a starting point upon which people's spiritual awareness can grow. If individuals have nothing, even that which they have shall be taken away. But if we can manage to sow something of the kingdom into their lives, a capacity for obtaining more is created.

So, in summary, the Lord measures us according to certain criteria. He is using daily life to make judgements as to where we stand in our relationship with him. So, if we have never had the opportunity of hearing the gospel, can Jesus nevertheless know how we would have responded if we had heard it? It is important to notice that anybody who is responsive in these categories would definitely respond and receive the message of the gospel when they encounter it. A Muslim, for example, who was reacting right in all the daily situations would definitely not persecute a Christian. Someone like that, meeting a true Christian, would become one. We should never then feel that we should leave people with the light that they have in case they reject Jesus. In fact they would not reject Jesus, they would accept him. So we must never be hesitant about preaching the gospel.

CHAPTER 10

THE MAINTENANCE OF THE MULTIPLICATION

This chapter, the last before developing some practical ideas in Part 2, looks at how we can maintain the momentum of church growth. One of the impressive things about the early church was how they managed to sustain the continued exponential growth of their membership. When the church was inundated with 3,000 converts on the Day of Pentecost, it would have been reasonable for them to take a year or two to consolidate. Actually that was just the beginning of what is estimated to have been over 500,000 new believers joining the church during the period of time covered by the book of Acts. There are regular updates recorded on how the church was growing. 'So the word of God spread. The number of disciples in Jerusalem increased rapidly' (Acts 6:7). The churches are described as continuing to increase (Acts 9:31). Some versions use the expresson 'the churches continued to multiply'. They maintained their multiplication through church planting; and churches were springing up all over the countryside. We are going to look at why church planting is still a strategic way of causing and maintaining church growth.

PRINCIPLE 120

Church planting provides variety

Church planting is an effective strategy for growth, even in areas where churches already exist. I am going to suggest several reasons for this. Firstly, our God is a God of infinite variety. He has created a world where every single human being is definitively unique. It seems the most obvious assumption to expect that the church should reflect this variety.

I personally think that it is wonderful that there are over 22,000 Christian denominations in the world. This merely serves to underline the fact that God loves a rich assortment. To want to make all churches the same is to react against nature and consequently against God's nature too. Nowhere does the Bible try to define exactly what a church should be like. It describes it as a body, but all bodies are recognisably different. Churches need to work out how to retain and display their uniqueness in the Lord. Church traditions are fine, but it is equally fine to strip them away or to change them. Many of our man-made expressions of church life are completely negotiable. Quite deliberately, there are so few biblical guidelines and models that we are allowed a total freedom for individual expression. We are crazy to insist on conformity to tradition or other things, when the Lord encourages spontaneity and variety. Church planting at least gives us the opportunity to wipe the slate clean from past customs and cultures, and enables us to start again. Interestingly, having been involved in church planting for many years I notice that we can still needlessly impose old forms and formats.

In the book of Revelation, seven churches of Asia are described (chs 2–3). As the Lord speaks to them, he describes the different qualities he sees in each, and tailors his message accordingly. The situations of these churches, and their assets and deficiencies, are all totally different. So, as the Lord looks at any church, he sees definite distinctives, some good and some bad. Every Christian has certain emphases which he believes are important and these are going to affect the kind of church which he plants. Because each leadership group is unique, the churches they lead will be unique too. These distinctives are part of the spice of life, and should be respected and encouraged.

PRINCIPLE 121

Church planting provides choice

Variety, on the one hand, portrays a truer image of the Lord, being the Creator of a vast spectrum of differences and, on the other, it provides multiple choice for those looking for a suitable church. Some years ago, we planted a church into Central London, where two other struggling churches already existed. One of these, a strict non-conformist church, was so upset about us starting there that they distributed a leaflet around the area describing us as a cult, warning people to stay clear. We telephoned the minister of this church and set up a meeting with him and the third local church minister. We talked through together some of our fears and prejudices.

One of the things that we suggested was that we each describe the kind of things we did in our respective churches to explain, for example, the style of our church meetings and worship, our target groups for evangelism etc. Having done this, I then asked them, 'Do you think that anyone who goes to your church would be interested in coming to ours?' They both let out a little chuckle and adamantly said, 'No, I don't think so!' I could also fairly safely say that nobody from our church would have been tempted to join their churches. Because we were so different, there was room for each of us, and they agreed that they could now see no problem with us existing alongside one another. They apologised for their leaflet and we ended up meeting once a month to pray for one another's work. Variety is important, because it is providing choice for non-Christians. Obviously, some people would be happier with one tradition or style while others would prefer another. Choice has to be a positive thing for society.

PRINCIPLE 122

Church planting increases the intensity of light

Revelation 1:12

The more churches there are in any given area, the more light is created there. This makes it easier for non-Christians to see truth more clearly and become more spiritually aware. I have often meditated on the picture in Revelation, where John turned to look for the voice that was speaking to him and saw seven golden candlesticks (Rev 1:12–20). The first things he saw were, actually, the churches, then he noticed Jesus walking between these lampstands.

The scene, depicted in the mind, is of seven candlesticks burning brightly and it is the light from these that allows Jesus to be seen. He is walking around between them. Initially the impression given is that he is only visible owing to the light provided by these candles. It is also interesting, in this picture, that Jesus is not in the churches but between these lights. To me that places Jesus in the world, walking around the community. Does the light shining from the churches allow non-Christians to see what the Lord is doing as he passes by? Perhaps the light from the candlesticks helps non-Christians to become accustomed to the light, leading them inevitably to see the glory of his face 'like the sun shining in all its brilliance' (Rev 1:16). For this reason it makes sense that we plant as many churches as we can. The more light there is, the more people will be converted, and then *all* the churches in that area will grow as a result.

In the 1980s, when Ichthus was one of the fastest growing churches in the country, it was surrounded by other denominational churches which were also among the fastest growing in their denominations. The same principle works for retail outlets. DIY stores, estate agents and restaurants have all discovered that they create more custom by clustering together. This grouping has become an accepted marketing strategy. Because there is a higher profile it attracts more customers and also gives the public a wider choice. When I have been asked if I would mind another church pioneering a plant into an area where I am also planting, I could honestly reply that I would be pleased if they would, because my church will also grow as a result of them being there.

PRINCIPLE 123

Church planting makes church accessible

The more churches are planted, the more accessible they become. This is particularly vital in the poorer estates where a large percentage of the people don't have their own transport. It is a good idea to put a church within everybody's walking distance. I reckon a biblical Sabbath day's journey is not a bad guideline, i.e. 890 metres. Ideally there should be a church within half that distance from any given point so that people can get there and back within the permitted limits. Imagine a town or an estate where churches were planted no more than 890 metres from each other. Wouldn't that provide an excellent base for evangelism? It is similar to the Challenge 2000 objective to plant a church for every 1,000 members of society. If we applied this principle to Hemel Hempstead, for example, every estate would need several churches still to be planted in them.

PRINCIPLE 124

Church planting has the lost as its priority

Romans 15:20

Paul talked about preaching Christ where Christ had not been named (Rom 15:20). We want to put churches into areas where at the moment there is not a living witness. Another one of my concerns, however, is that there can sometimes be several churches in an area but none of them is actually communicating the gospel to the non-Christians. In surveying an area to see where we should plant, we need to be able to ascertain how effective the witness of existing churches actually is. We must fulfil our mandate to the non-Christians even if it sometimes means treading on the toes of other Christians. Our priority is for the lost, to make sure that they are given every chance of receiving the gospel, and maybe that means planting a church into a non-evangelising church's patch.

PRINCIPLE 125

Church planting provides relevant evangelism

1 Corinthians 9:20

The idea of planting a church every 800 metres means that it would be possible to gauge the character of each estate in order to find the most appropriate evangelistic strategy. Like the Apostle Paul, we need to be all things to all men. To the Jews he became a Jew, so that he could win the Jews. To the Gentiles he became as a Gentile. As we live and work in an area, we seek to relate, in a relevant way, to the people who live there. Finding the right seeds to sow in each situation and the best manner in which to sow them is just part of the equation. The other factor to consider is how we can best identify with any particular community.

These concepts are sometimes referred to as 'contextualisation'. Within reason, we should adapt to the cultures and customs of our planned evangelistic environment in order to relate the gospel as much as possible into the context of the hearer. Some church growth principles suggest that we should only evangelise people like ourselves, because like attracts like. However, even if this is true in practice, I do not entirely agree with this as a biblical evangelistic strategy. There are occasions, for the sake of the gospel, when we try to win people who are not like ourselves, just as Paul did for the Gentiles. Maybe homogenous units (groups made up of similar kinds of people) grow faster than mixed groups, but our challenge must ultimately be to break down all divisions, whether of age, sex, status, religion or race and to build a fellowship, for example, from every kindred, tribe and nation.

An example of this from the early church occurred over the question of circumcision for the Greek believers. The early church eventually decided that it was not appropriate to enforce circumcision on the Gentiles and from then on this created an evangelistic, cultural distinction (Acts 15:1–35). Other things had necessarily to be fulfilled by both ethnic groups. Both, for example, had to refrain from sexual immorality and the eating of meat with the blood still in it. The propositions of the gospel will never vary, but there are many things such as the mode of worship or technique of evangelism which are cultural and which therefore could vary considerably even from one estate to another. It is a great shame that, on the mission field, missionaries carried a western form of worship, with western musical styles, into contexts where far more valid local styles could have been used. I would like to see some of our modern songwriters encouraging indigenous songwriters to use their own vernacular and musical styles, rather than just translating songs from one nation to another. Even within a nation, one area might suit a classical music or operatic approach to evangelistic communication while another would feel far more at home with gospel rap.

In any church planting situation, we need to assess what we can use from the given culture and identify those things which we need to emphatically change. Music is just one example, but there are other elements which can be adverse to the kingdom culture. For example, a 'stretch or starve' philosophy where you help yourself and look after 'number one', seems a little opposed to the basic philosophy of

Christianity. Although, we can adapt a certain amount of worldly culture to characterise our style and approach, there are nevertheless many areas of heavenly culture to which someone who is born again has to adapt. The mission field throws up all kinds of such ethical, culturally-based problems such as caring for multiple wives in a polygamous society, or the rights and wrongs of bribing officials in a bribery based bureaucracy, or being fair and just in a market bartering system, or dealing with intense national pride, or overcoming culturally inherited traits such as laziness, self-assertiveness or even materialism. As we contemplate church planting from one area into another, food, clothing, music, church decor, communication style and the content of activities are all possibly culturally adaptable.

PRINCIPLE 126

Church planting provides involvement in the community

Acts 6:1

The church doesn't just do evangelism, the church *is* evangelism. The visual aid of love, unity and hope from the church becomes the example for the neighbourhood. Society should be able learn these objective qualities by watching what is going on in the church. The practical care for one another, loving submission in the relationships and the servant heart of God's people couldn't be a better model for civilisation, as a whole, to follow. In the next chapter I suggest various evangelistic events which seek to bring non-Christians into the environment of the church, so that they can get a glimpse of genuine community at work.

Being a community within the community also becomes the base from which to serve the rest of society. The early church found areas in which to serve their community, such as caring for the widows and supplying their needs. This became such a task that they had to appoint seven deacons to deal with it (Acts 6:1). Getting to grips with the needs of those around the church is part of our pastoral role. Among any 1,000 people in any community there are an awful lot of pastoral needs. There is space for many more churches to be planted to be able to fulfil their caring vocation by coping adequately with these demands.

Jesus trained and taught his disciples in a context where other people could hear and watch him. He talked theology in the cut and thrust of the problems of life in the community. He used illustrations from their everyday life and culture identifying with their customs and traditions perfectly. The incarnation was not just into a human body, but into a particular time period and a definite cultural background.

PRINCIPLE 127

Church planting provides freedom for initiative/vision/gifting

Church planting allows pioneers to pioneer. It grants the visionaries freedom to implement their dreams and visions. Starting a new church provides all kinds of space and opportunity for individual initiative and gifting. In most churches there are those who are always straining at the leash, wanting to push into new ground, not happy with the way things are. These members are often the nuisances, the pains in the pastor's neck, because they are keen to experiment or to operate outside present frameworks and structures. Unfortunately, enormous amounts of energy are expended trying to contain these people. A better strategy is to release them, channelling their energy into something positive. Once let loose, these are excellent pioneers in the territory of church planting.

For others, church planting brings to the surface desires and energies hitherto latent or undiscovered. One of the churches we planted in London happened as a result of our being offered a building by the London Baptist Association. It was probably more a partnership in resurrection than an outright church plant. But as we took on the project, I was amazed at how quickly the team grew in their new-found responsibilities. We used a housegroup which had been meeting in our home at that time, many of whom were very young in their faith and some certainly struggling to keep their heads above water. But overnight they became an extremely dynamic team. They became so excited that some took their annual leave to do evangelism. Others even gave up their jobs to go into full-time church work, and they all suddenly found the incentive to live in holiness and pray with fervency. Not surprisingly the church grew very nicely!

The church planted at Colosse was not started by Paul or any of the other apostles. It began as a result of the revival at Ephesus. The churches at Hieropolis and Laodicea sprang out of the same revival, in the same way. Disciples who had visited Ephesus and been affected by what they had seen there, seem to have gone home and started churches spontaneously in their home towns. These untrained converts, who were not the recognised church leaders, just went and did it.

PRINCIPLE 128

Church planting provides task/team orientated churches

Matthew 28:18

It strikes me that there is a vast difference between a group and a team. A group is where people gather together for fellowship in face-to-face, inward-looking relationships, whereas a team exists to accomplish some kind of goal beyond just meeting together. A football team, for example, exists to play a game and win matches. Yes, the relationships are good fun, and the social life is great in the pub after the match. But that isn't their raison d'être. The team exists to accomplish a task on the field. They work hard at getting themselves fit and planning their strategies. Once in action, the whole team is absorbed with one overriding objective – to get the ball into the opponent's goal.

We enjoy our relationships in church life together but the reason we exist is to bring the kingdom of God into the world. There is nothing like church planting to turn a group into a team, where relationships, as on a battlefield, become shoulder to shoulder rather than face to face. Interestingly, we have discovered that the most outward-looking cellgroups, those which are particularly concentrated on evangelism, have often been the more effective pastoral care units. Perhaps this is because they provide an alternative objective which prevents people focusing too much on their own problems. The members of such a group are also more aware of the need for everyone to be fit for the task and so they perhaps look after one another more intensely. We get fit, and display our fitness, by applying ourselves to the task. When footballers are sitting around a 'pint in the pub' you can't tell who is fit and who isn't, but when they are chasing down a loose ball, you can soon tell.

Creating teams with tasks is the challenge for the leadership of the church. We need to get beyond being introspective. There was no element of self-indulgence when Jesus was training his disciples. He didn't seem to spend time getting them to 'open up', sharing how they were feeling or bringing up the hurts of their pasts. He led them into action-orientated service, focusing on others and their needs. This is how Paul described the mind of Christ in Philippians 2. 'Each of you should look not only to your own interests, but also to the interests of others' (Phil 2:4). This is the heart and lifestyle of Jesus and this was the way he operated with his team.

PRINCIPLE 129

Church planting provides localised spiritual warfare

Ephesians 2:2

There is no doubt that in any neighbourhood non-Christians are being manipulated by spiritual forces. Paul describes them as walking according to the prince of the power of the air (Eph 2:2). He goes on to affirm that, 'the spirit is now working in the sons of disobedience'. Our task is to so bring the atmosphere of heaven into an area that people's lives are influenced by the fresh air of the Holy Spirit.

We understand that our choices are essential in how the supernatural realm interacts with the natural one. That is, of course, why we pray. This is also how demons gain their entrance to possess individuals' lives. Both single choices and, even more powerfully, group choices, open the doors for spiritual activity. Jesus reveals that it only takes two or three people asking together for something to cause it to come about (Mt 18:19). Presumably, unholy alliances operate in a similar way so that if there are the two and three people making evil choices in our communities, wicked things will result. Our aim should be to influence these evil alliances, seeking to get them converted or to see them scattered and driven from the area. We have for years implemented a prayer strategy of asking the Lord to put us in touch with the enemy 'king pins' on our local estates. This is rather a dangerous ploy because you can stir up a lot of trouble! But we have seen some real darkness-to-light conversions in this field. These have included criminals, drug dealers and even self-confessed witches. When they become Christians, there is a significant shift in the spiritual dynamics of an area. We have also, as a result of prayer, seen the Lord remove significant enemy agents from our districts.

Another area to identify in spiritual warfare is whether, in the present or at sometime in history, there have been community decisions made which might affect the kind of demonic strongholds reigning in the various parts of the town. A typical scenario we have come across was where a bomb, dropped in the last World War, exploded on a local school. This wiped out the whole community's children at a stroke. You can imagine the anger and the bitterness felt by *everybody*, not just by those who had lost their children. It is not surprising that demons seek to exploit such situations. Although that atrocity happened more than a generation ago now, yet the same spirits of anger and bitterness were to be found controlling the present population. The people had changed but the territory was still controlled by the same demonic principalities. Understanding this gives us a clear strategy in evangelism to encourage the present residents to make different choices from those made in the past and to choose to live in an opposite spirit to this principality. They learned to live in forgiveness and love. The deliberate choices of two or three individuals can make a significant difference.

We can conclude from Abraham's intercessions for Sodom (Gen 18:21-33) that God would not have destroyed the city if he had found ten righteous people living there. In other words, the Lord would have shown grace to the rest of the town for the sake of a few righteous inhabitants. It seems that the spiritual dynamics change as we see people converted. If God's grace is drawn even to the unrighteous as a result of ten people becoming righteous, we have a terrific incentive to get on and evangelise.

Another essential lesson we learn in spiritual warfare is that the battle has to be fought and won on the battlefront. The demons were cast out by face-to-face confrontation during the ministry of Jesus. Maybe the mountain-top transfiguration was a key to victory, but the battle was fought and won in the valley as a demon in the little boy was encountered in hand-to-hand combat (Mk 9:2-27). We plant churches close enough to where people are in order to understand and beat the devil's strategy in each territory.

Paul seemed quite deliberately to take on strategic areas which were strongholds of the enemy. He passed through places like Samothrace and Neapolis to get to Philippi (Acts 16:11). Philippi was described as 'Little Rome' because of the Roman colony there. Paul was keen to enter into this hornets' nest, just as he also did at Ephesus (Acts 19) because that was how he would change the world. He also passed by Amphipolis and Apollonia to get a church started in Thessalonica. Taking these strategic places became an effective influence in evangelism. The Thessalonians 'became a model . . . The Lord's message rang out from you . . . your faith in God has become known everywhere' (1 Thess 1:7–8).

PRINCIPLE 130

Church planting because of building size

The advantages and disadvantages of owning church buildings is an interesting debate. Amazingly, the early church resisted the temptation to build Christian synagogues for the first 300 years of their history. They seemed content to meet in homes, public buildings, in the open air and even in the Jewish synagogues. This clearly demonstrated that church was a dynamic group of people relating together, rather than, as people refer to it today, a building with a sharp pointed tower. Remove these buildings from some of our communities and the world would see precious little evidence of the church! What does the community see of our church activity besides the building?

Although buildings are expensive both to purchase and to maintain, their public profile can be valuable. But we must find ways to use them fully in serving society. Unfortunately, so many have become white elephants, only used for a few sparsely-attended services and remaining dormant for most of the week. Church architects have a challenge to create multipurpose buildings which can best serve the needs of the community as well as double up as an auditorium for church services. We had, for example, one building where we managed to cram in a residential training programme for a dozen students, a nursery school, a full-time job club, and a very active church programme, all running side by side. Yes, it was a little crowded, but we felt we were getting the most out of the property.

The following paragraph asks a series of questions regarding the use of church buildings. These raise only some of the issues in this debate but, nevertheless, they are important to think through. I am not sure that there are definitive answers to these questions as every situation is different and each church's vision varies as to what they are seeking to accomplish. There are so many good models showing the advantages of big and small, hiring and owning, town centre and estate-based, sole use and shared use and so on, but here are a few discussion starters:

1. How big should we build?
2. Is there an optimum size for any given community?
3. Do you aim bigger by faith?
4. Does a smaller building automatically limit potential growth?
5. Does a larger congregation mean drawing people from greater distances?
6. Do large auditoriums then take Christians away from working in their own local communities?
7. Would several smaller buildings serve numerous communities better than one larger one?
8. Do non-Christians feel more at home in larger, more anonymous gatherings?
9. How can we stop the tendency of audiences to just attend larger services but not actively to participate in church life?
10. Is money better invested into people or church workers, rather than bricks and mortar?
11. How can bricks and mortar best serve people?
12. Would a shop on the high street be a better profile than a church building in an estate?
13. What is available in the town?
14. What can we honestly afford?
15. Is it better to buy little units in the estates and hire large units for celebrations?

PRINCIPLE 131

Church planting because of divisions and splits

Acts 19:9

Sadly, many churches get planted as a result of divisions and splits. This is not altogether bad, in that usually both halves of a split carry on and grow into viable units on their own. Their differences also underline the legitimately rich variety able to exist in church culture and life. Valid theological differences are, on the whole, healthy. These should provoke each of us to think issues through and to be fully persuaded in our own minds as to where we stand (Rom 14:5). To be free to emphasise certain pragmatic or theological distinctives is essential for believers to be true to their own revelation and leading. We should, however, never dishonour other believers, or churches, because they see things differently from ourselves. Spiritual maturity should allow us to agree to disagree and, if necessary, to work separately, while at the same time loving, honouring, respecting and relating to those who differ from ourselves. Everybody reaches theological conclusions from the information which is available to them. Because our sources of information differ, we are bound to reach differing conclusions. But these intellectual processes have nothing to do with the integrity of the individual's heart or the validity of their love for the Lord. Too often I think we are mistaking the true values of spirituality. God accepts, loves and uses his children, even when they come from totally opposite extremes of the theological spectrum. What right do we have to reject what our Father accepts?

This doesn't mean of course that certain emphases aren't wrong, or that we shouldn't try to help one another to understand or think through areas of difference. The Apostle Paul sought to shine as much light as he could into each synagogue he attended. He would argue and reason to the point where, either his hearers got converted or they threw him out. This makes a good model for those of us persevering in dead or dying institutional settings. Watch out though! They might drag you out and stone you! When Paul was thrown out he would start again with a new church plant somewhere down the road. 'But some of them became obstinate; they refused to believe and publicly maligned the Way. So Paul left them [at the synagogue]. He took the disciples with him and had discussions daily in the lecture hall of Tyrannus' (Acts 19:9).

Summary

Church planting is a risky business. Like all evangelism, you can never quite guarantee that people will respond to what you are offering. But the world needs pioneers who are willing to experiment and take the risks necessary to bring church to the people. Maybe we just start small, getting a foothold, like Paul when he finds a woman in Philippi who opens her heart to respond to his message (Acts 16:14). But this led on to her family being baptised, and then to a church being planted there.

Researching our town or estate, like Paul surveying Athens, when he discovered a key to use for his message (Acts 17:23), is the way that we become relevant in evangelism and spiritual warfare. Listening from history, from the public at large, from the local newspapers and from the Lord, are the sources for us to create short-term and long-term objectives in planting effective, relevant churches.

Finally, church planting is no different from starting your own business. I have often encouraged people to branch out on their own and to start their own company. I have also done this myself. To encourage such free enterprise is to be applauded in the business world. No one likes to see monopolies, the more choice and variety available the better it is. So why should we frown on energetic, adventurous pioneers starting up new churches? Why should older denominations hold a monopoly? Free enterprise challenges us all to make sure we are providing what is necessary to serve the community.

Part Two

101 Evangelistic Ideas

CHAPTER 11

THE METHODS OF THE MARKET-PLACE

Saturation evangelism

In advertising, the objective is to attract the attention of as many people as possible in a target group, in as many different ways as possible. This means trying to keep the name of the product in their minds. I wonder, how many times each month do the people of our town hear the name of our church? The following pages contain 101 different ideas which we have tried from time to time, in order to saturate society with our product – the gospel. Perhaps there is something here that catches your imagination – why not try it out? Or maybe reading these ideas sparks some even better ideas of your own. I am aware that some things work well in one situation which would not work somewhere else. So, some of these ideas won't work in your context. Trial and error are the keys to discovering what works well, or should I say trial and success!

Using initiative (Matthew 25:14–30; Luke 19:12–26)

The parable of the talents has always challenged me, in that each servant is left to use his own initiative as to how he uses what the master has entrusted to him. We all have responsibilities in serving our heavenly Master, and yet often our gifts and talents do not come with a detailed instruction manual as to how, where and when we are to use them. The Lord seems to expect us to use creativity and innovation to make things happen where perhaps ordinarily they wouldn't. This is essential if we are to break through in evangelism. We are rarely provided with opportunities on a plate and if we sit back and do nothing, in general, nothing happens. We all need to create ways of investing our God-given resources so that we can present back to God at the end of the day increased returns on his investments.

Being creative

The potential of human creativity, we are told, is unlimited. The business world proves this point clearly as improvements in this field happen at an incredible rate. In every area teams work hard at research and development. It is impossible to keep pace with the rapid changes in technology. It is so sad that the most unchanging institution on earth seems to be the church. All positive creativity comes from God and yet the church often projects an image of God that is static. The world should be understanding the Lord's creativity by watching the pace of change and development in his representatives – the church. Of course, the basic Christian truths and doctrines are everlasting and unchangeable, but we desperately need to do some creative thinking to develop our church methods and strategies. Our church services and forms of communication could do with a completely imaginative overhaul. We urgently need to do some brainstorming to improve our evangelistic approaches and to become far more innovative in our ways of serving society. Everything we are doing, we can do better, but the best has yet to be invented.

1) Market research

It is often extremely helpful to talk to the general public about what we are doing. Getting feedback, especially from the non-Christians, gives us a pretty clear picture of what is working and what is not. We need to gain an understanding of where people are coming from in the community. Why, up to now, have they not been involved in churchgoing? Communication is essential if we are going to meet the needs of society in a relevant way. Are we scratching where the people are itching? When we have planted a new church, we have often taken to the streets with a survey which asked basic questions like: 'What time would best suit you for a church service?' 'What would make you want to go to church?' 'What do you think we should include in our services?' 'What needs are you aware of in the community which the church could help to meet?'

2) Communications evening

To help us facilitate these last two points, in our church we have what we call a 'communications evening' every few weeks to hear suggestions from church members as to how we can be more effective. Our evangelistic objectives need to come from the grass roots of the church so that the members will then be motivated to work towards these agreed goals by implementing their own suggestions. We have often asked questions like: 'What sort of event would you be prepared to invite your neighbours or work colleagues to?' 'Are there evangelistic tools which could make personal evangelism easier?' 'Are there skills and talents in the church which could be better used in evangelism?' Everyone should be involved in this creative-thinking process to increase the church's motivation in winning the world.

3) Friendship evangelism

Sometimes a distinction is drawn between friendship evangelism and other conventional forms of outreach. Actually, all evangelism should be friendship evangelism in the sense that, whatever the contact point, relationship is the aim. I hope that converts who were originally contacted and befriended in an open-air meeting, would answer a questionnaire about their conversion by saying that they became a Christian as a result of friendship evangelism.

We all deserve friendship because this is how we were created to function. We are social beings. The popularity of TV soaps hangs on this. Unfortunately, they provide relationship without responsibility and so they become an attractive but unreal solution. In the real world, relationships are two-way. We rely on others for support and at the same time we are ready to help them. We live, however, in an increasingly fragmented society and it is all too easy to slip through the net. One day as I was doing door-to-door evangelism in London, I found a man who had not spoken to anyone for eighteen months. His firm had gone bankrupt, leaving him without a job. His self-esteem had plummeted and he had gradually ceased to have any real communication with others. I took him to church where he was welcomed into a loving community and where he felt instantly valued. His life was wonderfully transformed.

4) Clubs, societies, sports, courses

Give yourself a break and do something completely different! I have often advocated that Christians should make time for some non-church activity in their lives. They could join a squash club, for example, or the amateur dramatic society, or even the local evening class on bricklaying. In any town, the options are many and varied. It could expand our experience as well as improve our waistline, while at the same time giving us genuine contact with the unconverted world. It is so easy to get totally absorbed in church affairs, to be so busy that we pass the world by, like the priest and the Levite who passed by that poor man in the parable of the Good Samaritan.

I think that if we are too busy with church to meet non-Christians on their own ground, then we are simply too busy. If anything has to go, it should be the church activity which is curtailed, not the evangelism. For example, if we spend five hours a week in church-based activity, and most of us in fact spend a lot more, then it might be a useful experiment to halve that time and to spend a couple of hours nurturing relationships with a neighbour or two. It is of course an even better option to find the two and a half hours from alternative priorities in our lives.

Spending three hours with someone playing a round a golf gives plenty of time to talk. I have shared my faith on the golf course with all kinds of people, from managing directors of international conglomerates to the local publican. I enjoy their quips about divine intervention when I play a good or a bad shot. (Mostly bad I hasten to add!) I remember a fireman kneeling on a green with his hands together in an attitude of prayer saying, 'Lord, if this goes in, I will become a Christian.' It didn't!?! There is no better test of whether you have acquired the Christian graces than when you are losing to a non-Christian on the sports field. I am sure that non-Christians learn far more about our character when we lose than when we win.

5) Action cards

Prayer cards have always been an established part of missions. They encourage church members to pray for their unconverted friends. 'Action cards' develop this idea one step further by encouraging prayer for boldness actually to evangelise rather than just passively to pray for the unconverted. The action card encourages people to make a commitment to certain actions and then to pray that the Lord would open doors and create opportunities for these things to happen.

As you can see from the card example on the next page, sometimes these things are as simple as having a conversation with a non-Christian, not necessarily a gospel-orientated one, or giving a person a leaflet about the church. These are simple things, but they are often not done. The card provides the encouragement and the focal point to accomplish the task of evangelism. Through it we are asking the Lord, 'Help me to do what I need to do to win the lost.'

The 418 Prayer Project

Action Card No. 1	4	3	2	1	Names
1) Fill in names of 4 contacts 2) Pray for each of them 3) Pray that you can do each of the following 4) Tick the boxes when done					
1. Have conversation with non-Christian					Tick Boxes
2. Fill out information sheet					
3. Get more information through further contact					
4. Invite or be invited for coffee etc					
5. Share your testimony with them					
6. Serve them practically in some way					
7. Tell them about the Gospel Choir evening					
8. Give/sell them a ticket					
9. Ask them to get someone else to come					
10. Bring them along					

United Voices Gospel Choir

6) Networking relationships

It is not a bad idea, having invited someone to an event, to go one step further and to ask the person to bring another friend with them. Often they will feel more at home if they bring another non-Christian friend as moral support. Networking the circle of relationships of our converts is an excellent field to work, especially as they are, hopefully, already seeing the testimony of a changing life.

7) Being a good neighbour

You may have seen a TV programme called *Neighbours from Hell*. We are the exact opposite – 'Neighbours from heaven'. Our neighbours are worth investing in. There have been times when I have purposely popped round to borrow something from my neighbours, a ladder or a tool, because I want them to feel perfectly free to borrow from me. One of my neighbours died last year. We had shared many hours chatting over our lives and experiences. He would weep as I told him about God. He never came to church but I would say we often 'churched it' over the garden fence together. He regularly borrowed from me one of my most precious possessions – time. It was, however, time well spent.

Our neighbours see far more in us than we could imagine. We had a man in our church who was converted in a remarkable way. The major contributing influence to his conversion was just watching one of his neighbours, who happened to be a member of our church, when he got into his car to go to work in the mornings. He then watched him again at the end of the day getting out of his car and going into his house. He observed him for days, until eventually he went up to the neighbour and asked him why he was as he was. The Christian response which he received to that question brought an invitation to a longer discussion over a cup of coffee, during which he was led to Christ. So – 'Beware, your neighbours are watching you!'

8) Other church members knock on your neighbours' doors

There is no doubt that our neighbours do see something of

the kingdom of God in us even if only dimly. It is worth therefore capitalising on this. We have sometimes concentrated our door-to-door evangelism around the homes of church members, using them as a visual aid to discuss the Christian faith. Sometimes it is easier for others to evangelise your neighbours than it is for you.

9) Initiating neighbourly schemes

We have also been involved in helping neighbours to be more neighbourly. We have encouraged people to look after the interests of their neighbours' homes by starting up, for example, Neighbourhood Watch schemes. We have helped to initiate Tenants' Associations to encourage people to work together in rented accommodation in order to get their landlords and housing associations to fulfil their responsibilities. We have tried to kick start some self-help schemes, where we have offered to clean up lifts and corridors, which had been used both as a toilet and as a tip. The theory was that local residents would then take responsibility for keeping it clean.

10) Fringe contacts

There are so many people on the edges of church who don't ever quite get involved. There are those, for example, who come occasionally, perhaps at Christmas and Easter. There are parents of children who attend Sunday School or youth groups. There are friends of church members who have attended a service once or twice. There are people who have been contacted through the social and evangelistic programmes. These people will all see themselves as being associated with the church. Some of them would even refer to it as their church. Part of our evangelistic strategy is to win these fringe contacts for Christ and to bring them into the community of the church.

11) Use fringe contacts to train evangelists

I was very impressed by a programme being run by a church in Southampton, where they would ask their fringe contacts to help in a training exercise for the budding evangelists in the church. The fringe contact would be asked if they would host a visit from an evangelist-in-training. All they had to do was to act the 'typical non-Christian'. They had to let the evangelist present the gospel but to raise any objections and ask any questions they could think of in order to put them to the test. What would start as play acting would often become a real encounter. Often, these fringe contacts would be hearing the gospel for the first time. In that case, the exercise would become a real counselling to faith in Jesus.

12) Befriending schemes
It has been demonstrated statistically that if a person has seven or eight friends in a church then they will stay. So, we need to put all our energy into encouraging our members to relate to these fringe contacts. Like fishermen, we need to catch our contacts and to land them safely into the boat. Using systems like **Visitors Books** and **Welcome cards** (with slips to fill in) for getting the names and addresses of those who casually drop into the church is essential. The drop-ins can so easily become the drop-outs. We need to organise **befriending schemes, one-to-one projects, pastoral follow-up systems** to net people into the community of the church. Often, we shy away from the formal structured befriending schemes because we think that they are too artificial. We hope that it will all happen naturally. However, we cannot afford to leave things to chance, especially when dealing with the needy and socially deprived, who sometimes don't find it easy to strike up friendships or start conversations.

'Meet, greet and seat'
We need teams of welcomers who can meet, greet and seat each newcomer. Each stranger will struggle enormously when they first come into the environment of the church. Someone needs to show them the ropes, where to sit, where the toilets are. They need to know what is likely to happen in the service, who is who, how long the meeting is likely to last. (Well – be careful, don't put them off!) They need someone to talk to in order to take away the embarrassing vacuum of not knowing anybody.

13) Evangelism events

The church can encourage friendships by providing social events. Using church property as a venue where people can meet is a way of providing a useful service for society. Having the church at the centre of what goes on in the community is extremely valuable. It provides a trustworthy, protected environment, in which non-Christians can relax and enjoy themselves. The events listed below make evangelism good fun both for the members of the church as well as for those from the local community. Arranging evangelistic events as often as once a month keeps friendship evangelism on the church's agenda. Hopefully, the following twenty-three suggestions will provide enough ideas to furnish an evangelistic event for each month of the year.

14) Social events

1. Barbecues
2. Barn Dances/Line Dancing
3. Quiz Evenings
4. Family Fun Nights
5. Cabaret Meals
6. Sports Bonanza, e.g. It's a Knockout competitions
7. Athletics Competitions – Amateur Football League, Football in the Park
8. Aerobics/Keep Fit/Slimming classes

15) Day trips

9. London by Night
10. River trips
11. Coach to the coast
12. Picnics
13. Country ramble

16) Calendar celebrations

14. Valentine Souperdine
15. Pancake Parties
16. Anniversary Celebration – Town/Church/Event/ Individual
17. Easter Feaster

18. Bank Holiday Beano
19. Summer Festival
20. Harvest Hoe Down
21. Michaelmas Munch
22. Bonfire Banquet
23. Christmas Capers

17) London by Night

There is not enough space to comment on each of these listed above, and many are self-explanatory, but I can't resist remarking on two or three. We have really enjoyed the times when we have run a 'London by Night' trip. We were amazed to find out how many people living in London had never seen the City's tourist sights, which other people travel round the world to see. Hiring a bus to spend three hours looking at the beauty of London by night is spectacular. We have sold tickets from door to door and have sold out every time. It is excellent to spend an evening on a bus getting to know people and it is quite a challenge to communicate as much of the gospel as possible through the history of London in the course of the live commentary.

18) Canal trip

Hiring a canal boat for a six-hour round trip makes a wonderful summer's day outing. We pitch the price at a level so that even poor families can enjoy an entertaining day out. The money we take on selling tickets is usually given back to them in the form of a good buffet lunch on the day. We have from time to time done this on a Sunday and held a full church service on the boat. We have also arranged trips on the River Thames, which is a dramatic way to see London. Everybody enjoys a drink from the bar (orange juice, of course). Then, when we are furthest from home, we turn the boat round, close the bar and preach at them all the way home. It's great. You have a captive audience and the only way they can get away is by being baptised!

19) Barn dances

I've got two left feet, so if I can do this then anyone can. Actually barn dances are great fun. There is nothing like making a complete fool of yourself to get others relaxed. Sometimes we have sold so many tickets for these events that we have had to ask people to go and sit down in order to make a little room on the dance floor for other people to dance. Again, this provides an excellent opportunity to explain, at some stage in the evening, why we as Christians have really got something to dance about.

20) Process evangelism e.g. Alpha groups

Process evangelism encourages non-Christians to sign up for a course which, over a few weeks, will go through a series of subjects on the basics of the Christian faith. Alpha groups have had an astounding success. Everybody has heard of them and most people have now done one. We have run a similar course entitled 'Deeper Life'. In London, Ichthus use something called 'Startrite'. The evening class approach has a particular appeal and I am sure that it contains the germ of many creative ideas which have yet to be developed. The advantages of a course, as opposed to a 'one off' evangelistic event are firstly, the depth of relationships developed week by week; secondly, the huge amount of material sown into a person's life throughout the course; and lastly, the more informal, relaxed atmosphere, perhaps over a meal, which sometimes cannot be created in the church environment.

21) Home evangelism
It is not a bad idea for every church member to work towards planting a church in their own home. Failing that, they should at least think about how their house can be used for God's kingdom in some way or other. Perhaps they could run an open-door policy so that people living around them would feel free to drop in at any time for help or just a chat. Possibly they could use the concept of an extended family by helping children through fostering or adoption. Sometimes it is enough just to practise good old hospitality.

22) Spiritual house cleaning
From time to time we have got into what we call *'spiritual house cleaning'*. One day, a lady, not yet a Christian, asked us to come and exorcise her house. She and her family were terrified of the spiritual atmosphere in their home. Everyone had nightmares and, amongst other things, the curtains in the living room would often appear to be on fire. We took a team into the house and we worshipped and prayed in every room (yes – including the loo!) and then we prayed over the family, laying hands on each of them. This made such a dramatic difference that they then shared what had happened with the rest of the street. Over the next few days, other families asked us to pray around their homes too. It was great to be able to leave peace and blessing in those homes.

Recently we were asked if we could pray around the home of a lady who had just come out of a Buddhist cult. She phoned me a couple of days after we had exorcised her home. She was so excited that she laughed throughout the conversation. 'I can't believe it,' she said. 'I don't know how you do it. How can you change air?' She went on to explain that the whole atmosphere in her home had changed. The house was now filled with light.

23) Homegroup discussions

There are so many valuable tools such as **videos** and **tapes** to use as discussion starters. We have found that a discussion on a book is an excellent basis for dialogue. Giving a good evangelistic book to everyone in the street, with perhaps a note of how it has helped you written on the fly leaf, is an easy way to let your neighbours know where you stand. Inviting them to an evening where you get together to discuss the issues raised, allows you to develop the contact one step further. This has led to in-depth discussions with some of my neighbours whom I had never met before.

24) Talks on topical subjects

Having an invited speaker is, for many, less confrontational than a discussion. The topics need not necessarily be along spiritual lines. We have invited the local police to come and talk about home security, or a nutritionist to talk about a balanced diet. We have held evenings on 'Potty Training', even 'Beating the Kids'! However, we have also had talks on: 'Coping with Crisis', 'Understanding Suffering', and 'The Christian Response to War'.

25) Grill a Christian

How about advertising a barbecue where you can roast a Christian? This appeals to a lot of non-Christians. We used to do this in the bars at universities and colleges. We called these sessions 'Shoot the Christian', where we would give people thirty minutes to seek to destroy our faith. We would incite them, 'Fire your objections. Pull the rug out from under our beliefs.' They seem to enjoy attempting this and there is nothing quite like being put on the spot to make us clarify the reasoning behind our faith. It is also a great opportunity to make non-Christians think through on certain issues, which often are raised without being deliberated on, and to begin to understand life from a Christian perspective.

26) Home-based parties

There are many firms which have adopted the Tupperware approach to selling through parties in people's homes. Many things are now sold this way including children's clothes, make-up, Colour me Beautiful etc. These and a number of more Christian themes are excellent for gathering together friends and neighbours. Matthew's idea of a 'Repentance Party' (Mt 9:10) let all his contacts know where he stood right from the start. We have also run Third World craft evenings to let our neighbours know what Christians are doing to relieve suffering in poorer countries. A national sports match is another good opportunity to get a gang round to your house. You could even invite people round to watch a video or to see a demonstration of a new skill or hobby. Any excuse for a party! Don't forget your birthday and anniversaries.

Letter evangelism

27) Personal letters

Using pen and paper can make the daunting task of evangelism extremely easy. Even the Apostle Paul found that it was easier to say something in writing. He quotes others as saying of him, 'His letters are weighty and forceful, but in person he is unimpressive and his speaking amounts to nothing' (2 Cor 10:10). Have you ever felt that this is true of you? You can certainly assemble your thoughts on a page far more coherently than in conversation. In speech, on the spur of the moment, your mind can go blank and you may find yourself stammering in trying to find the right words. Because writing is premeditated, it is much simpler. Anyone can communicate this way.

I once worked with a Christian in France who was painfully shy. He was not confident when talking to people, but he got into the habit of carrying a notebook and pen around with him. Whenever he felt that the Lord wanted to convey something, he would write it down. He was constantly leaving notes, often with prophetic messages, under car windscreen wipers and through open car windows. His whole life was geared to hearing from heaven and communicating Christ to people. This should encourage us all to look for ways of communicating with paper to non-Christians. You can be far bolder in correspondence than in a face-to-face situation.

Letters are a very natural means of communicating gospel truths with close friends and members of your family with whom it is often difficult to raise spiritual matters in the course of everyday conversation.

28) Follow-up letters

Letters are also particularly effective in following up contacts made, for example, during door-to-door evangelism. Often when I have had an inconclusive or negative conversation with someone, I go home and begin to wish I had said things which I didn't think of at the time. Sometimes, in a case like that, I will write a letter. The fact that you care enough to put pen to paper is a powerful witness in itself. I recently had a long conversation with a lady and when I got home I felt the need to write to her just underlining the main points of my argument so that she could see clearly what I had been trying to say.

Once I knocked on a lady's door and she welcomed me

straight into her home. On her mantelpiece, taking pride of place, were six letters from a young American student who had spent some time in London on an evangelism training course, and who had come into contact with her. In her letters, the student had explained the gospel and because she had prepared the ground, the lady was ready to give her life to Christ there and then.

On another occasion, a lady slammed the door in my face almost before I had had a chance to speak. However, she looked so sad that I felt I had to write to her to tell her how sorry I was that I hadn't been able to tell her how much the Lord cared for her. She replied, answering my letter point by point. This was the start of a correspondence which lasted for some time, but at the end of every letter she asked me not to call at her house. I respected her wish and so I don't know whether she eventually gave her life to Jesus or not. I do know, though, that she got to understand the message of the gospel. The great thing about letters is that you are communicating on a very intimate level with people. Letters allow you to sow seeds deep into people's hearts. Of course, the Apostle Paul used this strategy a great deal. In fact, half the New Testament consists of his follow-up letters.

29) Circular letters

Another idea is to construct a letter, most of which can be printed, but to address and sign it personally to each family in the community. In this way, you can make a personalised letter or a prophetic statement to the whole neighbourhood. It involves going down to your local library or town hall and getting a copy of the electoral register. We have spent some fun evenings signing and addressing a few thousand envelopes and then delivering them by hand. One advantage is that it enables you to pray for everybody by name in your part of town. This sort of letter has produced the best response we have ever had to any publicity exercise.

30) Circular letters for closed countries

Letters can also be used to impact a society which is closed to any Christian witness, some Muslim countries, for example. Some years ago, we developed a concern for a certain country where there was no known church or Christian work. We had letters translated into the local language and sent them out using their national telephone directories as our source of names and addresses. Eventually, we started to reap the harvest of this long-distance sowing of the word. This has led to an ongoing programme of church planting in this country. Thousands of letters were sent to blitz this closed country from a distance.

31) Letters *from* non-Christians

From time to time we have asked everyone in the church to obtain a letter from a non-Christian, perhaps a neighbour or a work colleague, explaining why they don't go to church. This has proved to be a surprisingly successful exercise. We suggest that the church members should engage the sympathy of the non-Christian by saying something like: 'I am really embarrassed about this, I need your help . . . Sorry to have to ask you, but could you get me out of this hole?' They will take pity on you. It seldom fails. We have had instances where people have sat down to write the letter and then been unable to think of any decent reason for not going to church; so they turned up the following Sunday. Others put reasons which show that they have completely the wrong concept of what church is like. This gives an excellent opportunity to give a good positive church testimony. I had one man who said to me, 'Yes, I'll do that for you, but I think my neighbour upstairs ought to do this too, because she used to go to church but she doesn't now.' I asked if he wouldn't mind asking her to do this for me. It is great to get non-Christians doing your evangelism for you. Their letters resulted in a longstanding friendship, with many, many opportunities to share the Lord with them.

Open-air evangelism

32) Church on the street

Open-air meetings are a way of turning the church inside out in order to let non-Christians catch a glimpse of what we are like. Sometimes this overcomes non-Christians' erroneous, preconceived ideas about the church. Even just the visual aid of a group of happy people can be a powerful witness. We would sometimes take a company of church members through the depressing housing estates, stopping at various points to sing one or two 'happy clappy' choruses. Sometimes we would maybe dance a bit. The local residents, many of whom live in misery and isolation, get a view of churchgoers who are happy. They can also see genuine community in the relationships. This often changes attitudes. Even if they don't come along to church, at least they now have the idea that Christianity is quite a good thing!

We have seen several startling instances of the effect that such a witness could have. One day, a lady was having a row with her sister when she suddenly heard us singing. She looked down on us from her high-rise flat, stopped arguing with her sister and said, 'If those are Christians down there, I am going to become one.' She did! If you believe that the harvest is ripe, your presence on the estates allows people who are open to the Lord to surface

Marching around the streets with banners and singing is 'good PR' for the church. If people are seeking God, they are much more likely to go to a church whose name they know, or with which they have had contact already, even as a distant observer. I believe we must attract people, making it easier for them to contact us. (See 'Praise Marches' and 'Carnival Processions' later.)

One of our church plants had previously had a Boys' Brigade. When we moved in, we found all the brigade's equipment, including four snare drums and a big bass drum. We used these when we marched around the streets of Peckham. We would parade up and down Peckham High Street, carrying banners and banging the drums in simple rhythms. People would come out of the shops and stand six deep on the pavement to watch us pass. We found that they actually appreciated us being there.

33) Street busking
The musician busking on the street is often quite appealing.

It is only the fact that street musicians ask for money which causes people to hurry past. So let's play on the streets without asking for money. Someone playing the saxophone next to a sign advertising your church is as good an advertisement as you could want. I have often wished that I could play the trumpet because the prophetic release of Jubilee through the blowing of the ram's horn seems symbolically such a good expression of the release of the kingdom. I don't actually play the trumpet but even so I have sometimes taken one out during our open airs and have managed to make a very loud rude noise with it. It certainly seems to attract attention even if, musically, it doesn't bless many people.

34) Hit and run

We have often gone into the estates with teams and made a lot of noise for a short time with our singing. We would wave our banners and speak for a couple of minutes through a loudspeaker and then move on. There are places in London where you can reach hundreds of whole families in this way in one blast. We knew that when we moved on, they would be talking about us afterwards.

Although we call this 'hit and run' evangelism, it has been extraordinarily effective. In the north of England, I helped with a mission where we were trying to evangelise 5,000 homes on one estate. There was no time for us to reach every home by visiting door to door. We therefore developed a strategy whereby eight people walked down the street singing, while four team members walked behind. If people came to their windows to watch or came out into their gardens, one of the team of four would speak to them.

We have had some remarkable successes. One lady came out into her garden and the pastor handed her a leaflet with the titles of the mission talks on it. Her eye fell on the previous evening's talk, 'Jesus heals from hurts'. 'I should have been there last night,' she said. She revealed that her son had been knocked down and killed on a pedestrian crossing two or three months earlier. Horrifically, the previous year, on the same date, her other son had been knocked down and severely injured on the same crossing. The church leader encouraged her to come to that evening's meeting. When she didn't turn up, he was distraught that he hadn't prayed with her or even offered her a lift to the meeting. What was worse, he couldn't remember her name or exactly where she lived. All the terraced streets in the area looked so similar. The following day, he drove up and down the streets looking for her home and eventually, in despair, he stopped his car, knocked on a door at random and explained as best he could who he was trying to find. The householder was surprised. 'This is not the house of the lady you are looking for,' she said, 'but as it happens, she is here at the moment.' The pastor was overjoyed and after a lengthy conversation, arranged to pick her up for that evening's meeting where she came forward for prayer during the closing appeal. She explained to the two ladies who counselled her that she had been led to believe, because of the coincidence of the timing of the two accidents, that her son had been killed as a judgment from God. She was hurting and grieving because she thought that her son must have gone to hell.

One of the counsellors suddenly had a vision of Jesus holding the little boy. As she was wondering how to put this into words of comfort for the mother, they realised that all three of them had had the same vision. The lady burst into tears, and as she wept she exclaimed that she had been healed, and not just from the emotional hurts of the past. A growth on the back of her hand began to shrink and disappear as her tears fell on it. She was wonderfully healed emotionally, spiritually and physically.

Stories like this vindicate the effort that we put into street evangelism. The chances of finding that lady through door-to-door evangelism were minimal. If we don't provide the opportunity for people such as her to surface, they could remain forever locked up in their hurts and misconceptions.

35) Prophetic demonstrations
Although I have never done it, I have often had the compulsion to chain myself to the railings in the middle of

one of our poorest estates for a couple of weeks. After a few days, people would start to question what this was all about. Everybody would obviously think I was crazy. Then I could explain that we too think that people are crazy to remain trapped and imprisoned by their vices and sins.

All that crosses you out

One year, at a Sunderland University mission, a colleague stood at the entrance to the refectory with a huge cross, constantly repeating the one sentence: 'All that ties you down, breaks your back and crosses you out, Jesus took it all in himself.' 'All that ties you down, breaks your back and crosses you out, Jesus took it all in himself.' That repeated message still sticks in my mind today and I wonder in how many non-Christian minds it still echoes. When we went into the refectory, it seemed to be the topic of conversation at every table.

One Easter, at the Peckham market, we placed people at strategic points among the stalls just standing in silence pointing towards a huge cross which was visible from all over the market. Sometimes it doesn't take much to provoke people into thinking about spiritual truth.

36) Pictures/collages

Picture language is so powerful that it is worth taking pictures out onto the High Street. Simple, pre-drawn illustrations have a far more immediate impact than a person just standing preaching. If you are not good at drawing, a collage of magazine cuttings can do just as well. I have produced collages of various foods, famous people or material riches and even cosmetics. The spiritual application of these is fairly obvious. I would place little captions under each collage, for example: 'Look good on the inside' on a page portraying soaps, make-up and cosmetics. Or 'Be Somebody' pasted on the top of a page of famous people, with the caption 'You Are Somebody' along the bottom.

Message in a bucket

Street evangelism need not be complicated or elaborate.

Many church groups think that you have to do drama sketches and have slick preaching, but this is not essential. Have you ever tried putting a bucket down on the street with a Bible verse written inside it, and then standing looking into it? It is human nature to be curious and people will come along and stand next to you to peer into your bucket and read the verse. How you then initiate the conversation is up to you but everyone who passes by receives the message.

37) Ladder writing

One of my favourite open-air preaches is to use the Open Campaigners' Ladder Writing. This is a way of producing words quickly and easily out of a series of painted ladders. With single strokes of the brush, letters and words are formed before your eyes. I have often used pop song titles from the top 40 singles in the charts. It is amazing how many of these have titles which can be used to convey the gospel message. I offer a free pop music tape to the person who can guess the most singles titles on my sketchboard. This has always proved a crowd puller. I have used titles like: 'Real Life', 'I Still Believe', 'Turn Around', 'Better Best Forgotten', 'Love on Love', 'Is Nothing Sacred?'. Last Easter one of the hit singles was even called 'Can't Nobody Hold Me Down'. There are books produced by Open Air Campaigners explaining the techniques and giving suggestions for sermons.

38) Puppets

Puppets and ventriloquist's dummies are excellent in the open air. Adults as well as children find them entertaining. I have seen a large crowd gather just to watch stringed puppets dancing to simple canned music. It is also amazing what you can get away with when you are speaking through a puppet. You can be very direct with passers-by who take it in good part and with good humour, rather than taking offence. Somehow, when you use a puppet, your message will be more acceptable than it would be through straight preaching.

39) Human statues

I have been impressed by this new craze for human statues as a modern way of collecting money on the street. All the clothes and skin are sprayed with paint. They then strike a statuesque pose, remaining absolutely still for a number of minutes. When a tourist donates a coin, the figure moves to take up another pose. People will often keep feeding coins into the receptacle to make the statue move. The same principle, for example, could operate each time someone took an evangelistic leaflet.

40) Face painting

Alongside some of our open-air presentations, we have offered to paint the faces of children. Because this takes a few minutes to complete, the parents are usually around for some time to listen to what we are seeking to communicate. There are books which illustrate easy to copy face-painting designs and the paints are readily available.

41) Sketching faces

I always stop to watch street artists at work when they sketch people's faces. I have often thought that it would be a really good opportunity for Christian artists. Perhaps it would even be possible to use computer generated images which could then, be given to the customer free of charge with the slogan 'Made in the image of God'.

42) Open air videos and films

We have shown films in the street on a full screen as a Christmas Special. We chose a quiet cul-de-sac where we could set everything up without causing disruption to traffic and then knocked on all the doors of the surrounding houses and invited people to come and watch the showing of a short Christmas film.

Banners

43) Banners

Banners are one of the most effective ways of communicating an immediately understood message to everybody passing by. You can use the name of your church or find some pithy catchphrase which conveys your message. There are various books available to show how to make banners, but personally I think that there is nothing quite as easy or effective as an ordinary bed sheet sprayed with car paint. We have produced a series of banners by getting a personal computer to print off large letters (about point size 600, printed in outline to save ink). These are cut round and then glued with spray mount to a large white sheet – a full double bed size sheet is excellent. Then, using colours of your choice, spray over the letters and the surrounding areas. Once the paint is dry, you can remove the paper letters. This leaves behind white letters on a multi- or single-coloured background. This only takes a few minutes to produce and nevertheless looks quite professional. Mounting this sheet on a wooden frame holds it taut and means that it can be carried easily or set up on the High Street.

Producing banners from an overhead projector

Pictures and graphics can be produced on a banner by photocopying the desired image onto an overhead projector transparency, then projected onto the sheet and drawn or painted around.

Fast sign shops

In an age of computerised Fast Sign shops there is really no excuse for the church not to have excellent advertising hoardings, boards and banners. Most businesses see this as an absolute priority and we could learn much from their zeal in these areas. It is worth investing money in these realms of public advertising. You will find details of the shops in the Yellow Pages.

44) Display boards

Positioning display boards in a public place, the High Street for example, with photographs and explanations, gives a clear insight into our work. Photographs of church meetings show an outsider what he might expect to see if he came to a service. Pictures of people, along with their healing testimonies or personal stories of change, are always interesting.

We have used display boards to write up and display all the words of knowledge the Lord has given to us for people in the community. The board has contained a whole list of ailments, conditions and even people's names. A caption reads 'If your name or condition appears on this board, come and see us as we have a special message for you . . . from God'.

45) Drama

Street drama is as good a way as any of attracting attention and provoking thought for spectators. It is also good to mobilise the more dramatic among our church members and the creativity of our script writers. There are some excellent published Christian plays and sketches available for when our imagination runs dry. We will look at the use of sweatshirts etc. later, but for full effect we encourage the drama team to wear outfits which distinguish them from the rest of the crowds on the street.

46) Dance

Dance on the street is such an excellent expression of the joy and celebration of the Christian life. The kind of dance routines made famous by 'all girl' and 'all boy' bands looks great on the street (territory definitely for those younger than me). The harmony of movement and co-ordination, the life and vitality, all express spiritual values, as well as communicating powerfully through the lyrics of the backing songs.

47) Interviews

When television programmes such as *Songs of Praise* included personal testimonies, their viewing figures increased dramatically. There is a clear interest in real-life stories. Using our histories to demonstrate genuine life change is what many in the world need to hear. We have often set up interviews on the street to draw out the ways in which conversion makes a difference to an individual. Dialogue in front of a microphone is far more attractive to listen to than a straight testimony.

We have also interviewed non-Christians on the street in front of a video camera, asking their opinions on a range of issues. It is provoking just to ask the questions in some situations. This always gathers a crowd and gives the opportunity for people to listen in to the statements and explanations on camera. We have used some of the edited results of these interviews in evangelistic meetings. We have even run them as background viewing in bars at universities.

Posters

48) Poster hoardings

From time to time there have been some excellent national poster campaigns run by various sections of the church for mission outreach. The JIM Campaign was a good example from the past. There are also very good posters made available through CPO and others, for celebrating calendar events such as Easter or Christmas. But it would be good to see more poster campaigns run by local churches to communicate into the community. Hoardings are available for hire at stations and on trains. There are various advertising options on buses. These are fairly cheap per advertisement, although it usually requires a minimum number of ads. The bulkhead at the front of a London bus is even illuminated and couldn't be positioned better for commuters to see. Prices for these are now to be applied for through the various companies running them.

49) Lampposts
We have in the past gained permission from the local authority to place posters on the lampposts throughout our area. This amounted to hundreds of A2-size posters mounted back to back on hardboard and tied to strategic lampposts. It is not a bad idea to invest in AA or local authority road signs to point the way to your church. This gives more public credibility and is relatively inexpensive.

50) Private windows
Posters in the windows of church members' homes are good free advertising and they let all our neighbours know about our faith and our church. I remember one mission we ran in a South East London estate where I knocked on non-church members' doors and asked if I could stick a poster in their windows. I was surprised how many people let me do this. We had posters in homes all over the area. The general feeling was that everybody was involved with our church. This made people feel they were missing out on something, so they all came along. Especially those advertising our campaign in their windows came along to see what it was that they were advertising.

51) Church notice boards
The streetside church notice boards are another opportunity for communication. There have been some creative thinkers at work in some areas for this. Posters with slogans like 'Fight Truth Decay', or 'Carpenter Looks for Joiners', or 'Here For Good', are clever, thought-provoking and attractive.

52) Car stickers

We could take more advantage of the travelling advertising space afforded by our car windows. It is relatively inexpensive to have proper car stickers printed with maybe the logo of the church. Perhaps we should produce 'sign writing' for our cars, as they do for commercial vehicles. Everyone could carry a slogan, or the church name, on the side of their cars. This would give excellent advertising exposure for the church throughout the town, all the time.

Car windscreen visors

I used to have the words JESUS CHRIST IS LORD in large letters across the visor of my car windscreen. It was once trendy to put the driver's name and/or his girlfriend's emblazoned across car windscreens, so I decided to use this same idea evangelistically. I cut letters (about 8 cms tall) out of white plastic and mounted them on a dark green plastic backing strip. This adheres nicely when pressed on to glass. I used to get some interesting responses to this. On one occasion I was driving with Sallie through the City of London. As I drew up to a set of traffic lights I could see two policemen nudging each other and pointing at me from the opposite pavement. Before the lights had changed they had moved to the central reservation and, as I began to move away, they both stepped out into the road holding a hand up for me to stop. They then asked me to get my car off the road onto the pavement – not easy to do on a central London street. One policeman went to my wife's door and the other came to mine. As I wound down the window he asked, 'Is this your vehicle, sir?' When I admitted that it was, he then asked, 'And did you put this on your windscreen?' As I rather nervously said, 'Yes,' he went on to say, 'Well that's interesting because we are both Christians and thought we ought to say hello.' What a relief!

Leaflets

53) Handbills/leaflets/pamphlets
Producing A5 handbills to pop through letter boxes is a good way of keeping the church in people's minds. At a commercial price of about £45 for 2,000 handbills we could afford to distribute to every home in the area around the church at least once a month. The response to this is not sensational, some have suggested as low as 0.17 per cent. However, adding this to all the other forms of evangelism being done through the church, leafletting definitely adds something to the public profile. But it is not very effective as a strategy on its own.

54) Leaflets in shop windows
It is rather fun to walk into all the local shops with a reel of Sellotape and ask if you can stick a handbill in their window. Most shopkeepers are usually very community-minded, so if you ask permission to put an advertisement up for a couple of weeks just to inform the public of what is going on in the community, it is amazing how many will let you do this. Even if there is a company policy of 'no advertising', they don't like saying 'No' to your face. So, presume upon their kindness. If you leave it for them to display, they would probably conveniently forget, but if you offer to do it for them, the job gets done and you can choose where to put it. I usually stick it at head height on the door where everybody can read it as they come in.

55) Leaflets on counters and notice boards

There are a number of places where a pile of leaflets can be left for members of the public to take one. Here are a few suggestions: information centres, take away food outlets, sports centres, doctors' surgeries, cafés, Citizens' Advice Bureaux, and so on. It is also worth spending some time looking at what opportunities are available for handbills to be exhibited on notice boards, for example in libraries, hospitals, community centres, Local Government Offices (such as the Housing Department), colleges etc. I have had a Housing Department officer refuse me on one occasion on the grounds that it was unfair to other local churches. So I suggested that I produce a leaflet advertising all the local churches and their service times. He agreed to that and a poster saying 'Go to a local church this Sunday' was displayed from then on.

56) Cartoon stories

Producing leaflets is good for mobilising other areas of gifting in the church and harnessing them to the evangelism effort. Those with graphics skills, writing ability, artistic talents or just plain creative thinking can all contribute. Because reading is not the average person's most popular pastime we have tried to find some more novel ways of getting the message across. **Cartoons** and **drawings** are better for grabbing the public's attention. (Remember what we said earlier in the book about picture language?)

57) Crosswords, quizzes and 3D images

Crosswords, quizzes and 3D images are all good for getting the brain working. The more a person puzzles over finding answers, the deeper the message seems to settle. I am sure that is why Jesus used questions so much in his ministry. We have enjoyed the responses of passers-by on the street to our 3D image leaflets. They always keep them because they want to puzzle over the picture until they can see it. As we distribute them there are often people leaning against lampposts along the High Street struggling to focus on the message. We did one which said in the image, 'Jesus Saves'.

We had excited non-Christians coming back to us to affirm, 'I can understand it – Jesus Saves'.

58) Late news

Most newspapers have a **late news** section, an empty space often on the front page, which is run back through the printing machine when news comes to light after the first print run. I have copied this kind of section on to an A5 leaflet and put in my own late news, e.g. 'Prisoners Escaped in Peckham'. The article warned people to be on their guard because they might come across one of these escaped prisoners. The last paragraph described the kinds of prisons people had escaped from, such as loneliness, depression, alcoholism and fear. The morning we gave those leaflets out at the railway station, passengers came back out of the station to get a leaflet from us because everybody was talking about it on the platform.

59) Serial stories

Serial stories are a chance to sow a lot of material into people's minds during the course of several weekly editions of a leaflet. These can be given out at the stations, for example. Putting a leaflet into the hands of someone about to board a train gives them something to read, instead of the newspaper of the person sitting opposite. We have done this from 6.00 am–8.00 am outside our local railway station. The first one of a series has to be forced into people's hands, but the next week they come and ask you for the next part. The clever technique is to always leave the story at a 'cliff hanger' so that they are eager to see how the saga continues.

Literature Tables

60) Literature/book table on the High Street

It is so easy to set up a literature table somewhere prominent, and surprisingly effective. Recently, we wanted to use the *Jesus* video in our evangelism. We tried offering it as part of our door-to-door visiting programme but progress was very slow. Then we tried a 'free video offer' on a table in the High

Street. Within the first hour, several people came up and took videos, leaving us their names and addresses so that we could follow them up with an evangelistic questionnaire. Their response was much friendlier than the contacts we had had on the doors, because the choice and approach were in their hands. They were eager to discuss the video both then and on the questionnaire visit. All of them were affected in some way by it and some of these have found the Lord and been baptised since.

One Saturday in London we had sixty literature tables on high streets all over the South East. On that day, we didn't have sixty volunteers to man them. We just set them up with a note on them saying, 'Free Literature, please help yourself' and then went home to watch the football (I'm joking)! We went round to dismantle them at the end of the day. With so many people on each high street, everyone assumed that somebody nearby was looking after these stalls and so they didn't actually need to be manned all the time.

Not everyone can preach on the street or communicate on the doors, but a literature table is an exercise most can easily carry out. We have usually set out boards, back to back, with a thought-provoking message on them; these proclaim the message quietly and powerfully to the minds of every passer-by, while you just make yourself available to talk to those who want to chat.

61) Charity stalls

There are various charity galas in our town throughout the year and we usually try to be involved in them. This includes carnival days in the summer, a Victorian evening at the switching on of the Christmas lights, three Charity Market Days in the Hemel Market, and various Community Centre charity events. We mobilise our members to make jams, cakes and other home-made articles, and we also sell Christian books. It gives us an opportunity to explain what we do as a charity in the community. We don't make much money at these but we sure meet a lot of people! In fact, even the money we do make is sent to the Third World.

Giving to Bless

62) Sweets/balloons/teas/coffees

Whenever we are in the open air we usually like to give something away. In Hemel Hempstead we have to book the 'Charity Pitch' (a position reserved for charities on the pedestrian precinct, right next to the banks – now that's town planning for you). Most Saturdays some charity is there rattling tins at passers-by. It is good to be there not collecting like all the rest, but giving to the public. Maybe it is just **sweets** or **balloons** for the children, or **teas** and **coffees** for the adults, but being given something seems to cheer people up and soften their hearts to our cause.

63) Small gifts

We used to give **handkerchiefs**, with the church's emblem on them, to the prostitutes in the red-light district of London to try and show them genuine love and concern. The real concern came, of course, from the accountants at the end of the year. Can you imagine the church financial report with a section on 'gifts to prostitutes'? It is worth it, however, when we have seen some of them saved.

We had a couple of our girls evangelising from door to door recently and they were not being received very well. So, on their own initiative they popped round to the shops and bought a bunch of **tulips**, and gave one to each person they spoke to. It is amazing how people's attitudes can change through something so simple. We have had people in the church offering **pizzas,** even **glasses of wine** from door to door (I dare you!) with the result that people let them in to bless and pray for their whole family.

Last year we were giving out a leaflet about the parable of the sower. The idea was prompted by Jesus' words: 'To him who has shall more be given.' We felt we needed to sow something into everyone's lives. We simply told and applied Jesus' parable, but we then decided to affix some **sunflower seeds** to each leaflet. We stuck four or five seeds to each handout with a strip of Sellotape. It didn't cost anything, except a little time and a lot of muscle cramp, but people received these as though we were giving them something very special.

64) Gift of a tape

A few years ago we produced an evangelistic tape. These we gift wrapped and gave out from door to door as a present for Christmas. We produced thousands of them, so we needed to mobilise people who had never gone door to door before to help distribute them all. It was thrilling to see their responses as they returned home. They were so excited because everybody had been so friendly, welcoming and happy to receive this gift. They concluded that evangelism was a great way to spend their evenings. An important battle was being won here!

The tape itself was a short ten minute per side recording entitled *Recent Releases*. We used the title because we were distributing the tape at the time when all the new releases of chart songs for Christmas were being released. It seemed to be a good play on words as it described the stories of those recently released by the Lord. On the first side it carried a magazine style commentary on our church life. Vox pops (various one-line statements taken from people coming out of church and their reactions), succinct testimonies of healing from terminal cancer, a brain tumour and the re-creation of an ovary (previously surgically removed) as well as a couple of short testimonies of lives dramatically changed by their conversions. One of them had been a drug pusher and big time criminal, whereas the other was an ordinary lady from one of the local estates. The other side of the tape had a ten-minute gospel message and explanation of how to become a Christian.

65) Giving through social action
Giving can be in any number of different forms of which giving financially is just one. Using our time, skills, energy, belongings, homes etc. are all to be included in this area of giving. We want to serve people as best as we can, with what we have and who we are. (There are a variety of ideas developed in the section on Social Action.)

Marches and Processions

66) Praise marches/carnival processions
By covering a car with balloons, setting up a couple of boards on the roof rack advertising the church, and equipped with a loud speaker, you can speak to the whole community around the church in perhaps forty-five minutes. The Apostle Paul never had technology like this at his disposal! When I first was going to do this in the town where I now live, members of the church told me I couldn't do it. I said, 'It's OK I've been doing this for years in London.' 'That might be so, but you can't do things like that here!' they replied. However, they helped me get the vehicle ready but, as I expected, they refused to come with me. Instead, they drove ahead of me, stopping now and then to stand on the pavement to gather the reactions of the public as I passed by. It wasn't long before they were jumping up and down with excitement giving me the thumbs up sign.

67) Float in the carnival

This summer we won a trophy as a first prize in the town carnival. We produced a 60-foot caterpillar, which rhythmically moved along propelled by nine pairs of legs. This was accompanied by highly-decorated butterflies to make the point about metamorphosis. We were making a simple statement that people can change and that we all have hidden potential in Jesus.

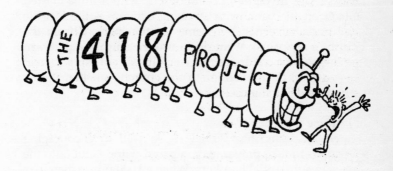

Last year we won second prize when we entered a lorry decorated as Noah's Ark. The theme for the carnival was 'Bygone Years'. Alongside the float we gave out an evangelistic leaflet which was a play on the theme 'It's so old it came out of the Ark'. This developed the line of thought in the age-old question, 'If God is a God of love why doesn't he stop all the trouble?' We were suggesting it was dangerous to ask God to do this because he did once!

Last December we also won first prize in the Christmas Carnival. We walked and danced to Graham Kendrick's 'Heaven invites you to a party'. We all dressed up, some as angels and shepherds in the Nativity story, and some as modern party-goers, banging drums, blowing whistles and waving streamers. We carried a great big festive banner sporting the logo of The 418 Project. As we were marching through the town centre we suddenly realised that we were the only organisation carrying a banner, which meant that to the thousands of observers the whole carnival looked like it belonged to our church. I think they were impressed!

One afternoon in London we ran our own church-based carnival. We had sixteen lorries decorated according to various themes, some had bands playing, while others were decorated with artistic displays. These processed through the streets of South East London making a lot of noise for Jesus. I was involved in building one with a three-masted galleon on the back, with smoking cannons – the lot! We wore impressive naval costumes of that period (from the local hire shop). We went on to use the ship as a platform and theme for a children's mission. This sort of thing is great fun and gives the impression to non-churchgoers that at least Christians enjoy themselves.

68) Praise marches
'March for Jesus' has served us so well in encouraging Christians to take prayer, worship and witness out onto the streets in substantial numbers. When 40,000 praise marchers descended on the centre of London you would have expected a little light from the kingdom to shine.

It was amusing to hear of a praise march in Wales where the police volunteered the information afterwards that there hadn't been a single crime reported during all the hours of the procession. There were only two possible conclusions to be drawn from this: one was that the light of the kingdom had, for those hours at least, driven away the darkness, or secondly it was the Christians who usually committed all the crime in that area and for that time they were otherwise engaged!

I don't intend to say anything on the organisation of such praise marches as there is already such good material available. My encouragement is that we need to do these marches more than once a year. We used to go around the estates in Southwark once a month and we saw some dramatic conversions as a result. One lady opened her window and threw a book at us. We thought she was persecuting us, so we were rejoicing and being, as Jesus said, exceedingly glad. But then she shouted down from her first floor flat: 'If you will sing number 47 in that book I will come to your church on Sunday.' I went over and picked the book out of the hedge. It was one of Her Majesty's Prison hymn books and she had stolen it from prison. Actually she had just been released from serving almost thirteen years as a sentence for torturing a fellow prostitute to death. Number 47 in the hymn book was 'I will enter his gates with thanksgiving in my heart' – she did! Not only did she come to church, she also later came to know Jesus in a powerful, life-transforming way. She was so wonderfully saved that she is today working full time in prison work. She is helping prisoners find both the Lord and a hope for their own personal transformation.

69) Silent march of witness

It seems an almost established part of Christendom to carry out a silent march of witness on Good Friday. I remember being involved in one such march in Sweden. It was very dramatic because the procession happened late in the evening, carrying lighted torches from the church down to the town square. We walked in silence. One member of the church was dressed as Jesus and carried a large cross. It became quite eerie. As we passed the pubs and clubs people came out and started hurling abuse at Jesus and spitting both at him and on the ground. It was suddenly like being back 2,000 years and actually watching the crowd rejecting Jesus. The celebration in the square afterwards was a little better received much to everyone's relief.

Services in Public Places

70) Church services in the park

We have been looking at ways in which we can bring the church into a sphere where it can be seen. Why not take church totally into the open? In my last church plant there were, fortunately, a few weeks in the year where the Community Centre was not available to us, due to dog shows and table tennis competitions etc. On these Sundays we took the whole church service into the local park. On some occasions in the past we have even set up a stage and made quite an event of it, with drama performances and user friendly presentations. What better way of allowing the public at large to understand what church is about?

71) Baptisms in the river

We have from time to time, temperatures allowing, baptised our converts in the sea, rivers, lakes and swimming pools. This seems to make the act of baptism a clear public declaration as in the days of John the Baptist and the early church. We baptised a lady two years ago who was converted from a life of prostitution and involvement with the occult. As she gave her testimony on the banks of the river, in the local park, she burnt her charms, tarot cards and the clothing she had worn as a prostitute in a metal bucket. She then went down into the water and buried her past in baptism. We then sprinkled the ashes of her past life on the water as she came up into resurrection life.

72) Funeral on the estate

I was asked on one occasion to carry out the funeral of a suicide victim, at the spot where he had fallen after jumping from a high-rise block of flats. The coffin was positioned where his body had lain. He was the local drug pusher and hated by the local community. He had jumped to his death just after slashing his wife's face a few times with the broken glass of a smashed bottle. It was, without doubt, the most difficult funeral I have ever taken. But it was an opportunity to make some public declarations to the community. On this man's behalf, we were able to apologise to those whom he had hurt, and on behalf of the community to express forgiveness towards this man for the evil he had brought into the area. A church was planted into this estate as a result.

73) Street parties

Exploiting national and local celebrations as an excuse to hold a party in the street is a fun way of getting your church known. Usually this is only possible if everyone in the street agrees to the road being closed off for the evening. On one occasion we knocked on all the doors in a particular street and everybody agreed to closing the road – except two people. There were about fifty households in total. Because these two refused, we were not allowed to close the street. It looked like we had to cancel, but then one of the families who had been positive about the street party got back to us and offered their back garden and their house instead. The bunting and pontoon lighting ran up and down the street leading into their front garden. The whole street turned out to this evangelistic party, except two!

Door to Door

74) Door to door

This is probably one of the most feared and hated forms of evangelism. Actually, I quite enjoy it. Of course I don't like rejection (I'm still learning to leap for joy) and I get even more discouraged when people are not at home. But on the

whole it is the best place to evangelise (it might seem a little obvious to say) because the non-Christian feels at home. I think it is important that the witnessee (there's a new one! i.e. the person we are witnessing to) feels totally comfortable. Their home is their territory, which is why some people feel confident enough to slam the door or tell you to get lost. But when they give you time they will probably be more relaxed than in any other situation where you might meet them.

The two approaches we have found most useful on the doors are:

75) Regular short visits

We have tried to give a regular, short visit (just a few seconds at a time), no pressure, no hard sell. With a smile and a one-line introduction to the church, we warmly welcome them to come to one of our services and then we leave. Doing this regularly, they know you are not going to take any of their precious time, so they can afford to be polite. After all, it takes about the same time to say 'Thank you very much' as it does to say 'No thank you', slam! Once they have been polite to you two or three times, they begin to feel they know you. Maybe then they delve a bit deeper with further questions. This kind of visiting is very easy to do. Everyone in the church could do it.

76) Questionnaires

The other area we have found very successful on the doors is using questionnaires. They seem to work amazingly well. People seem to have a fascination with seeing if they can answer our questions. We use these as conversation starters. In fact the following survey is excellent because it raises so many different points from which to launch off into discussion. We have found that the more genuinely you seek people's opinions, the more interested they are in your opinions. Using these surveys we have often only spoken to two or three people all afternoon because we have had such long in-depth conversations. Surveys are helpful because they prevent the unnerving eyeball-to-eyeball confrontation. The fact that you can both stand looking at the survey makes talking a whole lot easier. It is also so much easier to get their name, address and contact number.

The 418 Project
Survey

1. Do you belong to a church? NO ___ YES_____

2. Do you believe in God?   YES   NO   DON'T KNOW

3. Do you own a Bible?   YES   NO

4. Who do you think Jesus was? _____

5. Why do you think he died on the cross? _____
_____
_____

6. What do you think happens after death? _____
_____

7. What in your opinion makes a person a Christian?
_____

8. Would you like to know more about?

    Church _____   Becoming a Christian _____

    NAME _____

Address _____

Contact No. _____

---

77) Flashcards
We have produced a set of flashcards which explain the reason why we called our church 'The 418 Project'. The cards

explain Jesus' fourfold social mandate, i.e. his care for: 1) the poor, 2) the trapped, 3) the sick, and 4) the mistreated. Each of these cards has a prophetic point that we want to make about how Jesus' ministry can affect their lives. We put a set of these cards into everyone's hands who is involved in our evangelistic programmes.

Newspapers

78) Editorial articles
The potential for using the local press is going to vary considerably from area to area depending upon the religious attitudes of the newspaper editors. We are enjoying a real openness of the press in our part of the country, which makes a considerable change from the inner city areas of London where we were 'crucified' more than once on the front pages. In Hemel Hempstead, local journalists are pleased to profile anything which is happening in the community. Our church plants have had several articles and mentions, including a personal 'instant interview' with me when we started The 418 Project. We have also had a lengthy, almost full-page article, with colour photograph, to help support us in a campaign to try to get hold of a property for the church. We even had front page coverage when we were campaigning to see a husband of one of our members released from prison, because he had served more than his due sentence. They have also profiled our voluntary training programme a few times and actually appealed on our behalf for residential placements for our students.

One of the keys to getting coverage in the newspapers is firstly, to let them know well in advance of an event soon to happen. Next, ask for an interview with a reporter, make sure you update them on significant developments and suggest that a photographer might turn up on the day. Finally, if they don't turn up, send in your own article with a choice of supporting photographs.

79) 'What's on' column
Some of the newspapers run a 'what's on' column for local

events. It is worth keeping them abreast of all community or social events being run in the church.

80) Paid-for advertising/pages

As a last resort, should the other two areas suggested above fail, it is still possible to use the papers by buying space to advertise. This could range from a small advertisement to buying a whole page in which to place your own articles. We have been toying with the idea of sharing a page with local Christian businesses, whose adverts could sponsor the rest of the page for church-based articles.

Free Advertising

81) Corporate logo

There are so many ways we can advertise ourselves around the town by getting church members to carry our logo or church name on their clothing (e.g. T-shirts, sweatshirts), bags, pens, baseball caps, key fobs etc. There are nowadays a number of companies who will print your advertisement on whatever you like – imagination is the only limit! We have had sets of T-shirts and sweatshirts printed, particularly for the team serving in the open air or on our charity stalls.

82) Library computer databases

Another place to register ourselves is at the local library, where they carry all the details of local churches and charities on a computer-based information file. This allows any seeker to access data about the church by browsing through the library portfolios. These archives actually store a fair amount of information, so there is space to record quite a bit about the church's details and activities.

83) Local TV and radio

We have a local cable television company which carries pages of local news. There are pages which you can pay for to display your details, but they also do features on local activities for free. In fact, the company came and filmed a youth project we are involved with, and edited the video free of charge for us. We have been able to use this to raise awareness for the programme in the local schools. It has also been an excellent tool for fund raising. The same opportunities are available through local radio stations. Many of them run 'phone in' programmes. We should be more than ready to call in with Christian comment on current issues.

Telephone

84) Wrong number!

We had a remarkable conversion in London of a young man who was on a building site. He was trying to ring his boss to inform him that a JCB was being stolen from the site. In his panic he dialled the wrong number. He accidentally got through to one of the ladies in our church, who had the presence of mind when she discovered it was a wrong number to say, 'By the way, can I give you an invitation to a Christian meeting this coming Sunday evening.' Rather taken aback by this, he asked where the meeting was to be held. Sunday night he came along and found the Lord there. I never did find out whether they lost the JCB. The next time you get a wrong number, or a double-glazing salesman, don't get frustrated, see it as an opportunity for the gospel!

85) Helplines

We put helplines on all our literature. Even if people don't phone it, the fact that it is there tells them that we care enough to be available should they need help. One afternoon a lady called in saying, 'I'm desperate, I need some help,' so Sallie and I dropped everything and went round to see her. She opened the front door and led us into the lounge where there was an open Bible on the sofa. 'What's the problem?' I asked. She replied, 'I really need to become a Christian.' Those kinds of emergencies I can easily cope with!

Sometimes the leaflets we have put through doors remain on mantelpieces for months, on standby should the helpline be needed some time. Perhaps the call when it comes is as simple as: 'Could you walk my dog for me as I am not feeling well enough at the moment.' At other times the circumstances can be personally devastating for them, like bereavement, or the shock of having a serious illness diagnosed. They just need to talk to someone.

86) Recorded messages
Most of us are on the receiving end of dozens of recorded messages on the answer phone each day, but the suggestion here is an outgoing pre-recorded message that people can phone to hear, for example a thought for the day, or information about our activities, or a message which can help the caller know how to become a Christian. Dialling a pre-recorded message is a little more anonymous than having to have a personal conversation with somebody. Telephone technology is improving at such a pace that I am sure there are all kinds of rapidly developing opportunities which we need to keep abreast of.

87) Phone to phone
Telephone advertising is a form of evangelism for those with a good telephone manner. That's not me – I hate the telephone. Yet it is amazing how many companies use the telephone as the medium for contacting new business. We are all aware of this from the number of calls we receive. Companies are apparently prepared to phone 2,000 people a week to find just nine contacts. We often give up too easily before we get the positive contacts. If you don't like the idea of door to door how about 'phone to phone' as a form of out-reach?

Institutions

88) Old people's homes, hospitals, schools and prisons
I find maps so inspiring. Just to ponder over a map of the town and to identify the different institutions within its boundaries, I find myself asking the question 'How can we get the gospel into every area?' The list above shows the sort of organisations which present us with a positive challenge. How can the church infiltrate every sector of society? Some

of these, such as old people's homes, hospitals, schools and prisons, have long been on the agendas for church outreach.

89) Cinemas and theatres

In London we lived for a while behind one of the cinemas. I used to ask them what films were coming into the area over the next few weeks. I would then travel into central London and see those films in advance. If there was a usable theme or message in a film, I would write a little tract and we would go and give them out outside the cinemas as the audiences were going home. It is important only to emphasise positive messages from these films. Being critical of a film simply antagonises the cinema staff.

We had a cinema in the Elephant and Castle which used to show Turkish films in the middle of the night, after the usual film showing had closed down. We got hold of Turkish literature and would be there at three o'clock in the morning as they came out. Incidentally, we would do the same thing throughout certain, well known, fast food restaurants, which employed, almost totally, kitchen staff and cooks from Turkey. We would send five teams off in different cars, who would cover the whole of London on a Saturday. We drove from one high street to the next spending a few minutes in the kitchens of each restaurant. Because this didn't happen to them every day they were very open to receive us. It was great sharing with Muslims, who would not have heard the gospel because of their Islamic backgrounds. We handed out Turkish literature similar to that used at the cinemas. The potential for using demo tapes with spoken messages in their own language is also worth consideration.

We had a colleague who ran Bible studies in some of London's top theatres. He started one in a major show at the request of one of the actors. The actors and stage crew used to say that they always had their best performances when they had read the Bible and prayed together. Word got around and it was not long before he was running Bible studies in other theatres too. This became the forerunner of the organisation Christians in Entertainment.

90) Factories/offices/local football clubs

Industrial estates, office centres and local football clubs are penetrated by a few brave-hearted pastorally minded souls. I have been impressed by the way some have been able to get thoroughly involved in a secular sphere by offering themselves as chaplains. We had a friend who became the chaplain of the local football club in the days when they were racing up through the divisions. I think other clubs saw the spiritual bit as part of their secret, so they started employing chaplains for their clubs too.

I have spent time talking with chaplains in industry who offer pastoral care for those on the factory floor. They would even ask to have a 'Christian slot', sharing with the whole workforce – in work time. They would reason with the management that this is good for their business, because, for example, millions of man hours of work are lost due to depression or breakdown of relationships. The Christian message has a definite bearing on this and is bound to make a difference to their business. It also has obvious advantages in encouraging people to work with Christian ethics such as honesty, kindness, going the second mile and so on. I have been impressed by so much of the current literature about business management. So many of today's business principles are common sense biblical ethics.

Sometimes it is amazing just how responsive non-Christians can be when you ask them for permission to evangelise. Once we asked the manager of a McDonalds restaurant if we could present the gospel there. 'I must have any request in writing,' he replied, as if trying to put us off. When we wrote to ask for permission, he refused on the grounds that he needed to see beforehand what we were intending to do. So we sent a team along who performed our street-evangelism programme just for him as he sat behind his desk in his rather cramped office. They sang and shared and juggled at him until eventually he said, 'How long does this go on for?' They told him they could do about twenty minutes if he wished. 'No, I was thinking more like two hours!' he replied. 'At lunchtime on Saturday.' So when the restaurant was at its most crowded, for a couple of hours they did their presentations in short bursts followed by questionnaires around the tables.

Local Shopfront

91) Bookshop/charity shop

A presence in the shopping precinct seems an ideal profile for the church and in a way this puts us more in contact with the public than a lot of church buildings do. There are so many good bookshop/coffee shop schemes across the country. The charity shop has also become extremely popular in recent years. Ichthus have been running one to help sponsor their Christian schools programme.

The 'second-hand shop' and the 'sell it through us' concept both provide a vehicle for recycling goods in a throw away society. These shops provide cheap goods for the poor and an avenue for the Christian who has two coats to be able to easily sell one and give to the poor. One of my concerns in dealing with the second-hand market is how you prevent it becoming a fencing house for criminals to sell on their swag. But then perhaps contact with this criminal element is a potential means of mending broken ways, and it would be great to be able to return stolen goods to their original owners. That would really serve society!

We ran a little shop in the early days of Ichthus to raise money to send to Third World development projects. This shop was always a good contact point with the general public. We also opened a **launderette** in one of the most crime-ridden estates in Europe, in North Peckham. It was a kind of prophetic statement that we wanted to clean up people's lives. It was very high tech, fully computerised, to save having cash on the premises. It also had an affiliated coffee shop so people could sit and talk while their clothes spun round and round.

92) Christmas Cracker (Oasis Trust)

Christmas Cracker is worthy of mention as it has worked very successfully for us in the past. The idea is to take over a restaurant for the evening. The menu is run as usual, with the normal staff on duty. The only difference is that the meals are sold for twice the normal price. Half goes to the restaurant but the other half is sent to the Third World. Surprisingly, this caught the imagination of the public and on these evenings the restaurants were packed. Using hotels and restaurants for **businessmen's lunches, dinners** and even **breakfasts** has always worked well, as has the relaxed meal together with an after dinner speaker. I ought to add that these are just as successful with businesswomen's lunches too!

93) Pantomimes

Ichthus has run two or three really successful pantomimes during the panto season, hiring a local theatre for a week of nightly performances. Written and performed by local talent, sporting titles such as: *Malice in Underland* and *Snow Joke*, these sell-out presentations have been excellent as first time contact for friends, neighbours and family members. Such ventures exercise so many talents such as writing, composing, stage management, lighting, dance, singing, acting, costume, prop production and artistic skills. Not only are production resources mobilised but the rest of the church also is motivated in advertising the show and selling tickets.

Pubs

94) Hiring pub rooms/saloon bars

The pub seems one of the most natural meeting places in British society. I am sure that Jesus would have carried out much of his ministry down at the George and Dragon, if he had chosen to come in our century. Having been brought up 'tee total', I was led to believe that pubs were evil places. I remember the first time I went into one I felt so uncomfortable, like a fish out of water. But I learnt an important lesson in that I realised that this is how non-Christians feel the first time they walk into a church. For this reason we have hired pubs for evangelistic evenings and for Sunday church services too. It is most important that the outsider feels comfortable even if we feel a little uneasy in this environment. For many this is their territory and they can relax in this environment. What better venue to bring in the kingdom and influence lives than in a place where the lonely and the sociable gather, or where the depressed go to drown their sorrows.

I have always thought that Christians should own and run pubs. We could help regulate those who drink too much and take a share in influencing the heart of local society. I have also thought we should run our churches along the lines of a pub. Often our churches are so cold and unwelcoming. I think we need to employ some pub interior designers to refurbish the inside of our church buildings. It is rather amusing that pubs have been desperate to get hold of our old church pews, just as desperately as the churches have wanted to get rid of them. But they use them totally differently from the way we have used them. It is amazing how cosily they can arrange our cast offs which were so cold in a church setting. We have sometimes run evangelistic services with people arranged around tables, to break up the formal meeting feel. What a difference it makes to be sitting facing people rather than looking at the back of their heads!

One thing I have never dared try is something one of our well-known evangelists has done, that is to hire the room above the pub and set a sign up on the bar downstairs which read 'Striptease upstairs in five minutes'. Everybody would get their drinks and disappear upstairs. Then, when the room was full he would stand up and preach on 'being laid bare before God'. I would imagine this was followed swiftly by a lynching.

95) Running a pub

Ichthus, having used pubs for years, eventually bought one. The Brown Bear, in Deptford, is still run as a pub, with one significant difference – it doesn't sell alcohol. In fact it had a sign up outside which read 'Who needs alcohol anyway?'. This not only houses church services, pub-style, but is open as a drop-in centre for people to take friends to and chat, or dance in the disco. It is run like most youth venues in clubland. For example, there are bouncers on the door who will frisk you for drugs or weapons as you go in. I think this says to young people that this is worth going to!

96) Befriending in the bar/guitar at the bar

We have often encouraged our evangelistic teams to go and spend an evening in the local pub. In fact some evenings we have organised people to be in every pub in the area. We would make this a non-pressured evening of evangelism and suggest that the members of the team just sit in the bar with their drink (tomato juice!) and see what happens. Invariably they would return with exciting tales of open doors of opportunity and in-depth conversations. How about spending an evening a week at your local?

Another trick we used to play with unerring success was to walk into the bar and leave a guitar resting against a table and then go and get a drink. It would not be long before someone would ask if this guitar belonged to us. Then they would ask us to give them a tune. We would say that we couldn't without the landlord's permission. They would then go and ask for permission for us. Because this was their local pub and they were probably there every night the owner was hardly likely to say no. We have then sung various songs with an evangelistic cutting edge. I once did this with a group of young people in four pubs in a row on one evening and it worked in every one of them. We have also seen this work in cafés too.

Youth Work

97) Youth drop-ins
There are so many exciting things happening among young people today that I don't feel qualified to speak into this area, seeing I am fast advancing in years. I am, however, on a youth committee in our town, which is seeking to set up a safe haven drop-in centre. This is running drop-in lunch clubs in the schools, which are proving to be a winner with the staff and the young people. Maybe fifty to ninety will turn up to be part of a relaxed, informal, game-orientated lunch break. This is not 'in your face' evangelism, it is more relationship building which is nevertheless run openly by Christians.

The schools, at the moment, seem very open to outside input, from both the community and the church. We need to meet the demand while it is presenting itself. The churches in Hemel Hempstead now sponsor two workers who take classes and assemblies as well as helping to organise the Christian groups which are growing in most of the schools.

98) Youth competitions
We recently ran a townwide computer competition, hosted by one of the computer stores in the town. The Final was hosted by the town's leisure complex, Leisure World. Around 200 young people took part. The excellent prizes, which were all donated by local businesses, were presented by the mayor of the town. There are a host of other areas where competitions can be organised. There is a Christian football league, run by a friend in our town, which mobilises many young people, Christian and non-Christian. In fact the

basis of entering the competitions is that each team has as many unsaved as saved team members. We have also enjoyed going to the local park on Sunday afternoons and challenging the young people there to a game of football. Yes, I did get involved! I played almost every Sunday for a year and half up to last year. Admittedly I am almost completely over the hill now, and middle-age spread is spreading. Perhaps I should take part in one of the growing number of evangelistic aerobics classes which offer to enable me to shed a few pounds and trim and tone up my physique. One afternoon we hired the local athletics track and ran an athletics knockout competition. Every athletics event imaginable was represented.

99) Youth church
It has been good to see the growth of youth and children's churches in this country. We know from the Bible that the Lord uses the young (Acts 2:17), and it is good to see them taking responsibility and being involved in ministry today. YWAM's King's Kids have opened our eyes to the way children and youth can hear from heaven and pray with faith, which is a total challenge to our older generation. We need to develop these channels, and it is probably here where revival is most likely to break out. Ichthus has been running a children's church called the Popcorn Church for the last few years, and we have started one recently called 'The 418 Kids'.

100) Children's work
When Jesus says of children 'the kingdom belongs to such as these' it seems a very appropriate domain to be involved in. Children are not only open and receptive in their early years but they are also specifically described as the vehicles for supernatural revelation (in Acts 2:17f). If the church has had any expertise during the last couple of generations this is the realm in which we have probably triumphed the most. The following are a few suggestions for work with children:

1. Holiday Clubs
2. Reading Clubs

3. Camps and Holidays
4. After School Clubs
5. Adventure Groups
6. Sunday School
7. Children's Church

101) Websites
The rapidly-growing influence of the Internet presents the church with a new evangelistic challenge. To run a church web page is a way of disseminating information about our activities and what we believe. The astounding growth in the computer industry, where they now claim that over 5,000 personal computers are installed every day, presents an expanding field of influence. The opportunity for interaction, questions and answers through open letters on e-mail, is another unparalleled opening.

Visit *The Evangelism Handbook* Web page for some photographs and descriptions of methods on evangelism profiled in this section. The address is:

how.to/evangelismhandbook

Information about The 418 Project is available at:

http://come.to/the418project

The Ichthus Fellowship Web site can be found on:

www.ichthus.org.uk

EVANGELISM IN THE EARLY CHURCH

Michael Green

A comprehensive evaluation and reappraisal of the
main aspects of evangelism in the early church –
concentrating on the New Testament period but providing
also a topical treatment of evangelism up until the middle
of the third century.

This edition, with a new Foreword, introduces the reader to
the latest finds and developments in scholarship,
concluding with an analysis of the implications of the
redating of the Magdelen papyrus: could the Gospel of
Matthew be an eyewitness account written by a
contemporary of Christ?

*I cannot conceive how anyone could read this book without
having his evangelistic vision renewed and zeal kindled.*
John Stott

A notable achievement
The Church Times

The indispesable basis for a consideration of modern evangelism.
I Howard Marshall

Michael Green is an accomplished communicator of the
Gospel, an ordained minister of the Church of England and
the author of numerous books including *Freed to Serve, I
Believe in the Holy Spirit, Who is this Jesus?* and, for Eagle,
My God and *Jesus.*

0 86347 157 9

JESUS

MICHAEL GREEN

Whose name is most used as a swear-word?
Who has more than a third of the world worshiping
him 2000 years after his death?
Why do we date our calendar from his birth?

Michael Green believes that Jesus is God's son, a 'perfect expression of the God we cannot see' who longs to know him. In this short, evangelistic book he examines what makes Jesus so special, looks at his claims and objectives and the ways he has been misunderstood down the years. The book closes with a simple invitation to face up to the challenge of a crucified and risen Jesus.

Jesus is the perfect little booklet to give to anyone seeking to know more about the truth and life of Jesus. It is illustrated throughout with full colour pictures.

Michael Green has spent his life sharing the Good News about Jesus: as a teacher, a clergyman and as an Adviser in Evangelism to the Archbishops of Canterbury and York. He is the author of numerous books including *Freed to Serve, I Believe in the Holy Spirit, Who is this Jesus?* and, for Eagle *Jesus* and *Evangelism in the Early Church.*

0 86347 198 6

MY GOD

MICHAEL GREEN

Why is God's name used more often in pubs than churches?
Is God relevant?
Does he even exist?

Michael Green is convinced that God does exist and that
we can actually find out quite a lot about him, not least of
which that he wants us to befriend him.

In a few short, sharp chapters Michael Green unveils what
he has come to know and to experience about God during
his life as a teacher, pastor, evangelist and writer.
My God is illustrated throughout with full colour pictures.

Michael Green has spent his life sharing the Good News
about Jesus: as a teacher, a clergyman and as an Adviser in
Evangelism to the Archbishops of Canterbury and York. He
is the author of numerous books including *Freed to Serve, I
Believe in the Holy Spirit, Who is this Jesus?* and, for Eagle
Jesus and *Evangelism in the Early Church.*

0 86347 041 6